# New
# Management
## in Human
## Services

# New
# Management
## in Human
## Services

## SECOND EDITION

Leon Ginsberg
Paul R. Keys
*Editors*

NASW PRESS

National Association of Social Workers
Washington, DC

Jay J. Cayner, ACSW, LSW, *President*
Robert H. Cohen, JD, ACSW, *Executive Director*

Linda Beebe, *Executive Editor*
Nancy Winchester, *Editorial Services Director*
Marcia Roman, *Staff Editor*
Ida Audeh, *Copy Editor*
Susan J. Harris, *Proofreader*
Louise Goines, *Proofreader*
Angland Creek Indexing, *Indexer*

**Library of Congress Cataloging-in-Publication Data**
New management in human services / Leon Ginsberg, Paul R. Keys,
    editors. -- 2nd ed.
        p.    cm.
    Keys's name appears first on the earlier edition.
    Includes bibliographical references (p.  ) and index.
    ISBN 0-87101-251-0 (pbk.)
    1. Human services--United States--Management. 2. Social  work
administration--United States.  I. Ginsberg, Leon H.  II. Keys,
Paul, 1954-    . III. National Association of Social Workers.
HV91.N46  1995
361.3'068--dc20                                                    95-25243
                                                                        CIP

Printed in the United States of America

# Contents

# Preface

anagement is
one of the most rapidly changing human sciences. How
organizations are managed has a dramatic impact on
their effectiveness, whatever their mission. Whether
they are businesses providing adequate products to the
marketplace while earning a profit for their owners or
health and social welfare agencies commit-

ted to maintaining the well-being of vulnerable people, the achievements and
failures of organizations affect the lives of everyone.

Managing human services organizations is not easy. It is often true that
organizational managers are neither as satisfied with their jobs nor as well com-
pensated for their work as employees in other sectors. And management is
always an imperfect process. There are so many things that can go wrong for
organizations, internally and externally, that even the best management may succeed only partially.

Management and managers are often under attack. It has been popular to
criticize *bureaucrats,* usually defined as employees of large government organizations. It is rare for anyone to defend these people as performing important
tasks that help others with the essentials of their lives. When the term *bureaucracy* is broadly defined, it can probably be applied to most of the people,
including human services workers, who are employed by social services

agencies. Those who direct and provide supervision in human services organizations are probably among the most dedicated of all workers in the United States, although they are often undervalued. The editors and authors of this book acknowledge their value and offer suggestions and commentaries in the following chapters to help them improve their performance. Many of the authors and both of the editors have been or are managers in human services organizations. Therefore, the contents of this book reflect real experiences in the world of management as well as a positive attitude about those who are engaged in that important work.

Many of the concepts reported here are taken from classic as well as contemporary management theory. It is reassuring, as several of the chapters make clear, that many of the most pervasive, newer management concepts are based on and follow from much earlier ideas about managing. New approaches and new theories of management are developed almost daily. However, most of them are solidly rooted in the classic ideas that also inform this book.

The first edition of *New Management in Human Services* was published in 1988. We recognized that management had been, for several years, the most important and, in many ways, most neglected topic in the human services. We had, from the perspective of teachers of social work management and of managers in large social welfare agencies, frequently heard that social work schools were not effective in preparing practitioners for the jobs most graduates eventually assumed as supervisors or directors. For these graduates management skills are even more crucial than the clinical and service skills so central to social work education. We also recognized that the social work articles on management frequently seemed to lag behind other management literature; social workers were teaching concepts that business and public administration had rejected years earlier as almost mythological. We wanted to bring the newer theories into the social work management literature—especially the lessons from Japanese management and from the "excellence" concepts of Tom Peters and Robert Waterman.

By the 1990s, even the "new" management we espoused began to look old. There had been much newer theories of management developed and explicated, although the works of Peters and Waterman and the Japanese lessons continued to be central to modern approaches to organizations and are included and emphasized in this second edition. However, many concerns that had been important in the first edition were no longer as central as they once were. New ideas that should be included in any discussion of new management approaches had not yet been developed or had not been emphasized in the first edition. And the practical issues of management had also changed. There has been a near revolution in organizational structures from "tall" structures with multiple layers of management and supervision to "flat" organizations and team management in which fewer people supervise more workers and in which the middle levels have been reduced or eliminated. Technology that includes personal computers, electronic mail, the Internet, pagers, and cellular telephones has changed the ways managers and workers perform their tasks in all sorts of organizations but, perhaps, most dramatically in the human services. Traditional concepts, that once seemed unlikely to ever change, such as "offices" and "working hours," now often seemed superfluous. Human services workers could and often do perform their responsibilities with only rare visits to their offices and diverse locales. Meanwhile, the nature and composition of the workforce became much more diverse, including many more women and people of color as managers. The growing diversity of the population was reflected in the growing diversity of the employment patterns in all organizations, especially those in the human services organizations. More people of various ethnicities and physical abilities were engaged in the work of human services organizations. Management was different and new again, perhaps more so than when the first edition was prepared.

Therefore, we proposed to the NASW Press that a second edition was needed. They agreed, and this volume is that new version of *New Management in Human Services*. Little other than the title is the same in this edition. Two chapters of continued value and relavence, by Joseph Bevilacqua and Felice Davidson Perlmutter, are all that are republished from the first edition. A few chapters have been updated and revised, but most are on new subjects and written by new authors. There are more women authors and an emphasis on organizational diversity, as well as attention to forms and techniques of management developed in the 1990s. Total quality management, which has become one of the most important and influential management ideas of the current era, is covered in several chapters, in addition to some of the more pervasive management concepts.

We think the book will be useful to human services managers and to students of human services management. Management content is now a requirement for social work students at both the baccalaureate and master's-degree levels, and we hope this book will help faculty and students learn more about new management concepts. We also hope that the other human services fields—counseling, nursing and other health care fields, education, psychology, public administration, rehabilitation, and others—will find this work useful in their own educational activities. We use this content in continuing human services management, and we believe others will find it helpful for such teaching.

Our thanks go to the authors of the chapters for their scholarship, dedication, and cooperation. Their efforts are the primary substance of this work.

At the University of South Carolina College of Social Work, support staff member Joyce Shaw has been instrumental in manuscript preparation. Graduate assistants Kevin Colligan and Jeanne M. King also helped organize and process the manuscript. The National Network for Social Work Managers was instrumental in setting priorities for new management areas that needed major emphasis. NASW Press editor Marcia Roman was project manager and has done excellent work. Director of Editorial Services Nancy A. Winchester reviewed the final draft of the book and made several suggestions that improved it. As with the first edition, NASW Associate Executive Director for Communications Linda Beebe has been enormously helpful with every element of the book—from the original conceptualization to all of the details of content, format, and design. We are indebted to her for her attention and her peerless publishing skills.

*September 1995*                *Leon Ginsberg and Paul R. Keys, Editors*

# Challenges for Leaders of National Human Services Organizations

David S. Liederman

Leadership 18 is a group that links the chief executive officers (CEOs) of the 18 largest national membership organizations in the human services nonprofit field. After 11 years at the Child Welfare League of America (CWLA), I am now the oldest member of the group in terms of seniority. Running a national human services organization is a tough job. You have to keep one eye on the mission and the other on the bottom line. You have to provide high-quality services to your members, work collaboratively with your board, and keep staff morale high. You have to crisscross the country, keynoting conferences, addressing leadership gatherings, and attending annual meetings. You have to meet the press, inspire the troops, and work with colleagues in other national organizations. And you have to remember everybody's name! You have responsibilities to yourself, to your organization, to your members, to the human services field, and to the nation at large. Following are some of the challenges we all have to face or questions we all have to answer sooner or later.

## RESPONSIBILITIES TO YOURSELF

> How do you keep your focus, maintain your health, keep your energy level high, and control stress while you continue to operate at breakneck speed day in and day out? Where do you find your personal and professional support systems?

On the personal level, your supports are the people who care about you and who insist that you take time for regular exercise, sensible eating, and whatever kind of leisure activity recharges your batteries. Professionally they might be a group of your peers, like Leadership 18 or the National Assembly. You have to make a commitment to these vital relationships, to give as well as take. That's only the beginning.

## RESPONSIBILITIES TO THE ORGANIZATION YOU LEAD

> How do you keep your organization viable in a time of growing competition and dwindling resources when the only constant is change?

You have to be a leader. Vision is the major difference between managers and leaders. To lead, you must envision the future: not in its precise details—that would limit the possibilities—but with enough clarity to be able to set the direction for those you lead. If you can summon the vision, keep it in focus, translate it into a mission, and communicate it effectively, you can inspire others to follow you.

But a vision, no matter how compelling, is just smoke and mirrors unless you can marshal resources behind it. People in the human services used to flinch from talking about money, but those days are past.

Keep track of the money! Fiscal accountability goes hand in hand with honesty and integrity. Then, beyond everyday good management, financial leadership requires an active, entrepreneurial approach. Leading-edge organizations and the leaders who run them are open to change. If a new venture furthers the mission, or if it generates resources to accomplish the mission and is generally in keeping with the mission, it might be a good idea, even if it's not something the founders could have envisioned.

> How do you make sure that the governing board shares your vision and your flexibility?

Wise administrators take a hand in the selection of board members, and especially of the board chair. They make sure that people join the board for the right reasons, bringing the right skills and the right qualifications. Ideally, the administrator can depend on the board chair to find ways to expand the organization's resources, play a role in establishing its mission and its policy, and handle board politics and personalities. The chair knows that the administrator can do an outstanding job of running day-to-day agency operations.

As an administrator, you should be able to draw clean lines between your role and that of your governing board. The role of the board and the role of the administrator must be complementary, a partnership. Job descriptions must be clearly defined and spelled out in writing. When each role is well-defined, each side is strong, and each pulls its weight, the organization benefits. When one player is stronger than the other, the relationship is out of balance and the organization suffers. Regular evaluations by both sides are essential.

How do you ensure that the best and the brightest leaders in your field
are working for you and running your member organizations?

Leaders actively recruit the best people. At CWLA our executive search program is on hand when member agencies need a CEO or have other high-level vacancies. We do not stop there. We have leadership training programs that attract and equip senior managers and allow us to identify talented leaders. Our members appreciate these services, and they also give us the opportunity to bond leaders in our profession to the mission of our national organization.

Leaders cultivate and mold talent and facilitate growth. They inspire and they enable. They provide a climate of care and challenge, an environment that supports learning and rewards creativity. Andy Miller, former national commander of the Salvation Army, said something once that I've never forgotten. "You can encourage the people under you or you can crush them," said Andy. "It's your choice. But remember: You have to work with what's left." A word about turnover. Obviously, excessive turnover of key staff is always a bad sign, but a certain amount of turnover is healthy. It presents the opportunity to do some restructuring; to elevate staff members who are ready to take on new leadership responsibilities; or to attract new talent, new energy, and new ideas. Every change is an opportunity if you're open to the possibilities and you seize the moment.

How do you create a management team and other structures within your
organization that leave you time to play your national role, knowing
everything will stay on track in your absence?

Leaders inspire and demand loyalty to themselves and to the mission of the organization. This should not be equated with the sycophant allegiance that tyranny demands and gets. As Reg Murphy of National Geographic said recently, "The day of the boss is over. The day of the leader is here." Leaders pick trustworthy people, they trust them, and they are trusted in return. They share responsibility in management teams with others who share their vision and whose strengths complement their own.

## RESPONSIBILITIES TO THE MEMBERS

How do you communicate your vision in a way that makes member executives feel part of something bigger than themselves and bigger than their own organizations—part of a powerful national movement that yields benefits they can't otherwise provide for their constituency? How do you keep every member satisfied that they're receiving full value in exchange for their dues?

As we approach the 21st century, membership in national organizations is more critical than ever for our member agencies, but executives may find it harder to justify the expenditure. Members expect a range of tangible benefits, and it is up to you to provide them. Above all, they want to experience success at the national level and to be able to take credit for accomplishments beyond their immediate scope. At CWLA we see proof of this every time we rally our members on a public policy issue that affects children and families. They respond eagerly, obviously excited at a chance to shape child-friendly national policies. When they succeed, as they did with last year's significant family support and family preservation legislation, they are energized for the next challenge.

How do you provide visibility for the issues that matter to your members? They want to see their point of view reflected in the media.

Having a spokesperson who gets national media coverage makes your members feel like they're in the ballgame. However, it's never easy to get coverage. You need a solid game plan to attract the attention of jaded editors and producers who think only the bad news sells. You need hard news, something they haven't heard before or new evidence for something they've known all along but couldn't prove.

This means devoting resources to a media strategy. Many times funding for public relations is the first thing to go when an organization feels the pinch. Keep it at the top of the priority list, in good times and in bad.

> How do you help member agencies position themselves strategically in
> their own communities, so they can survive any eventuality?

You advocate the same rule of thumb that guides your national organization: Be open to change, but never lose sight of the mission. A few years ago, a successful leader was one who could keep programs running and compete successfully for funding. Today much more is required. Success hinges on defining and redefining the agency's niche and knowing who its partners are. Some agencies I know have lost large, long-time funders. The loss forced them to a strategic re-examination of their mission and their niche, and they came out far ahead in the end. But that did not happen by accident.

Even better than a quick reaction, of course, is the ability to foresee trouble or opportunity and plan proactively—without losing sight of your mission. For the leader of a successful organization, at any level, periodic course corrections are standard operating procedure.

## RESPONSIBILITIES TO THE HUMAN SERVICES FIELD

> What responsibility do we have, as leaders in the human services field,
> to maintain the highest levels of integrity for ourselves and our peers?

As managers of organizations that depend on public support for both their mandate and their resources, we must keep faith with the public, for pragmatic as well as ethical reasons. Should we open a serious discussion on the level of salary and benefits appropriate for executives of national nonprofits? Are there limits on which we could agree?

Even after Aramony's problems at the United Way, there's still a lot of reluctance to have this conversation. I think we need to raise the question of accountability, at least among ourselves. I ask this next question of myself first, so I think it's a fair one.

> Have I been in charge long enough? How do executives of national
> organizations know when it's time to move on?

In rare cases, our own foolish actions determine an abrupt end to our tenure. Some administrators, like Father Tom Harvey, formerly the executive director of Catholic Charities USA, set time frames for themselves. Even though he was doing a great job, Father Harvey moved on when the time he had allotted ran out. The Salvation Army puts short term limits on its top position. Is there an upper limit we might all agree on, in the same way we agree on a compensation ceiling? Or should each case be decided on its individual merits?

## RESPONSIBILITIES TO THE NATION

How do national human services organizations provide collective leadership on behalf of all their clients—leadership that reflects the interrelatedness of the problems we all confront?

Dave Cooney, CEO of Goodwill Industries International, Inc., got us off to a strong start when he drafted "17 Characteristics of a Successful Society," a document that Leadership 18 has discussed at recent meetings. The group is still trying to refine the list. The three characteristics that have received our highest priority so far belong to a society where

- social problems like alcoholism, drug use, child abuse, and spouse abuse are virtually eliminated by reduced stress, proper prevention, and adequate treatment.
- each person has full access to education and training to achieve his or her potential in contributing to the growth and flexibility of the workforce.
- violence, racism, sexism, age discrimination, ethnic tensions, and discrimination against people with disabilities are eliminated as a result of increased public knowledge, active social resistance, and government intervention when necessary.

If we can imagine it, we can achieve it. The members of Leadership 18 represent the nation's largest social services organizations. If we can submerge our own interests and merge our energies behind an overall vision of what's good for America, then agree on a public policy agenda and a major public campaign to promote that agenda, the face of this nation could be changed forever. The challenge is to move from a general philosophical statement to a practical, step-by-step agenda. I really believe that if we can do this, the resources will follow.

This common commitment is especially urgent today because the mood of the public is increasingly hostile to constructive social change. Americans must be convinced that short-range investments in children, families, and communities pay long-range dividends for everybody. But first we have to agree among ourselves. Can we meet that challenge? If we can't, we can hardly expect our political leaders to solve our problems.

# Chapter 1

# Concepts of New Management

**Leon Ginsberg**

The social work profession has a long-standing commitment to improve and better understand the management of the services it renders. Before the general acceptance of the term "social work," one of the earliest names for the profession was "social administration." Some venerable schools of social work, such as those at the University of Chicago and Temple University, are still called schools of social administration. This text uses the term "management," instead of "administration," to include administration, supervision, and other processes.

The methodological debates in social work have historically focused on the relative merits of the various frameworks for evaluating and conceptualizing social work practice. Is casework or group work the more effective approach to direct services? Should social work curricula be organized according to the traditional triad of casework, group work, and community organization, or is a binary division such as macro and micro conceptualization more useful? What are the relative merits of the functional, diagnostic, and behavior modification approaches to direct practice? Should community organizers take confrontational, planning, or capacity-building approaches (or some combination of them) to their work?

Debates about the best approach in social work may be off the mark. Two other elements of social work, namely, social welfare policy and management, seem to transcend all forms of practice with clients and yet play a crucial role in meeting human needs. If social policies for the provision of services are absent or inadequate, there is little chance that services will be available to clients. Rent for offices, cash for assistance, arrangements for housing, and salaries for staff are a result of social policies.

Moreover, management makes it possible to implement such policies. Without management, it is doubtful that services could be provided. In many cases, the nature and quality of the services would be even more heavily influenced by the nature and quality of the management than by the laws (in public programs) or board decisions (in voluntary programs) that create the services.

Whereas the importance of well-prepared and ethically committed practitioners cannot be overemphasized, the quality of the management under which they operate must also be acknowledged. Management can impede or enhance their work, expand or contract the nature and extent of services they provide, and increase or retard the availability of those services. For example, capable mental health managers, who direct the agencies in which the largest numbers of social workers are employed, can often make it possible (or impossible) for discharged hospital patients to survive in their communities. Skilled public assistance managers can determine the degree of ease with which aid is provided and the complexity of applying for and receiving services. Similar examples can be cited for the diverse fields of social work—corrections, community planning, and programs for people with disabilities, among dozens of others.

Therefore, the quality of human services management, especially what is discussed in this book under the rubric "new management," is an important, too-often neglected, element in service processes. Several other books cover social work and human services management from various perspectives. Some of those most closely related to this book are by Brody (1993); Crow and Odewahn (1987); Rapp and Poertner (1992); Skidmore (1994); Tropman, Johnson, and Tropman (1992); Weinbach (1994); and Yankey and Edwards (1991). Austin (1995) has written a comprehensive overview of social work management theory and practice, including its historical development. He described the approach of early social work theorists to management and applies several concepts of management to social work.

## SOURCES OF MANAGEMENT CONCEPTS

This book is about modern management theory and practice, referred to more succinctly as "new management." This term refers to some of the newer concepts of making organizations work efficiently, especially those developed by Peters and Waterman (1982) and others whose work is discussed throughout this book. New management theorizing also results from questioning the assumptions and approaches underlying traditional management theories that no longer appear to be valid. In essence, new management is based on systematic, scientific observation of what directing organizations *is* rather than on a priori ideas specifying ideal models of what management *should* be, as developed by some earlier, more classical writers.

### Management in various settings

One of the issues that frequently arises in discussions of management is the generic versus the specialized nature of the field. Does it make a difference where one is managing, or are the processes the same? In the 1950s President Dwight D. Eisenhower appointed top business executives to manage major government departments. The belief then, among many, was that a skilled chief executive officer would be effective in any large organization, whether it was General Motors or the U.S. Department of Defense. Even in more recent times, some social welfare agency chief executives are taken from business management ranks, on the assumption that the processes and the requisite skills are similar. There is an ongoing debate in management about whether those who direct organizations ought to have special knowledge of the effort they administer—vehicle specialists for auto manufacturers; social workers for social agencies; educators for colleges and universities—or whether the skills are interchangeable. The issue is unsettled, because there are both positive and negative examples in both kinds of circumstances. Systematic study has not been conducted to answer the question in an authoritative way.

Some concepts of new management result from what some writers have called a "managerial revolution" (Jary & Jary, 1991), especially in connection with the development of management as separate from ownership. This is a product of organizations becoming more complex; of absentee shareholders owning organizations, instead of individuals and families (which has been the traditional mode); and the technical nature of modern organizations and all other organized human endeavors.

Management tasks are carried out by managers, whose styles vary widely. Many seem to manage by instinct, partly because they want to but often because they lack formal education in the art of managing as such.

In the professional literature, there is no consensus regarding what managers really do and to whom they actually respond—higher-level managers, constituents, customers, the press, staff, or others. The norm is that professional managers or other employees direct almost all types of organizations, including businesses, human services, professional associations, financial institutions, and schools and school systems. That development has created a phenomenon called a "management class."

Management theory and skill are the by-product of the explosion of management jobs and management activity. The traditional owner–employers such as farmers, shopkeepers, and individual professional practitioners have been replaced by giant agribusiness conglomerates; international retail chains that are interconnected with advanced electronic communications; and groups of physicians, lawyers, psychologists, and social workers, some of whom are affiliated with large health care corporations such as health maintenance organizations. When owners or practitioners manage, they operate as they choose. If they are successful, they survive. Although many owner–managers are formally educated in management, many are not. Trial and error or family traditions may determine how they operate. Many seek and use the services of consulting or training organizations. However, the basic development of management theory resulted from the managerial revolution and its creation of the need for specifically educated and skilled managers who could serve many different kinds of organizations by applying general managing skills.

Perhaps the most important of those is an attitude that there are fundamental, unchanging truths about management. In fact, management is now understood to change with the circumstances on the environment. The times change management. Social values change management objectives and styles. What may be effective in one context is not necessarily effective in another, for neither organizations nor the environments in which they exist are static.

It should also be recognized that organizations have a political dimension. One social work writer, Burton Gummer (1990), has published a book about the politics of social administration. He and Richard Edwards coauthored one of the chapters of this book on a similar topic. Gummer believes and demonstrates the reasons for the belief that every aspect of organizational life has a political dimension. Matters such as personnel selection, financing, and program implementation are all affected by both internal and external political environments.

Internal organizational politics are central factors in how programs are administered. The power of employees in the organization, the power of unions, and the political environment of the organization all place requirements and limits on the manager's functioning. Politics also have an effect on the organization's environment. For example, affirmative action programs, which were in the process of being changed at the time of publication of this book, arose from a specific political environment in earlier years, just as the changes—in effect, weakening—of affirmative action in the 1990s is a response to changing political values and environments. Political values and political decisions lead to basic changes in the ways human services programs are conceptualized and delivered. How and to what extent a society will assist disadvantaged populations are largely issues of politics. Child care services, particularly day care programs for families receiving public assistance, and work requirements for those receiving aid are central and current examples of political values changing and informing human services programs.

As one example of change in the organizational context, consider day care, which until recently was viewed by many social welfare organizations to be an unfavorable part of the delivery system. Social welfare programs were designed to make it possible for parents, especially mothers, to remain at home with their children. However, for many Americans the workforce and family life changed dramatically. Today, the only complaints about day care are that some programs are inadequate and that funding is not sufficient to provide this service for low-income clients. Similarly, mandatory work programs for public assistance recipients were considered not long ago to be violations of client rights. Today they are considered both acceptable and curative of poverty.

### An early advocate of new management

An early theorist and writer about human relations in management was Mary Parker Follett (1973), who is remembered by those who have preserved and recently republished her work as a social worker (Graham, 1995). She is described as having been active in fields such as "vocational guidance, industrial relations, civic education, and settlement work" (Syers, 1995, p. 2585). One of her major achievements was the development of after-school recreation and education centers in Boston. She distilled a number of psychological concepts of leadership, employee motivation, and conflict resolution in organizations from her social work experiences. Many of her concepts were the forerunners of the human relations school of management (Graham, 1995) and even the Peters and Waterman (1982) excellence principles, because she wrote about human behavior and human need, rather than the mechanics of organization and production.

In the 1920s Mary Parker Follett advocated ideas that are still important today, such as less hierarchical organizations, listening to line workers, and less authoritarian management (Linden, 1995). In fact, she propounded many of the same new management approaches that are highlighted in this chapter. Although some believe that her writings were ignored in the 1930s and 1940s because they did not fit the current interests of the times, Linden (1995) suggested that Follett was given less attention than she might otherwise have received because she was a woman writing in a field dominated by men. Her own collected papers provide the original sources on her contributions (Follett, 1973).

## Government sources of management ideas

**The military.** The military has been a source of many management concepts. The popularity of books such as *Victory Secrets of Attila the Hun* (Roberts, 1993) indicates how important the management of military operations has been in the development of management theory. Similar to other organizations, military units require careful coordination, direction, effective execution, and a clearly defined mission.

Traditional military formations have been handed down from generation to generation. Highly specific tactics have been developed over centuries and passed on. In the course of implementing them, military commanders periodically discover that the nature of combat has changed and revise the theories they inherited to match those changes. Frequently, those changes follow military disasters. American movies often show disciplined, carefully aligned, brightly uniformed British troops being slaughtered by loosely organized, surprise-oriented, modestly clothed American troops, who subsequently won independence in the American colonies. The highly structured American Cavalry is often portrayed as losing to bands of irregularly organized Native Americans. In any case, the straightforward mission of the military unit often seems attractive to human services managers. Armies have one mission—to close in and destroy the enemy. Everything they do is geared to achieving that mission, including their medical services, their music, and their military justice programs.

**The Office of the President.** Some of the fundamental ideas of management came from efforts to improve the executive branch of the U.S. government (Fox, 1973). Franklin D. Roosevelt's Committee on Administrative Management, appointed in 1937 to streamline executive operations and led by Luther Gulick, enunciated many of the classical management concepts discussed in this chapter. One of the practical effects of the effort was the development of the Executive Office of the President. Also out of that innovation came the Bureau of the Budget and a number of other structural changes that helped systematize the president's work. Some of the articles produced by committee members, such as Elton Mayo (1946) and Mary Parker Follett (1973), were written in a modern mode (that is, what has become known as the human relations approach).

Many of the original sets of concepts that have now become traditional management ideas came from an article by Luther Gulick entitled "The Theory of Organization." His effort was part of the work of the Committee on Administrative Management to help develop an executive staff to help the president discharge his responsibilities. Gulick's summary of the characteristics of organizations (cited in Spero, 1973) became the framework that pervaded organizational theory for decades to come. He wrote about organizational factors such as structure, purpose, place, clientele, and process. He also wrote about such essential factors as the hierarchical structure of organizations, the distinctions between staff and line functions, and the organization's span of control. Gulick and Unwick (1937) developed the term "POSDCORB," a common and widely used conceptualization of managerial functions, which stands for planning (P), organizing (O), staffing (S), directing (D), coordinating (C and O), reporting (R), and budgeting (B).

In more recent years, the notion of a list of management functions was further developed and presented by others, especially the popular textbook writer Koontz (1990), whose *Essentials of Management* is widely used in educational programs for managers and in higher education programs. Earlier editions of Koontz's text, coauthored with others, reduced the term "managing" to five functions: planning, organizing, directing, supervising, and controlling. Their list has also been adopted by writers on social work management; for example, Weinbach's (1994) *The Social Worker as Manager* is organized around the Koontz concepts.

### The faith in science

New management is rooted in what would now be classified as the essence of the older management theories: Frederick Taylor's (1947) *Scientific Management*. Employees were viewed almost mechanistically. Removing human discretion was a major feature of good management, according to Taylor and his supporters. If people could be properly matched to tools and machines and put in situations in which they would perform exactly and precisely as desired, then management would properly control its work. Of course, such mechanical and technical approaches are still central to modern concepts such as quality control and, therefore, "Taylorism" cannot be dismissed as a philosophy of the past. In fact, it remains fundamental to all management, both traditional and modern. Other Taylor ideas, such as relating work as closely as possible to payment, are also important in today's management. People want to be paid, and financial compensation is a powerful—perhaps the most powerful—motivator in work environments. Such modern innovations as profit-sharing and the use of other means to persuade employees to identify with the profitability of the company are rooted in Taylor's recognition of the importance of money in motivating workers.

In some ways, the scientific management approach stems from a widespread desire to make a science of everything. This tendency gained strength with the publication of Charles Darwin's (1900) 19th-century theory of natural selection and with the spate of major medical and biological discoveries that seemed to hold the promise of solving many fundamental problems. There seemed to be a scientific explanation for everything and a scientific solution for every problem, if one only looked hard enough and used the proper method. Vaccines were found for diseases such as rabies and, later, polio. Sulfa drugs and later penicillin were discovered and, for the first time, showed that infectious diseases could be treated and cured. In some ways, social work was a product of those beliefs; in its early days, some called it "scientific charity." However, the great scientists of the 20th century seemed to question such excessive optimism. Fox (1973) suggested that scientific management as an approach declined with the general decline of dogmatism brought about by the discoveries of Albert Einstein and Werner Heisenberg, among others, which helped refute the mechanistic and deterministic model of the physical world. The scientific management approach and similar "scientific" longings were based to an extent on the classical Newtonian view of the world as a mechanism. Ideas such as Einstein's theory of relativity and Heisenberg's uncertainty principle offered new ways of analyzing the physical world and, correspondingly, clues to understanding the social world.

**Hawthorne experiments**
The Hawthorne experiments were conducted at the Hawthorne Works of the Western Electric Company in Chicago from 1927 to 1932. The primary researcher was Professor Elton Mayo (Dickson, 1973; Etzioni, 1964). In these experiments, workers were studied, interviewed, and observed in test rooms.

The best-known part of the study was its illumination experiments. Physical factors such as the intensity of illumination at the work sites, which was a central variable in the Hawthorne studies, were found to be less important than social and emotional factors, a fact that ran counter to the intuition of the times, which was that physical factors made a great deal of difference in worker productivity. Researchers wanted to determine whether a relationship existed between variations in lighting and efficiency. They used two groups:

an experimental group and a control group. When lighting was increased, the experimental group showed an increase in productivity, but so did the control group, which did not experience the increased lighting. When the lighting was decreased, both groups again increased their productivity. The researchers concluded that lighting or illumination was just one of several factors affecting output, and perhaps not the most important.

The researchers concluded that people were motivated by factors other than their paychecks. For example, individual attitudes as well as the role of the supervisor were found to be important motivators. In several interviews and observations, researchers found that the feelings of the workers toward their supervisors and their loyalty to one another in the work situation vied with economic gains as motivators. In other words, simply changing the physical features of the work environment was not enough; emotional and psychological factors came into play.

The knowledge gained from the Hawthorne experiments led management theorists to understand the implications of human factors in management, namely, that the attitudes and sentiments of workers were important and that the feeling of belonging and of being a contributing member of an enterprise made a difference. When some workers were singled out as an experimental group, they were motivated to work more adequately and more effectively, a phenomenon that was later called the "Hawthorne effect" and has important implications for the ways in which management operates.

### Human relations school of management

One of the consequences of the Hawthorne experiments was the development of the human relations school of management, which is attributed by many to Elton May, who led the experiments (Heyel, 1973; Jary & Jary, 1991). Proponents of the human relations approach believed that careful application of human relations knowledge about working with people, group dynamics, and human motivation would lead to effective and efficient organizations. In fact, such measures as training managers for sensitive work with their employees, employee newsletters, and service pins have been widely used in management for over 50 years. The Wal-Mart stores have regular pep rallies as a means of increasing the devotion and improving the performance of their employees, for example.

However, certain kinds of management sensitivities may be more important than others, and many of those are of the kind Taylor (1947) would have identified as central to worker concerns—that is, the motivation of employees is largely economic, in one way or another. Managerial measures to promote loyalty to the organization are often most successful when they are combined with such material concerns as salary, fringe benefits, or job security. When an organization responds to employee emotional needs with practical benefits such as more generous leave policies, sharing profits, and providing scholarships for employee children, the blend of human relations and economically based rewards are more likely to engender loyalty, devotion, and productivity.

An important practical consideration is devising ways to thwart disgruntled employees from sabotaging organizational efforts. Not only might sensitive human responses to employee feelings improve productivity, but they may also prevent the diminution or destruction of the organization's basic efforts.

### Managerial grid

One of the best blendings of the human relations and scientific management approaches is found in the works of Robert R. Blake and Jane S. Mouton (1964), who developed the managerial grid as a means of graphically demonstrating the importance of both people and production in any organization. The most recent version is called the Leadership Grid (Figure 1-1). (In social work, production means the delivery of services and the operation of programs.) These are the important dimensions of any organization. Although the objectives of an organization may be closely related to production, the organization must be sensitive to and concerned about the people who develop and carry out productive activities.

In their book and in the seminars that are organized around it, the authors have been quite clear and specific about what they mean. They cited organizations and the characteristics that may make them too heavily oriented to one or the other of the dimensions. An organization that is overly oriented to production may be a sweatshop and may undergo heavy personnel losses. However, an organization that is too "people oriented" may produce very little and may lose its orientation to the customers' needs and its own needs to meet its objectives. Clearly, the two dimensions are not contradictory or incompatible—an organization may be both productive and concerned about its employees.

The dimensions of the grid are measured along two axes, and the various points at which the axes may intersect define various kinds of organizations. A 9,9 organization—one that is equally and highly concerned with both dimensions—is ideal. A 1,1 organization does not take care of its employees or its customers. A 5,5 organization is balanced but not ideal because it is only half as concerned with its employees and its productivity as it could be. A 9,1 organization reduces the human factors to a minimum, and it probably experiences extensive personnel dissatisfaction and turnover. A 1,9 organization

FIGURE 1-1

# The Leadership Grid Figure

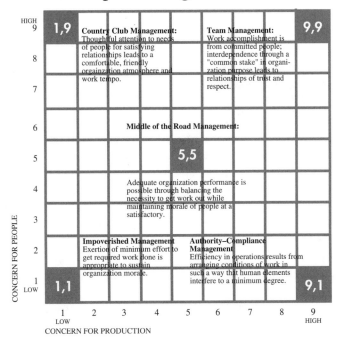

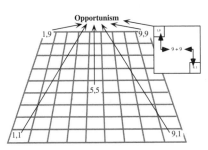

In Opportunistic Management, people adapt and shift to any Grid style needed to gain the maximum advantage. Performance occurs according to a system of selfish gain. Effort is given only for an

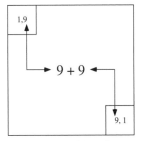

**9+9: Paternalism/Maternalism**
Reward and approval are bestowed to people in return for loyalty and obedience; failure to comply leads to punishment

*Source: Blake, R. R., & McCanse, A. A. (1991). The leadership grid® figure. Paternalism figure and opportunism. In R. R. Blake & A. A. McCanse (Eds.), Leadership dilemmas—Grid solutions (pp. 29–30). Houston: Gulf Publishing. © 1991 by Scientific Methods, Inc. Reproduced by permission of the owners.*

probably satisfies all staff, but if it is profit driven, it may fail; if it is a non-profit organization subject to external surveillance, it may find itself without funds or support.

Perhaps the most effective use of the managerial grid is in training and consciousness raising for managers and employees. Exercises, retreats, and other training programs that use the grid can help the organizations assess and plan for change.

Human services agencies may find the grid useful with appropriate modifications. One of the difficulties with using it as it is presented by its authors is the use of the term "people" to discuss employees. For human services agencies, showing concern for people (clients) and serving those people is productivity. That is, when human services agencies produce, they produce concern for people. Therefore, an appropriate adaptation is to conceive of the "concern for people" axis as "concern for employees" instead.

Agencies that deliver human services can overemphasize one dimension or the other, just as a profit-oriented business might. In fact, with billings becoming the basis of the budgets of increasing numbers of health and mental health services and with the trends toward private practice, an excessive emphasis on financial productivity, to the exclusion of employee concerns, may prevail. On the other hand, some organizations may overemphasize the concern for employees. Without the pressure to perform services in order to survive, many organizations may become more concerned about the needs and sentiments of their workers than about the clients they serve, just as businesses may.

Consumer complaints about unanswered social agency telephones, employees who always seem to be unavailable, and other forms of neglect or maltreatment signal that an organization is more concerned about people than productivity. Of course, one sees the same kinds of things in retail operations—employees who are constantly interacting with one another about their leave time, their complaints about their working conditions, and their compensation, but interacting little (if at all) with customers.

The managerial grid is a useful device for understanding and training employees. It helps bridge the dichotomy between scientific and human relations approaches in concrete ways.

### McGregor's X and Y theories

McGregor's (1960) theories are another example of the blending of the human relations and scientific management approaches. McGregor divided organizations into those that are "new" and followed a theory Y orientation and those that are "old" and oriented to theory X. Theory Y maintains that people find physical and mental effort to be as natural as playing and resting, and people exert self-direction and control to pursue organizational goals. Theory X maintains that people dislike and avoid work and that they must be threatened with punishment to perform.

McGregor also suggested that people work to satisfy their egos and achieve self-actualization and are not motivated solely by material rewards; most people want to accept responsibility and are capable of imaginative and creative efforts. He was concerned that the abilities of employees were only minimally being used.

## REALITIES OF MANAGEMENT FUNCTIONS

Perhaps the most important impetus for the development of new management concepts in the human services and the profit-making sectors has been the realization that the functions long associated with management have not been the real functions of managers for years. That is especially true of top managers in the corporate sector, many of whom spend most of their time studying potential acquisitions, mergers, and ways to influence government regulations, which have varying effects on organizations.

### Changing understandings of supervision

A basic rule of management states that a finite number of people can be supervised by one supervisor. This rule is implemented in military organizations, where one squad leader may be assigned to eight troops, a platoon leader to a few squad leaders, and a company commander to three platoon leaders. These decisions about ratios of managers to subordinates are not necessarily based on empirical research. Convenience, tradition, desires for symmetry, and preferences of decision makers are often the bases for structuring and staffing organizations. An additional person or two in a squad or a few extra supervisees may have no effect on the organization—or the ratio may be too great. In some circumstances, even lower supervisor-to-supervisee ratios may be desirable. It is unlikely, however, that unchanging, persistent ratios are required. The same kind of pattern is followed in traditional social welfare agencies such as public assistance and child protective services, in which a supervisor is assigned to every five or six line workers.

Current understandings suggest that the supervisor-to-worker ratio depends on the work being done and the qualifications of those who perform it. Experienced physicians may need no more than occasional mutual consultation with colleagues and little or no supervision. The same is true of experienced and well-prepared social workers. However, people with undifferentiated educations—soldiers, workers in restaurants and retail stores, and workers in other organizations with minimal educational requirements and rapid personnel turnover—may need careful supervision.

In organizations that are staffed by professionals, as most human services organizations are, traditional supervision is unnecessary and inappropriate. Professionals in social work, medicine, law, counseling, nursing, and most other fields that require postgraduate education often know more about what they should do and how they should do it than the organizations' managers, who, in turn, do their work by hiring capable people and providing them with wide latitude to carry out their tasks.

## Environmental changes

There are major environmental changes in U.S. management in the fields of human services and business. Many have written about the effect of "downsizing," a phenomenon that began in the 1980s and continues in the 1990s, and its impact on business, the professions, and human services programs. Bearing in mind that all organizational life is interrelated, one can easily see that if the business sector shrinks, then tax revenues would diminish, and with it money for education and social welfare. Moreover, when those areas lose employees, as they typically do because they are labor intensive, tax receipts further decline, which causes a downward spiral for organizations. Clearly, under such circumstances more services must be provided with fewer resources, which is a management issue par excellence.

## Technology

In modern times, many factors have contributed to the expansion of what organizations could achieve and the ways they could achieve it. Technology, for example, has been a major factor in the recent developments in management. Human services management may have assimilated modern technological developments as quickly and as effectively as other fields such as manufacturing. Not many foresaw the potential for management of the silicon chip, which led to the development of the computer. Needless to say, computer technology has been the single most important change for all management, including human services management. Innovations in this field have improved every aspect of human services management from monitoring client services to enhancing communications both within organizations and among them. Moreover, whereas the computer systems of the 1960s and 1970s were the responsibility of highly specialized computer programmers, experts, or "data entry" clerks, workers today in almost all fields are computer users.

Although one cannot overemphasize the importance of technology in modern organizations, one ought to use it with caution. Many organizations may overspend or overuse computer technology. Computer specialists may convince managers to develop programs and generate reports that have little or no significance for the organization. Effective managers are as cautious about expenditures on information as they are about expenditures on other equipment. In many cases, computer services are contracted out to firms that specialize in such work. Doing the work may be more expensive than the eventual product is worth to the organization. An unusually cynical approach to computers was taken by Robert Townsend, a highly successful business CEO best known for his work with Avis auto rental, in the first edition of his book *Up the Organization* (1970). He advised managers that computers become obsolete as soon as they are unpacked. He warned executives that their computer experts have a tendency to spend their time and the company's resources developing their computer expertise for their own use. Although Townsend changed his tone in the second edition, *Further up the Organization: How to Stop Management from Stifling People and Strangling Productivity* (1984), his earlier words have the ring of truth, and his views are shared by many other CEOs.

## Continuing necessity of bureaucracy

A structured and orderly bureaucratic organization as defined by Max Weber (Etzioni, 1964) and others is an essential element of organizational life. Of course, people in organizations know that strict adherence to a hierarchy often is dysfunctional, and the bureaucratic element of organizations can be harmful. In many organizations, people spend too much of their time disputing territorial boundaries of authority or protecting their "turf." Although the hierarchy and the specificities of job description may be more flexible than was originally conceived by Max Weber (Etzioni, 1964), the principle of maintaining some unity of command is important, and failure to maintain a division of labor can lead to conflict and to some functions not being performed. The need for an organizational structure that separates tasks and maintains distinct responsibilities is probably as important as it always was. Understanding this issue is crucial to understanding organizations, which are great social inventions. The implications of this for management are obvious. The orderliness, the rules, and the division of labor are all elements that make it possible for organizational objectives to be achieved.

Bureaucracies also make it possible for people to be substituted and for work to continue even when key people are absent or unable to perform their duties. A well-organized bureaucracy ensures that clients are served efficiently and treated equitably. Furthermore, it is not likely that the concept of entitlements would be possible without bureaucratic organizations. The opposite of the bureaucracy is the organization based on sentiment, in which employees distribute services on the basis of their feelings about the applicant or the worthiness of the applicant's statement of need. With entitlements, only those who meet certain specific criteria are eligible for help.

The assurance that all applicants will be treated equally is important for public confidence and justice. Some people do not like bureaucracies because that uniform treatment is uniformly unfriendly, but that is a small price to pay compared with the alternative.

Bureaucracies do not have to be bad and do not have to treat their customers or clients uncaringly or brusquely. Many friendly and compassionate bureaucrats also operate professionally and within the regulations of the bureaucracy. However, appropriate, professional, and civil treatment are required, whereas friendly treatment is not.

### Psychology of workers and managers

One defining issue for new management is the importance it places on understanding and molding managers' personalities. Better understanding of human psychology and application of this knowledge to enhance management effectiveness have led to the development of modern management concepts. One popular idea in management has been Abraham Maslow's (1968) concept of basic human needs. Maslow postulated the existence of a hierarchy of needs (preference ordering) that people seek to satisfy. Not all needs have to be satisfied fully before the next level of satisfaction is reached, and people are likely to have some satisfaction, as well as some deprivation, of all their needs at a given time. However, people are probably motivated to satisfy the most basic needs before seeking the more advanced. The levels are physiological needs, safety needs, love/belonging needs, esteem needs, and self-actualization.

Motivating workers involves helping them meet their needs, especially those that are basic, with the recognition that other needs also play a role. These concepts were discussed earlier in the context of human relations approaches to management, the managerial grid, and McGregor's theories X and Y.

Etzioni (1964) defined other characteristics of successful modern managers. First, effective managers typically need to deal, often in the span of a few hours, with major long-range issues such as influencing legislation and public policy, resolving immediate personnel details that may have large implications for the organization, and handling press inquiries. Managers only infrequently have well-planned days. Emergencies and other new priorities develop that may require the manager to make immediate shifts in plans, to cancel meetings, to travel to other cities, and to otherwise shift gears with little or no notice. Adaptability and skill in quickly assessing and reacting to new problems or issues, as well as skill in making and sticking to long-range plans, are important characteristics of modern managers.

Second, successful managers tolerate frustration and can delay gratification (Etzioni, 1964). Modern managers must think in terms of long-range goals, not just immediate outcomes, which necessitates a long-term tolerance for relatively slow achievement of objectives.

Third, successful managers are achievement oriented; they have a strong urge to achieve both material and symbolic rewards. Complacency or general satisfaction with the status quo often hampers a person's ability to manage effectively. Discontent, striving, the desire to obtain more, and comparable qualities appear essential to modern management effectiveness.

### Whose organization is it?

One of the other major changes in modern organizational life is the recognition that businesses, social agencies, financial institutions, religious organizations, and virtually all other organized human endeavors are subject to some control by standards set by the larger environment. Previously, managers assumed that they were the absolute masters of their own organizations, but today they are constrained by external controls and regulations in areas such as the physical environment, employee relations, and customer treatment. Pollution, denial of employee rights, employment discrimination, and exploitation of customers are all forbidden by a network of legal regulations. It would be perilous for managers to neglect their obligations under the law. The uncontrolled operation of organizations as may have been the case in the past no longer exists.

**Employee rights.** A major management issue at one time in the United States was the right of workers to organize and collectively bargain with management over issues of salary and working conditions. This issue was resolved in the 1930s and 1940s with the enactment of the Wagner Act and the Taft–Hartley Law. More recently, other kinds of rules have been developed to protect employees and to regulate management–labor relations. Wage and hour laws are now clearly defined; discrimination in employment is forbidden; and generally, preferential treatment on the basis of color, religion, ethnicity, or age may not be given. Throughout the world, organizations, particularly businesses, have been held responsible for larger social goals than their own profitability or survival. Spain and Portugal, for instance, require organizations to work to preserve family life through housing, health care, education, and recreation programs. That is also true of many nations that are heavily influenced by the Roman Catholic Church, such as Colombia, where companies are expected to contribute amounts equal to or exceeding their payroll to programs of recreation and other services to their employees.

Human services agency managers are no different from the managers of business and other kinds of organizations. They must also follow the rules on nondiscrimination, affirmative action, protection of pensions, and social responsibility.

**Affirmative action.** Among the changes in the regulations governing employment are a variety of statutes and rules forbidding discrimination and requiring equal employment opportunity and "affirmative action." These requirements developed in a context of social and demographic changes. Many newcomers immigrated to the United States from Third World countries, and the potential for discriminatory behavior against them is comparable to that experienced in the early 1900s against such groups as Chinese, Irish, Italians, and Jews. The changing demographic composition in the United States requires not only vigilant law enforcement to deal with discrimination but also sensitive managers. As Roberts (1993) put it, "A shift in the ethnic, racial, and cultural composition of the work force pressures managers to exercise greater interpersonal skills than were needed in the past" (p. xiii).

Affirmative action requires organizations to give representatives of all groups employment opportunities. When candidates are equally qualified, people of color or women are often given the vacant positions, in part to compensate for past discriminatory behavior of the organization. The groups most typically protected are women, older individuals, African Americans, Hispanics, Native Americans, Asian Americans, and people with disabilities. Some believe that affirmative action can result in "reverse discrimination." This is not the intent of the law; in no case are unqualified people to be hired instead of those who are qualified. However, persons who meet the minimum requirements—not necessarily those who have higher grades on their transcripts or civil service scores—are considered equally qualified. In fact, members of different racial and ethnic groups are often more qualified because of special knowledge of their own communities, language skills, the ability to handle especially sensitive issues (for example, women with rape victims, older people with clients) and other characteristics, than members of the majority groups.

In any case, modern managers, whatever their organizations, must be aware of and comply with regulations on equal employment. They must be careful to avoid discrimination in services to clients, in employment, and in every other element of their personnel work. These issues are even more important in human services programs, partly because of a tradition of support for minority rights and partly because disproportionately large numbers of clients usually are women or elderly or from ethnic minority groups.

A corollary concern is sexual harassment—unwanted sexual advances or a climate of sexual tension caused by sexual jokes or innuendos (Weil, Hughes, & Hooyman, 1994). Effective managers must be aware of and able to overcome sexual harassment in their organizations.

**Employee security.** Among the growing responsibilities of managers is protection of the workforce. Increasing numbers of employees are assaulted by other employees and clients, as well as by people outside the organization—examples include attacks on offices with guns, the bombing of such buildings as New York City's World Trade Center and the Oklahoma City federal building, and ordinary thefts. Human services organizations, which deal with people with mental illness, child protection issues, and assistance grants, can engender angry clients. Therefore, security desks in office buildings, identification badges, the increasing use of locked doors, and other security measures have become common in most organizations and are the responsibilities of managers.

## POPULAR MANAGEMENT CONCEPTS

### Total quality management

Among the most well-regarded and widely used new management approaches is total quality management (TQM). TQM developed from the quality control movement and technology developed by W. E. Deming (1986; see also Creech, 1994; Dobyns, 1994; Gabor, 1990), who is credited with revolutionizing management and quality and whose ideas were a powerful influence in Japan, where he lived from 1990 to 1993. TQM goes beyond simply guaranteeing quality by monitoring activities and production and by pursuing continuous quality efforts.

Originally, efforts to maintain quality were confined to inspecting products before they left the plant. The process of sampling products and projecting the observed deficiencies to the entire production run was used to help control quality. One of the features of TQM is the development of "quality circles," in which workers in the organization come together to promote quality and to reinforce each other's pursuits of quality. The idea of TQM has taken hold in many organizations, including many human services organizations. The chapter by Morrissey and Wandersman in this book describes the application of the TQM model in a health care setting; see also Dale and Cooper's (1992) *Total Quality and Human Resources: American Executive Guide.*

The human services guide by Ammentorp, Gossett, and Euchner-Poe (1991), *Quality Assurance for Long-Term Care Providers*, provides information on the methods and instruments that can be used to maintain quality assurance in nursing homes and other long-term care facilities as required by the Omnibus Budget Reconciliation Act of 1987. This book offers assessment tools for evaluating the quality of life of residents and the quality of care provided by staff.

TQM has evolved from such processes as inspection, quality assurance, and quality control, which have been used not only in industry but also in human services organizations. In fact, quality control is a major factor in the administration and evaluation of such programs as Aid to Families with Dependent Children, Food Stamps, and Medicaid. States that do not satisfy the quality control requirements of the federal government for avoiding errors in those programs may be financially sanctioned. Although many may confuse errors in granting assistance under these programs, which may result from failure to check a financial source or other detail, with fraudulent receipt of help, the consequences for the states may be a loss of funds as a penalty for failure to operate a program of sufficient quality. Important sources on the subject for human services managers are Affholter and Kramer (1987) and Kramer (1987), based on panel studies by the National Academy of Sciences.

Martin (1993) believed that a quality crisis in human services is part of the reason for recent political attacks on social welfare programs and that implementing quality management approaches should help overcome that crisis. He also provided a guide for human services agencies to determine their ability to implement quality management programs. Martin proposed the following criteria: careful involvement by clients and their families in operating the program; a commitment to fine-tuning the agency and its services, even when things appear to be going well; collection of data for making decisions about changes; continuous training for staff; management communication in all directions (top–down, bottom–up, and sideways); a view of managers and supervisors as consultants whose job is to help staff do their jobs; and emphasis on teamwork.

Concepts of TQM are similar to those mentioned by Peters and Waterman (1982): a focus on the customer of the organization's services; involvement of everyone in the organization in the pursuit of quality; a heavy emphasis on teamwork; and, above all, encouragement of all employees to think about and pursue quality within the organization. Mistakes are viewed not as events to be covered up but as learning opportunities. Workers are discouraged from passing problems or errors along to the next level and are instead encouraged to focus on clearing up whatever problems they can before they are magnified. In an organization that practices TQM, everyone is on the quality team, and everyone is responsible for and encouraged to pursue quality results.

### Peters and Waterman's principles of excellence

Among the most popular of the new management concepts has been that developed by Tom Peters and Robert Waterman (1982) in their landmark book, *In Search of Excellence: Lessons from America's Best-Run Companies.* The high regard they are accorded is probably due to the fact that their findings are empirical. They and their colleagues in McKenzie and Company studied the best-run companies in the nation at the time (some of which have subsequently failed). Their concepts seem to fit well into the more fluid, situational management that has evolved in recent years. The responsive, frequently changing, form-modifying organizations of the late 20th century probably spawned these principles of excellent operations. Perhaps the most spectacular success–failure story involved People Express airline, which competed well against other airlines for several years before it was absorbed into a larger airline. People Express had the virtue of centralized operations (Newark, New Jersey) and proved there was a market for travelers who did not want to buy all the services that most airlines provided. Originally, the airline charged for checking luggage and for snacks and meals and apparently had less-than-efficient reservation and information systems. However, it had begun to cope with even this last problem by installing a sophisticated computer system shortly before it was absorbed by other airline companies. People Express was a model of the application of the eight principles of an excellent corporation defined by Peters and Waterman (1982): a bias for action; closeness to the customer; autonomy and entrepreneurship; productivity through people; a hands-on, value-driven approach; a "stick to the knitting" mode of operation; simple form, lean staff; and simultaneous loose–tight properties.

Peters and Waterman (1982) cited Domino's Pizza as another example of an excellent company; it continues to thrive, although it may not be as competitive now as it was when Peters and Waterman studied it, partly because Pizza Hut and other large pizza franchises have adopted some of Domino Pizza's programs (such as rapid home delivery). That fact does not suggest that the original ideas were poor; rather, it may prove their virtue.

Although Peters and Waterman's eight basic principles were written for businesses, they have ready application and significance for voluntary and public social welfare organizations as well. Although the ends are different, in that businesses necessarily focus on earnings and agencies focus on other indicators of success, the eight principles are means to ends that are appropriate for any kind of organized endeavor.

**1. A bias for action.** Peters and Waterman (1982), both of whom have written new books (Peters, 1987, 1992, 1994; Waterman, 1987), found that the best organizations are those that act instead of thinking about acting, planning for action, or studying possible activities. This principle—a bias for action—is important for social workers. Social workers probably have an even greater need for action, perhaps because action so often is stifled by immobilized organizations. One consequence of community priority studies and planning projects is that planning and study often do not lead to action. Organizations that identify and quickly act on an obvious need and an advantageous change in their programs often succeed more dramatically and for the longer term than do those organizations that continue to ponder what action to take, if any. Not all actions are necessarily beneficial, however, and organizations should not squander their resources on frivolous projects that have little possibility of success. However, taking an occasional risk or acting without complete information—because complete information is never available—often makes good sense for a social work manager.

Studying and assessing needs often is less effective than simply trying out an idea because research may generate misleading results. Often a pilot study or a small demonstration program that tries new ideas or programs will succeed more readily and more permanently—with later modifications—than will a perfectly designed attempt based on an ideal planning effort. Some of the most successful social agencies have been those that identified and attempted to respond to new needs, such as assisting clients with AIDS, dealing with the growing problem of homelessness, and finding ways to serve national and international migrants in the United States. Sometimes simply allowing a worker to try a new approach or service to a new community is an excellent way to determine whether the activity is worth more effort and agency resources. Successful organizations and their managers have a bias toward acting on a community's needs, on opportunities, and on new developments.

Peters and Waterman (1982) found that organizations reap rewards for action, although some actions have negative results. Innovative actions seem to keep employees motivated and optimistic. Customers and clients seem to respond positively to innovative and constantly changing organizations. For example, the director of a youth corrections facility that reevaluated and changed its comprehensive treatment approach every few years indicated that simply modifying the approach seemed to keep the staff and the youths involved and focused on treatment, although he had no evidence that one treatment approach was significantly better than any other. The author's experience as a director of activities for a community agency substantiates the virtue of action. The agency had two objectives for large-scale youth programs. The first was a winter vacation camp for one week in December, and the second was a three-week day camp in the summer. For the winter vacation camp, postcard surveys were sent to parents to assess the need for the project. The bulk of the responses indicated that such a program was not needed. When summer approached, the author mailed an announcement of the summer day camp with details on costs, the site, and the program, rather than conducting a survey. The response was sufficient for the program to be held that summer, and the camp has continued operating for three decades. A study or a long period of planning might have doomed the program, whereas action brought it to fruition.

**2. Be close to the customer.** Organizations are becoming more aware of the importance of being responsive to the needs of their customers. Successful manufacturers often seem to be those that can best assess and meet the demands of their customers. At times, that ability is more important than the quality of the products manufactured. IBM, for example, continuously monitors the use of its products by its customers and responds promptly and effectively to the need for service (Peters & Austin, 1986; Peters & Waterman, 1982).

The principles of excellence are as important in social work management as they are in the management of manufacturing, financial, and sales organizations. In the proprietary practice of social work, they are even more crucial. However, the concepts and language have to be better identified with and adapted to social welfare organizations. For instance, the principle of being close to the customer is easy to understand when it is applied to an organization that sells products. The example of the IBM staff staying close to customers by frequently visiting the offices of customers who purchase their equipment and quickly responding to customers who need help is reasonable. However, what if the service is Aid to Families with Dependent Children, food stamps, or the secure incarceration of criminals? In those circumstances, social work managers must understand that clients are not always customers. A number of other groups are the "customers" of the social workers who provide those services. Thus, the social work manager must determine who is purchasing the agency's services. Is it the agency's board of directors, the state legislature, or the federal government? This consideration does not mean that the manager should not be close to and concerned about the *recipients* of service, who are the clients. However, the real customers—the people who buy the service and pay the bills—may well be others. Therefore, the manager must stay close to members of the agency board or the state legislature or federal government officials who supervise the program and who purchase the services that are provided.

Other characteristics of closeness to the customer include being available for appointments and answering telephone calls and answering one's mail. Most managers can communicate directly with those who contact them. In a few situations (for example, public assistance agencies, which receive large numbers of detailed, technical inquiries), responses can be delegated to specialized correspondence or communications staff. However, all organizations and all managers should make sure that every telephone call and every letter is answered and that every request for an appointment is honored.

**3. Autonomy and entrepreneurship.** Excellent organizations also prize autonomy and entrepreneurship among their employees. They allow workers to try new ideas and programs. They listen carefully to and are supportive of innovative ideas. Excellent organizations often are short on discipline and long on imagination and creativity. Managers in these organizations support the workers' search for new and better ways to serve clients. The workers may spend less time carrying out orders or following policy manuals or procedural guides than their counterparts in more traditional organizations. Head Start, crisis intervention, case management, family day care, partial hospitalization, employee assistance programs (EAPs), and workfare are all innovative social work programs that started with workers who were allowed to develop their ideas on the basis of their observations of people's needs.

Furthermore, the best organizations often pick the best innovative ideas from their smaller counterparts and build on them. Even some large corporations find their best ideas in smaller organizations and among the customers with whom they work. Modern hotel chains are patterned, in many ways, on the innovative lodging designs of Holiday Inn, a chain of motels that was first established in Memphis, Tennessee. Before the development of the Holiday Inn corporation, there was a vast distinction between motels (which usually were owned locally, located away from downtown areas, and oriented to motorists) and hotels (which were large, downtown structures, some of which belonged to national chains). Some of the giant international hotel operations, such as Hilton and Sheraton, appear to have emulated Holiday Inns in their current practices—for example, by locating outside city centers and building smaller hotels with accessible parking.

Social agencies are different from businesses in that they try to avoid competition and duplication. If money is being made in the soft cookie industry, other companies justifiably get involved and do all they can to sell their versions of the product. However, if one agency is providing high-quality alcoholism treatment to everyone who needs it at a fee that is based on the clients' ability to pay, other agencies will not enter that field and try to compete because that would scatter the few resources available for helping people who abuse alcohol (current practices in health care may be changing that).

However, autonomy and entrepreneurship can be fostered within organizations and within the constraints of the planned, nonduplicative ideal of the human services industry by allowing workers to find their own ways to deal with the problems of the agency's clients.

Agencies frequently seek out and pay for the best possible social workers thay can find but then try to place those social workers in the tight constraints of agency discipline. Workers are required to practice in precisely the same ways as their peers and under the close supervision that often is found in social work programs.

An imaginative agency gives capable workers the freedom to find new ways to serve through groups, through consulting with community agencies, through sponsoring programs with related agencies and professionals, and through instituting programs in churches and other related institutions that may have better access to clients. An effective organization not only will find good social workers who have some initiative but will give them the opportunity to demonstrate their abilities through independent and innovative actitivies.

Of course, the agency remains accountable for the ways in which it expends its resources. Accountability is addressed frequently in the literature on social work management (Carter, 1983) and is a reality that managers of voluntary as well as public agencies must confront regularly. Observers of new approaches notice that those who manage are immobilized by the need to be accountable to such a degree that they stifle the imaginations and productivity of their employees.

**4. Productivity through people.** A related principle of excellence is productivity through people, which states that excellent organizations make their mark by effectively using the talents of people. These organizations do so by keeping employees happy, letting them know that they count, using their ideas, and giving them some role in managing and profiting from the company. This principle follows McGregor's (1960) notion of theory Y organizations—those that believe people can be counted on to help and that rely on their people for assistance and ideas. Too many organizations treat employees as if they were human forms of machinery or hardware and thus fail to get the best out of their workers. Rewarding employees, recognizing them, and perhaps helping them benefit financially are methods used by excellent companies.

Managers of large organizations can personalize their relationships with employees and improve their employees' morale by maintaining direct contact with them. In one large state government organization, the state director interviews all final candidates for positions. These candidates are recommended through the chain of command after a careful screening process that is based on pre-established criteria and an internal merit system. The final interview and official selection are made by the top manager. This manager rarely rejects the recommendations he receives. However, his final selection communicates to the entire agency staff that he cares about all the employees and that they are ultimately responsible to him for their employment. Such an action gives him an opportunity to meet everyone at least once and helps him retain the loyalty of a large number of employees.

In another large state government organization, the director sends a personal letter to each employee on the anniversary of the employee's appointment to a position in the agency. Employees know, of course, that the director's letters are prepared from a schedule, although they are personally signed. However, the action communicates to them that the top management knows when they first started working and considers each anniversary of their appointment significant. Some large agencies have a similar program for their employees' birthdays. Birthdays and beginning dates of employment are important milestones for employees, although they are essentially symbolic and have no special organizational meaning. Furthermore, employees recognize that the management cares enough to pay attention to something that is primarily of interest to them as individuals.

Symbols of position are important to some managers and staff at other levels in organizations. In some federal government agencies, careful attention is given to the size of offices and furnishings so that people of the same rank are treated equally and better than those who are subordinate to them. These and other noneconomic rewards for staff, such as service pins, patches for uniforms, and recognition in employee newsletters, often mean much more than employees are willing to admit.

**5. Hands-on, value-driven approach.** Peters and Waterman (1982) noted the importance of the hands-on, value-driven approach to management. They stated that organizations must know their values and work to pursue them. Effective managers, they suggested, remain close to the organization and work to make sure that the values of the organization are pursued.

If that value in social work practice involves helping clients become independent, then everything needs to be assessed through a screen of moving clients from dependence to greater independence. If the value involves improving clients' mental health functioning, then that value becomes the screen through which the organization measure its success. Whatever the values—social work agencies pursue many different kinds of values in many different ways—the manager's focus should remain on the achievement of those values.

**6. Stick to the knitting.** In presenting the principle "stick to the knitting," Peters and Waterman (1982) cautioned businesses against diversifying into fields they do not understand. The same principle may be applied readily to social agencies, even though these agencies may need to change their direction, particularly when the nature and the degree of social problems in their communities change.

Thus, an agency that is doing well should not abandon its successful activities for others that may seem attractive but that may not promise success. An effective agency that provides direct services may find itself hopelessly underused by the community when it tries to convert to a planning, advocacy, or standard-setting agency. Similarly, an agency that is effective at organizing services and planning for the resolution of human needs may be lost when it attempts to provide direct services. In another example, a health care organization may be tempted to provide mental health services but encounter many problems when it tries to add a service that is different from the immunizations, family planning, and other public health programs it provided. An agency that provides day care services to preschool children may have difficulty operating an after-school program for school-age children. None of these examples means that an agency should never change its roles or add functions. Instead, efforts to do so should be studied carefully, all the implications should be analyzed, and existing successful services should not be dropped before the new efforts prove successful.

**7. Simple form, lean staff.** Another principle of excellence is that organizations should have a simple form and a lean staff. The more complex one makes an organization and the more layers one encounters, the more problems one is likely to have in accomplishing anything. Multiple levels of supervision may unnecessarily complicate an organization. At times, it seems as if social work organizations reward key staff by giving them more people to supervise or more power over others. In fact, an excellent organization tends to minimize supervision and maximize goal-related work by all staff members.

Keeping the staff lean and small makes good sense not just to save money, but to avoid the complications of a larger staff. Many managers have discovered, to their surprise, that a larger staff does not really enhance the functions of the organization but, instead, makes it more difficult to achieve their agency's objectives. There is some evidence that hiring additional people complicates the manager's job because he or she must find ways to occupy them.

When I first became commissioner of welfare in West Virginia, I found that a number of dedicated people were working hard at jobs that no longer seemed necessary. Perhaps the jobs continued without their being evaluated or perhaps there may have been more employees than useful work for them to do. In one situation, an employee was preparing a detailed monthly report on a small program. The report may have been needed in the past but it no longer was. Therefore, the report-writing position was eliminated and the employee was moved to a job in the same city, serving clients with no reduction in salary. However, the new position was in a local office, rather than state head-quarters, a fact that the employee initially resented. In social work programs, focusing on the operational, client-serving levels and reducing the concentration of resources at the headquarters levels is consistent with modern management concepts. Many positions in headquarters are simply not needed. Sound management often requires one to appraise carefully the need for the people who surround the top levels of the organization.

More and more organizations are complying with this idea. Line workers in services and manufacturing as well as human services are retained, whereas supervisory and managerial positions are reduced. Modern technology has made many of the supervisory structures and positions that existed in the past unnecessary.

**8. Simultaneous loose–tight properties.** The last of the eight principles of excellence is that an organization must have both loose and tight properties. In other words, there must be a strong hand running the organization and a strong central direction and dedication to objectives within it, but the organization must give its workers the opportunity to work independently and exercise some autonomy.

Many organizations go too far in one of the two directions. For example, the author recalls an organization that was so eager to have professional social workers that it hired as many as it could and let the social workers work wherever they wished. This occurred in those wonderful days in the 1960s when there were many social work jobs and not nearly enough social workers to fill them. However, the organization made an obvious error in turning over its direction to the needs of potential staff rather than meeting its own needs. By the 1980s, the agency faced the same problems and successes as others in social welfare. There were now more social workers to employ and fewer dollars with which to employ them. The more formal and structured patterns of the modern era meant that the agency had to define its needs carefully and create positions on that basis while eliminating those positions that no longer were needed. The early loose patterns were balanced by tighter arrangements.

A combination of enough looseness to provide for flexibility and imagination within the staff and enough control to make the organization fit together is a critical principle. Being able to control, let go, take command, and delegate are all parts of effective, modern management.

Peters and Waterman's (1982) principles of excellence are among the most widely used of the modern management concepts in U.S. businesses. A careful study of the principles, along with conscientious applications to social work management, can improve the functioning of most social agencies.

Although the principles discussed by Peters and Austin (1986) and Peters and Waterman (1982) were initially developed with profit-making businesses in mind, it is useful for social work managers to think of their enterprises in some of the same terms. In fact, the writers frequently mention nonprofit and other service organizations, as well as government agencies, in their works. More and more social welfare positions are becoming business related and businesslike. Many social workers now engage in full- or part-time private practice. Others serve proprietary hospitals and nursing homes. An increasing number are employed by businesses to operate EAPs or work with agencies that contract with businesses to provide such services. Even the voluntary, nonprofit, and government social work programs, however, have many of the attributes of businesses; third-party reimbursements are often important income sources for them. They must balance their expenditures and resources, deploy personnel advantageously, change their operations in light of changing needs and conditions, take action when it is needed, relate effectively to customers, and pursue the activities they know how to do best. Therefore, modern management concepts are highly relevant to social work managers, as well as to their counterparts in business and industry.

### Seven habits

Another of the more popular concepts oriented to managers of recent years is Covey's (1994) *Daily Reflections for Highly Effective People,* in which he discusses seven habits: be proactive; begin with the end in mind; put first things first; think win–win; seek first to understand, then to be understood; synergize; and sharpen the saw.

These concepts are similar to those of other writers mentioned in this chapter. They emphasize the importance of communicating, setting, and working toward goals, being action-oriented, and self-renewal. They are in the mainstream of modern management thinking, and Covey's books have been best-sellers for years.

### Management by objectives

The best management is management that can pursue and reach its objectives. Modern emphasis on missions and objectives has, perhaps, supplanted the debates over specific management for specific settings. If the organization's objectives are clear, effective managers ought to be able to pursue and achieve those objectives. Objectives are diverse. The objective may be profit for businesses; the delivery of services for some social agencies; and social control for law enforcement agencies. Therefore, debates about the differences between, for example, public administration and business administration are really about the differences between objectives rather than differences between management styles.

One example of the recognition of the centrality of objectives was the development of the concept of management by objectives (MBO; Albrecht, 1978), which is as popular as the managerial grid and other analytic and training systems. Managers at every level are trained to work with and evaluate their subordinates according to agreed-on objectives, and those objectives become the content of supervisory conferences. The developers of MBO suggested that decisions about compensation and promotion be excluded from the process.

One of the difficulties associated with managing by objectives or understanding management effectiveness in relation to objectives is that organizations sometimes fail to state their objectives or else they misstate them. In the public arena, there are occasional contradictions. Some corrections staff and even corrections agencies may believe that their primary objective is the rehabilitation of offenders, although they acknowledge their dual responsibilities for helping offenders and protecting the public. However, state legislators may view the public's protection from offenders as the primary objective and rehabilitation as secondary, if it is an objective at all. One public assistance manager may view the manager's role as ensuring that all those who are eligible receive the services to which they are entitled, whereas another may view the same role as being focused on limiting to the bare minimum the number of people who receive assistance. The differences in the likely managerial behaviors of the two are obvious and demonstrate how differing understandings of objectives may lead to different behaviors.

## Principles for human services managers
Some of the fundamentals of management can be distilled into a list that makes sense for social workers while applying the basic concepts of business management to the human services settings.

**1. Maintain a focus on goals.** A goal orientation is more difficult for social work managers than for managers in business because there are often multiple and conflicting goals, as has been mentioned in some of the earlier discussions in this chapter. Serving clients is one objective, but, at times, it is difficult to determine exactly who the client is. In child protective services, the statutes are designed to protect children from abuse or neglect. However, there is a related goal of keeping parents and their children united. Protecting mentally ill people from harm is a clear objective but, in some cases, mental health programs are designed to prevent people with mental illness from harming others. In other cases, mental health organizations work to keep people who might be considered mentally ill from being improperly hospitalized.

In some cases, human services managers rise and fall on their ability to help their chief executive officer remain in power. That is especially true in government organizations, in which human services managers serve at the will of a governor, a mayor, or even a president.

Maintaining a focus on goals probably means, above all, knowing who one's boss is and following the demands of that boss in one's management of a program. The boss, baldly defined, is the person or persons who can terminate the manager's employment. Therefore, knowing what the boss expects is a part of knowing one's goals and keeping them in mind. Helping the boss look good is an infrequently stated but important function for managers.

The statutes, policy manuals, or, in the case of voluntary organizations, mission statements and board directives for the organization provide other goals the manager needs to understand. National organizations also often have national policies that are applied to state and local units of the organization. In any case, effective managers devote extensive thought to the objectives of their tasks and are always careful to remain mission focused in their work.

**2. Deal with multiple publics.** Just as the manufacturing company must be concerned about government regulators, consumers, suppliers, and the media, among others, the human services manager must be aware of and deal with a variety of publics. For human services managers, those publics will always include clients, but they will also include the media, government organizations, advisory or governing boards and their individual members, funding organizations including foundations, and related organizations in the same field and in the same community. An effective manager is aware of multiple audiences and the need to deal with them. Sometimes the audiences' wishes conflict with one another. Mediating among the various goals of the various groups is often a central task of the human services manager. For example, agency rules and professional mandates may require confidentiality. The media may want facts, and the public's perception of the organization may be powerfully affected by the media reactions. Being able to interpret the agency's confidentiality requirements while continuing to relate effectively to the media is often a challenge for managers. In another example, a powerful individual board member may have objectives that differ significantly from those of other board members. Keeping the board member involved and think-ing as well as speaking positively about the organization is frequently another managerial challenge. Public agency managers often find themselves caught between the wishes of the executive and legislative branches of government. Although they work under the direction of the executive branch, legislative actions can have a profound influence on the organization. This kind of bal-ancing is often a source of frustration for managers. Perhaps the most negative outcome—which is more typical than would be desirable—is for the conflict-ing publics to agree that the manager must be replaced.

**3. Be positive.** There is nothing quite so ineffective as a manager who is gloomy about the organization's future. An effective manager, although realistic, tries to remain positive about the organization, its effectiveness, and its mission. An effective manager monitors the environment, adjusts the organization, and even makes major changes in its mission and service delivery system. But the effective manager tries to see the bright side of things, viewing problems as opportunities for trying something different or making necessary changes that might have been impossible had the prob-lem not developed.

**4. Understand the appropriate level of management.** Managers operate at various levels. The manager at the operational or supervisory level is typically focused on the task at hand and on the cadre of employees carrying out the work of the organization. Dealing with issues such as personnel practices, work schedules, and the like is the typical preoccupation of that level of management. The sec-ond level of management is focused on meshing responsibilities among the parts of the organization, coordinating the various divisions, and attempting to operate the program in as smooth and effective a way as possible. That level of management also concentrates on looking for issues that require resolution and proposing changes that may be required.

The higher-level manager stays in touch with the larger environment—the community, the state government, funding organizations, and regulatory bodies. An effective upper-level manager devotes less time to the internal operations of the organization and more time to monitoring and working with the larger environment. That is why state or local agency directors may know very little about the internal functioning of their organizations but a great deal about the legislature, the local United Way, or other crucial entities.

**5. Work with the staff.** Some of the earlier ideas of classic, scientific manage-ment suggested that employees were more or less like machines and that, in fact, the more like machines they could be treated, the better off the management of the organization would be. Reducing the human factor seemed to be the desire rather than building on and working with it.

However, it now is widely believed that employees can make the organization work or cause it to fail. Loyal, committed employees can convince clients of the worthwhile nature of the agency; can assist in fund development; and can help the media react positively to the organization. Disgruntled or angry employees often have the opposite effect. Experiments in industry that allow employees to work as a team to complete a task, even a task such as constructing an automobile, have gained favor in the management literature. Staff training and development, humane and concerned supervision, soliciting ideas from employees rather than imposing regulations on them, and similar activities have all contributed to more effective organizations.

Providing rewards to staff, including tangible rewards such as salary increases or bonuses, is an effective means of motivating. So are special parking places and better offices. Rewards such as plaques, service pins, and recognition in employee newsletters also have merit. Helping staff attend professional meetings or participate in training sessions are also examples of how organizational goals can be pursued while motivating employees.

**6. Understand the effectiveness–efficiency continuum.** An ideal organization is both effective and efficient. An efficient organization is one that uses the minimum amount of resources to achieve its objectives. Holding down costs, providing more service without adding staff or other expenses, and otherwise getting the most for the expenditure are all examples of efficient operations.

Of course, managers must be cautious when seeking efficiency in their efforts. Humane wages, for example, are important for maintaining employee morale and for avoiding turnover among employees. Although it is poor management to pay lavish wages, which might be defined as significantly more in salary and benefits than a comparable employee would be able to earn in a comparable organization, it is also unwise to skimp on wages.

An effective organization is simply one that meets its objectives—that carries out its mission ably. It is possible for an organization to expend so many resources on achieving its objectives that it is highly inefficient. Just reaching the goal is typically not justification enough for calling an organization sound or competent, because it may do so much to reach its objectives that it is not a solid organization in the long run. For example, some fundraising organizations raise significant amounts of money but at such great cost that very little of what they raise is used for the services they provide. An organization that spends half or more of the proceeds of its fundraising efforts to finance those efforts is neither efficient nor effective—although it can argue that it has reached its financial goals.

**7. Know the absolute bottom line in management.** In the management of organizations, the absolute bottom line is money management. Effective managers have always understood that. In some cases, however, program-oriented human services managers make the error of treating financial issues as the province of specialists. They turn over the financial decision making and financial management to accountants or other fiscal experts. However, by doing so, they abdicate the main feature of modern management—obtaining, managing, and monitoring financial resources. Nothing, of course, takes place in organizations unless it is associated with money. To try to manage an organization without managing its finances is impossible. If someone else is making financial decisions, then the manager is not really making the key decisions about the organization. Paying attention to the absolute bottom line is essential to any management.

**8. Sponsor and participate in management training.** One of the major management activities and innovations in recent years is training for managers and for organizational staff. The training of managers is a multibillion dollar industry. It apparently works as a good investment for organizations because it improves the performance and therefore the productivity in both the profit-making and nonprofit sectors. In government agencies that receive federal funds, professional training of staff members is encouraged.

Training occurs on almost every subject from interpersonal relations and leadership to technical instruction on completing forms, policies, and regulations. Training is also provided on methods of service, diagnoses of problems, especially in mental health, and many other subjects that touch the operations of organizations. Some training is provided by externally selected firms that specialize in management training. In other cases, management training is a product of internal staff assignments. Programs can range from weekly brown bag lunches in agency conference rooms to retreats at major resorts or special training centers with nationally known presenters. Some organizations, particularly large organizations, maintain full-time training centers with well-developed technological training materials, housing facilities, and food services. Some organizations, including those in the human services, maintain training staffs who coordinate and sometimes provide training and maintain training records on each staff member.

The almost universal legal regulation of human services workers through licensing and other forms of regulation has increased the amount of training in which workers and managers participate. Most state regulation programs require those who are regulated or licensed to earn specific numbers of educational hours as a condition of maintaining their licenses.

**9. Remember the basics.** Some management concepts are not quite as esoteric as they may seem. Such principles as answering telephone calls, mentioned earlier, may be more critical than the specific management models one adopts. Other fundamentals that deal with appearance and dress—being appropriate and neat and avoiding the unusual—seem to work for the large corporations and probably for human services organizations as well. What one does about men's facial hair may depend on the community and clientele. Beards are "in" in some settings but "out" in others. Mickey Mouse neckties are probably only taken seriously when top executives of the Disney corporations wear them. Molloy (1975a, 1975b, 1988) offered excellent, empirically derived suggestions for dress and appearance in his books on dress and success.

## CONCLUSION

Managing effectively is such a difficult task that there is always opportunity for perfecting management skills or finding new systems for motivating and leading staff. The challenges are enormous, success has handsome rewards, and failures are devastating.

## REFERENCES

Affholter, D. P., & Kramer, F. D. (Eds.). (1987). *Rethinking quality control: A new system for the food stamp program.* Washington, DC: National Academy Press.

Albrecht, K. (1978). *Successful management by objectives: An action manual.* Englewood Cliffs, NJ: Prentice Hall.

Ammentorp, W., Gossett, K. D., & Euchner-Poe, N. (1991). *Quality assurance for long-term care providers.* Newbury Park, CA: Sage Publications.

Austin, D. M. (1995). Management overview. In R. L. Edwards (Ed.-in-Chief), *Encyclopedia of social work* (19th ed., Vol. 2, pp. 1642–1658). Washington, DC: NASW Press.

Blake, R.R., & McCanse, A.A. (1991). The leadership grid figure. Paternalism figure and opportunism. In R.R. Blake & A.A. McCanse (Eds.), *Leadership dilemmas—Grid solutions* (pp. 29–30). Houston: Gulf Publishing.

Blake, R. R., & Mouton, J. S. (1964). *The managerial grid.* Houston: Gulf Publishing.

Brody, R. (1993). *Effectively managing human service organizations.* Newbury Park, CA: Sage Publications.

Carter, R. K. (1983). *The accountable agency.* Beverly Hills, CA: Sage Publications.

Covey, S. R. (1994). *Daily reflections for highly effective people.* New York: Simon & Schuster.

Creech, B. (1994). *The five pillars of TQM.* New York: Trema/Tallon.

Crow, R. T., & Odewahn, C. A. (1987). *Management for the human services.* Englewood Cliffs, NJ: Prentice Hall.

Dale, B., & Cooper, C. (1992). *Total quality and human resources: American executive guide.* Cambridge, MA: Blackwell.

Darwin, C. (1900). *Origin of the species by means of natural selection, or the preservation of favored races in the struggle for life.* New York: P. F. Collier & Sons.

Deming, W. E. (1986). *Out of the crisis.* Cambridge, MA: MIT Press.

Dickson, W. J. (1973). Hawthorne experiments. In C. Heyel, *The encyclopedia of management* (2nd ed., pp. 298–302). New York: Van Nostrand Reinhold.

Dobyns, L. (1994). *Thinking about quality: Progress, wisdom, and the Deming philosophy.* New York: Random House.

Etzioni, A. (1964). *Modern organizations.* Englewood Cliffs, NJ: Prentice Hall.

Follett, M. P. (1973). *Dynamic administration: The collected papers of Mary Parker Follett.* New York: Pitman.

Fox, W. M. (1973). Scientific management: Taylorism. In C. Heyel, *The encyclopedia of management* (2nd ed., pp. 923–930). New York: Van Nostrand Reinhold.

Gabor, A. (1990). *The man who discovered quality: How W. Edward Deming brought the quality revolution to America.* New York: Random House.

Graham, P. (1995). *Mary Parker Follett—Prophet of management: A celebration of writings from the 1920s.* Boston: Harvard Business School Press.

Gulick, L., & Urwick, L. (1937). *Papers on the science of administration.* New York: Institute of Public Administration.

Gummer, B. (1990). *The politics of social administration: Managing organizational politics in social agencies.* Englewood Cliffs, NJ: Prentice Hall.

Heyel, C. (1973). Management movement: Leaders in thought. In C. Heyel, *The encyclopedia of management* (2nd ed., pp. 512–515). New York: Van Nostrand Reinhold.

Jary, D., & Jary, J. (1991). *The HarperCollins dictionary of sociology.* New York: HarperCollins.

Koontz, H. (1990). *Essentials of management* (5th ed.). New York: McGraw-Hill.

Kramer, F. D. (Ed.). (1987). *From quality control to quality improvement in AFDC and Medicaid.* Washington, DC: National Academy Press.

Labor–Management Relations Act of 1947, 18 U.S.C.A. §610 et seq. (Taft–Hartley).

Linden, D. W. (1995, January 16). The mother of them all. *Forbes,* pp. 75–76.

Martin, L. L. (1993). *Total quality management in human services organizations.* Newbury Park, CA: Sage Publications.

Maslow, A. H. (1968). *Toward a psychology of being* (2nd ed.). New York: Van Nostrand Reinhold.

Mayo, E. (1946). *The human problems of an industrial civilization.* Boston: Harvard Business School.

McGregor, D. (1960). *The human side of enterprise.* New York: McGraw-Hill.

Molloy, J. T. (1975a). *Dress for success.* New York: Warner Books.

Molloy, J. T. (1975b). *The woman's dress for success book.* New York: Warner Books.

Molloy, J. T. (1988). *New dress for success.* New York: Warner Books.

National Labor Relations Act, 29 U.S.C.A. §§151 to 161 (1935) (Wagner Act).

Omnibus Budget Reconciliation Act of 1981, P.L. 97-35, 95 Stat. 357.

Peters, T. J. (1987). *Thriving on chaos: Handbook for a management revolution.* New York: Alfred A. Knopf.

Peters, T. J. (1992). *Liberation management.* New York: Fawcett Books.

Peters, T. J. (1994). *The pursuit of WOW: Every person's guide to topsy turvy times.* New York: Vintage.

Peters, T. J., & Austin, N. (1986). *A passion for excellence: The leadership difference.* New York: Warner Books.

Peters, T. J., & Waterman, R. H., Jr. (1982). *In search of excellence: Lessons from America's best-run companies.* New York: Harper & Row.

Rapp, C. A., & Poertner, J. (1992). *Social administration: A client-centered approach.* New York: Longman.

Roberts, W. (1993). *Victory secrets of Attila the Hun.* New York: Doubleday.

Skidmore, R. A. (1994). *Social work administration: Dynamic management and human relation-ships* (3rd ed.). Englewood Cliffs, NJ: Prentice Hall.

Spero, S. D. (1973). Public administration. In C. Heyel, *The encyclopedia of management* (2nd ed., pp. 807–822). New York: Van Nostrand Reinhold.

Syers, M. (1995). Mary Parker Follett. In R. L. Edwards (Ed.-in-Chief), *Encyclopedia of social work* (19th ed., Vol. 3, p. 2585). Washington, DC: NASW Press.

Taylor, F. (1947). *Scientific management.* New York: Harper & Row.

Townsend, R. (1970). *Up the organization.* New York: Alfred A. Knopf.

Townsend, R. (1984). *Further up the organization: How to stop management from stifling people and strangling productivity.* New York: Alfred A. Knopf.

Tropman, J. E., Johnson, H. R., & Tropman, E. J. (1992). *Committee management in human services: Running effective meetings, committees, and boards* (2nd ed.). Chicago: Nelson-Hall.

Waterman, R. H., Jr. (1987). *The renewal factor: How the best get and keep the competitive edge.* New York: Bantam Books.

Weil, M. O., Hughes, M., & Hooyman, N. R. (1994). *Sexual harassment and schools of social work: Issues, costs, and strategic responses.* Alexandria, VA: Council on Social Work Education.

Weinbach, R. W. (1994). *The social worker as manager: Theory and practice* (2nd ed.). Needham Heights, MA: Allyn & Bacon.

Yankey, J., & Edwards, R. (Eds.). (1991). *Skills for effective human services management.* Silver Spring, MD: NASW Press.

# Chapter 2

# The Imperative of Professional Leadership in Public Service Management

Joseph  J.  Bevilacqua

In the future, public services, particularly those services that involve social work, will face a new set of challenges. The traditional roles of family, community, and health care, for example, will have to assume new patterns of assistance in dealing with the interdependence of generations, with profound diseases such as AIDS, with homelessness, and with the structural poverty brought on by economic dysfunction (Wilkinson, 1987). These issues will push the human services systems into greater political ferment and, consequently, affect future practice. The question of professional leadership will have to go beyond the confines of any one profession or discipline.

*This chapter was originally published in Keys, P. R., & Ginsberg, L. H. (Eds.). (1988). New management in human services (pp. 283–289). Silver Spring, MD: National Association of Social Workers.*

Because the public sector is large and comprehensive, it will play a continuing role in managing these aspects of life. To meet the challenge, government service will require stronger advocates and professionals who are well trained and respected.

It is interesting to note that Paul Volcker, the former chair of the Federal Reserve Board, plans to devote a significant portion of his retirement to building a stronger base of both support and respect for government service (as reported in Hunt, 1987). Additionally, John Gardner, a leading American philosopher and public official, also has focused on the importance of developing leaders who can cope with ongoing as well as emerging problems in government (Hechinger, 1987).

Social workers are drifting away from public service and are beginning to emulate models of entrepreneurship in human services. The development of public leaders will require a return to the traditional value of services rather than profits. The social work profession must recapture the social ideology that values the sustenance of human beings—an ideology that social workers may have lost by allowing the balance of psychosocial concerns to tilt toward the psychological and away from the social.

## THE DRIFT

The trend is away from traditional social work values. Social workers cannot allow themselves to develop into a profession whose mission is simply to avoid doing harm, and they also cannot afford to condone the idea that the state is hostile to individuals and that litigation is the only way to make the state behave.

In government service and education programs, discussions of some real and continuing problems in the practice of social work are avoided. Professional social work education teaches far too little about the chronic mentally ill and provides far too little professional labor for their care (Davis, 1987). Apparently, social workers focus less on public issues than on the microproblems of individuals and families—those who are more likely to be able to pay for the services they receive. Paradoxically, as more community care is required for people, social work is moving away from its traditional role as a participant and leader in community care. At a time when care is increasingly home based and voluntary and informal groups are moving into community caregiving, social work is becoming more office based and emulating the professional models of medicine and law. Skills that are necessary for group work and planning, which are central to good psychosocial programs for the mentally ill and for helping the chronically mentally ill become employable, are becoming less identified with social work, even though the concepts emerged from the social work tradition. Private practice is becoming the goal and the occupation of many professional social workers, which poses a problem because too much of private practice is unavailable to the indigent.

## THE ENVIRONMENT OF PUBLIC SERVICE

The environment of public services has become less attractive to new and developing professionals. Although there is a tradition of life-long employment in the civil service positions of many human services agencies, the tenure in office for top leaders is brief. State commissioners of mental health, for example, average two years on the job. In 1987, 22 states changed mental health commissioners, according to the National Association of State Mental Health Program Directors ("The Editors Interview Harlan Cleveland," 1982). That pattern is replicated in departments of social services and other human services programs.

### The management environment

Working with chief executive officers—governors—is also a new challenge for top leaders in the human services. Once they are elected, politicians assume centrist positions; they are not as free to take risks. Human services issues are unpopular with governors and have only minimal clout with voters. What a governor achieves in the area of human services rarely has a positive effect on his or her career. Frequently, however, it has a negative effect, when human services programs are seen primarily as problems and not solutions.

The problems in public agencies are so diverse and so complex that they can be mind-boggling. The typical governor, in a single day, may have to deal with major issues of architecture and finances involving millions or even billions of dollars, as well as individual case matters that affect only a few people. All that work takes place in a glass bowl, with the press, the legislature, clients' families, staff, and all the other constituencies of a public official watching closely.

In this era of declining real resources for the government, there is also great competition for the funds that are available. The competition with highway programs, education, and other services makes it difficult for governments to allocate funds on the basis of need, particularly to the human services. In many states, lawsuits have been filed to bring programs of mental health and support services to needy citizens.

### Importance of the public sector

Despite all its problems, the public sector remains the keystone of all other human services. Only the public sector can and must treat people in need equitably and insist on their right to equal treatment. Because the services are designed to alleviate poverty and hunger, as is the case with social services, or to treat problems of physical or mental illness, as is often the case with public health and mental health programs, equality of treatment is an absolute in government service. All people have a right to treatment, and anything less is a legitimate basis for litigation. The government remains the one sector of human services systems that cannot say no to people who are eligible for help.

The public sector also can promote and enforce standards in such fields as education, child care, and health care. Only the government has the sanction and the resources to ensure that adequate standards are met. Were it not for those standards, which even today are not as fully enforced as they should be, the treatment of people who have social and emotional problems would be even less adequate than it is.

The government can deal with need in other ways as well. For instance, it can, and generally must, serve as the organization of last resort for dealing with individuals who have nowhere else to turn. In doing so, individual and group needs emerge. Government agencies can and do conduct research to identify trends in needs and developments; they can fund demonstration models that develop efficient approaches to helping others in ways that can be replicated by larger systems as well as voluntary agencies. Perhaps what is most important, the public sector serves as a forum for policy discussions within the agencies themselves, within legislative bodies, and within the court systems. As Thomas Jefferson said, "The care of human life and happiness, and not their destruction, is the first and only legitimate object of good government."

## ROLE OF SOCIAL WORK

The social work profession is a facilitator of leadership in public service. Traditionally, social work has provided the link among services and the services themselves to those people who need them. Social work has provided that same link among service providers, so that together, they can make the best care available at the lowest possible cost. Social workers are a profession of organizers and planners, not just treatment providers.

Social work also plays a crucial role in the development of services because it works with people as they relate to the environment in which they live. Problem solving takes place most effectively when it occurs within the context of the larger environment.

Social workers also are oriented toward working through systems; they recognize the impact of working in an interdisciplinary fashion. By working together with people to solve problems in an effective way, they build on their own capacities to solve problems.

Social workers are optimistic; for example, they view the cup as half full, rather than half empty. They value self-determination, which they express in work toward enhancing clients' strengths, rather than focusing on weaknesses and pathology. This model is increasingly important in public service. As a profession, social workers have a long tradition of working with the community at large—with lay citizens, volunteers, and boards. Social workers are dedicated more to service and action than they are to study and analysis. That is, social workers have a bias for doing rather than for simply thinking or projecting solutions.

### LEADERSHIP

Many believe that the essence of leadership for the future will be the skill of pulling together expertise, not in developing more expertise ("The Editors Interview Harlan Cleveland," 1982). Expert information already is available in many areas, including the technical areas of human services. What is needed now is the ability to blend that expertise so that social workers will be better able to implement good programs. Social workers recognize more and more that the real problems are interdisciplinary—that no one discipline has all the answers. The profession of social work is not threatened by that awareness.

Indeed, social workers are situated ideally to work in an interdisciplinary world. Their focus on consultation, information and referral, and case management is a good indicator of their commitment to the interdisciplinary approach.

Social workers also have focused on similar concepts that are important for the development of leadership in the future. Social workers practice what they know about maximizing strengths. They know about helping people develop self-confidence and the will to improve before they try to change those people. All these factors point to leadership, and the factors will be influential in making social work prominent in public service in the future.

Throughout many years in public service, the author has developed several beliefs about the necessary conditions of leadership. They are as follows:

- Believe in what you are doing and have the vision to understand its importance.
- Assume and understand that risk is part of the game and that effective leaders lose as well as win their battles.
- Recognize that there are no secrets in public service—that anything one does or says may become public knowledge almost immediately.
- Get out into the public and be known on the street and in the community. Do not be a shadowy, isolated figure.

- Do not wear green eyeshades. You have specialists in accounting, so you do not need to be one yourself.
- Recognize that ambiguity is part of the job. Many more situations are ambiguous than are clear and precise.
- Have a good personal support system of family, friends, and colleagues.
- Search for and hire able people who are loyal and who share your values. They are important to your success.
- Encourage celebrations of success but avoid bureaucratic rituals. That is, honor devoted employees but do not let these honors become ritualistic. Celebrate milestones in the agencies; work to make them genuine celebrations in which people want to participate.
- Develop a broad base of support to lead effectively.
- Work for, obtain, and use political support.
- Pay attention to the consumer—both listen and respond. The recipient of services may know more about what your agency does and should be doing than anyone else.
- Develop and maintain a connection with institutions of higher education. Universities have the objectivity and the information to help you succeed in ways that would not be possible without such connections.
- Work for significant and visible success early in your tenure on the job. You will be able to build on that success.
- Do not take the credit—not all or even most of it. Defer to others and spread the credit around. Everyone will assume that you are largely responsible for what happened, but others will appreciate your willingness to let them share in the glory.
- Do not maintain a dogmatic position. Have convictions, but understand that there are many ways to achieve the same fundamental objectives.
- Communicate in a straightforward way. Do not dodge the truth or use complex terminology to avoid saying what you mean. Everyone should hear from you in a straight and direct manner.
- Love your job but recognize that you are only a temporary occupant and will someday have to give it up. Be totally dedicated and be willing to drop out when the time comes.

## REFERENCES

Davis, K. E. (1987). *The challenge to state mental health systems and universities in Virginia: Preparation of mental health professionals for work with the chronic mentally disabled: Final report.* Unpublished manuscript, Virginia Commonwealth University, School of Social Work, Richmond.

The editors interview Harlan Cleveland. (1982). *New England Journal of Human Services, 2,* 8.1.

Hechinger, F. M. (1987, August 18). Help wanted: Leaders [About Education]. *New York Times,* p. 20.

Hunt, A. R. (1987, July 24). Paul Volcker: The ultimate public servant. *Wall Street Journal,* p. 20.

Wilkinson, G. (1987). *National planning assumptions and select key implications for United Ways.* Paper presented at the Annual Meeting of the Profession, National Association of Social Workers, New Orleans.

# Chapter 3

# MBA, MPA, MSW

## *Is There a Degree of Choice for Human Services Management?*

Anthony A. Cupaiuolo, Grant Loavenbruck, and Kim Kiely

The merits of the master of business administration (MBA), the master of public administration (MPA), and the master of social work (MSW) degrees are compared with respect to human services management. The following interrelated questions are addressed:

- Do business, public administration, or social work graduate schools show more interest in human services management than they did in the past?
- Do any of the accrediting bodies associated with these disciplines show more interest in human services management than they did in the past?

- Are graduates of these professional schools considered to be adequately prepared for management positions?

Management innovation (including the reinventing and reengineering of organizations) is the subject of articles in the contemporary management literature as well as the popular press. In particular, the concept of total quality management has demonstrated real staying power; it was initiated by W. Edwards Deming after World War II and was used effectively by the Japanese before it was "rediscovered" in the United States toward the end of the 1980s. Generally, ideas are developed in the corporate sector and then are adopted by the public and nonprofit sectors. Human services organizations should apply these ideas with caution, however. Their mission, functions, and values differ significantly from those of corporations (Cupaiuolo & Dowling, 1983), and their ability to adapt management practices effectively from the private sector requires an awareness of, and sensitivity to, the characteristics that distinguish them from that sector.

Richard Hoefer (1993), a University of Texas social work professor, conducted a major empirical study that focused on two questions:

- What skills do current administrators of nonprofit organizations consider to be important?
- What type of degree program, if any, do these administrators believe is best suited to teach these skills?

One hundred human services agencies in the Chicago area were randomly selected for the survey; 44 responded. The majority (63 percent) were nonprofit, 27 percent were government organizations, 7 percent were for profit, and 3 percent fell in the "other" category. Most of the surveys were completed by the agency executive or by someone else in an upper-management position. Respondents were asked to rank the importance of 37 skills, attitudes, and knowledge areas to human services organization administrators at the entry level, middle level, and top level. They were also asked their opinion regarding the academic training that was most useful at each level from among the following: no management degree, master of social work (administrative track), master of public administration, master of business administration, and other.

It is interesting to note that a significant percentage of the respondents (29 percent) did not have advanced degrees. The remainder had advanced degrees in a fairly wide range of fields: MSW (12 percent); MBA (7 percent); education (7 percent); public health (7 percent); divinity (7 percent); MPA (5 percent); and unspecified or other (26 percent). The diversity of the advanced degrees held by the respondents would tend to preclude results that might have been biased because of the preponderance of any one type of degree. The actual results of Hoefer's study are discussed in the following sections for each of the three degrees.

## MBA DEGREE

### Overview

In the first edition of this book, it was predicted that the rapid and continuous increase in the number of MBA graduates was about to come to a halt (Cupaiuolo & Miringoff, 1988, p. 44). The emergence into adulthood of the baby boomers alone could be expected to result in a decline in the growth of MBA programs and even lead to a decrease in the absolute number of students and the elimination of some programs. The October 1987 stock market crash could serve as a reality check for potential MBA graduates who believed it was axiomatic that they would convert their sheepskins into megadollars on Wall Street. One might also assume that endemic corporate downsizing even in such traditional bastions of stability such as IBM would further erode the value of the MBA degree. Add to these facts of life the recession of the early 1990s, and there would seem little doubt that the MBA degree had lost its luster.

Nevertheless, business schools are generally thriving, despite all predictions to the contrary. Not one MBA school has closed its doors; in fact, a record 84,642 MBAs were granted in 1992, representing an 8 percent increase from the year before. There does not appear to be any change in sight; many of the more prestigious schools are reporting increases in number of applicants (Bongiorno & Byrne, 1994).

Meyer Feldberg, dean of Columbia University's Business School, foresees the possibility of another surge in MBA education as applicants stream in from developing countries. He suggested that the top 20 schools could get as many as 400 to 500 applications from China alone (Bongiorno & Byrne, 1994). According to Thomas P. Gerrity, president of the Wharton School of the University of Pennsylvania, "Applications from Latin Americans have been growing at the rate of 20 percent a year for the last five years" (Brooks, 1994, p. 4).

The reason that business graduate schools continue to be so successful in recruiting students is that their graduates continue to be successful, at least when success is measured in dollar terms. For example, of the 4,608 MBAs in the class of 1994 who responded to a *Business Week* survey, 594 (13 percent) indicated that they already knew that they would earn $100,000 or more in total compensation in their first year of work (Bongiorno & Byrne, 1994). According to that same survey, the principal career paths of the MBAs include consulting (46.3 percent), finance (13.6 percent), investment banking (8.8 percent), general management (5.1 percent), and marketing (3.7 percent).

What do the business school trends suggest about human services management? Business schools do not appear to focus on human services management or nonprofits in general, and newly minted degree holders show no particular need or interest in seeking careers in human services management. In fact, the *Business Week* survey revealed that only a little more than 5 percent of the business school graduates are interested in general management in any field. Indeed, why should they be, when more lucrative career paths beckon (Borgiorno & Byrne, 1994)?

### Utility for human services management

The following information is based on an informal survey and discussions with business school colleagues. There is some indication of increasing interest on the part of business schools in health management. This is undoubtedly driven by the growing emphasis on managed care as a means to reduce or at least slow down the growth of health care costs. It is perfectly logical for an emerging health care industry that has cost containment as its goal to welcome MBAs and consequently for business schools to develop special health care management programs. The marketing of managed health care would also be a skill associated with business education.

The MBA socialization process is at best irrelevant to human services and at worst inimical to them, because it fosters a materialistic ethic. Does the future look any different? If the latest *Standards for Business Accreditation* provides any guidance (American Assembly of Collegiate Schools of Business, 1994), the answer is apparently negative. According to the *Standards*, graduate schools of business should include instruction in the following core areas: financial reporting, analysis and markets, domestic and global economic environments of organizations, creation and distribution of goods and services, and human behavior in organizations.

Unquestionably, some of these areas are relevant and necessary for human services organizations; however, no specific reference to nonprofit organizations appears anywhere in the 1994 *Standards,* unlike the 1986–87 edition. Whereas this omission may not necessarily represent a decreased emphasis in graduate business schools on nonprofit management, it certainly cannot be construed as an increased interest.

Business school graduates' apparent lack of interest in fields outside the corporate sector stands in sharp contrast to the view of the MBA degree in Hoefer's (1993) survey. At the middle level of management, the MBA degree is perceived as second only to the MSW degree (administrative track), with 23 percent favoring the former and 27 percent, the latter. At the top level, 29 percent consider the MBA to be the preferred degree.

It is not clear whether the preference for MBAs is due to actual skill levels, to stereotypes of business managers as icons of productivity and efficiency, or to the perception within financially hard-pressed nonprofits that MBAs are better at fundraising and spend money wisely. Although business schools and their graduates may not be focusing on human services organizations, these organizations seem to favor them.

## MPA DEGREE

### Overview

The MPA degree is the most difficult of the three degrees to describe, mainly because it has come under many different influences historically and because its institutional locus is so diversified. Just as the institutional locus of public administration programs varies greatly, so do the orientations and focal points of these programs; therefore, it is difficult to render general observations about the nature and utility of the MPA degree (Ellwood, 1985).

In its *1994 Directory of Programs,* the National Association of Schools of Public Affairs and Administration (NASPAA) stated:

> The purpose of the professional master's degree program in public affairs, public policy and administration is to prepare individuals for positions of leadership in public service. A career of leadership may involve management and/or policy at the several levels of government, in non-profit agencies and in private sector areas where knowledge of government is important. (p. 5)

Before looking at the relevance of the MPA degree for the management of human services organizations, it is worth comparing the trend in MPA and MBA enrollments. After experiencing a brief downturn between 1979 and 1983, enrollments in public administration programs that are members of NASPAA increased by 26 percent between 1983 and 1994 (from 21,128 to 26,679 students). During the same period, MPA degrees granted rose 27 percent, from 6,190 to 7,867 (NASPAA, 1994).

### Utility for human services management

MPA programs differ widely in their objectives and emphases. However, NASPAA promulgates standards for the common components of the curriculum of programs in public administration and affairs regardless of their orientation. According to NASPAA's (1992) *Standards for Professional Master's Degree Programs in Public Affairs/Policy/Administration,*

The common curriculum components shall enhance the student's values, knowledge, and skills to act ethically and effectively:
in the management of public service orientations, the components of which include:

- human resources
- budgeting and financial processes
- information, including computer literacy and applications

in the application of quantitative and qualitative techniques of analysis, the components of which include:

- policy and program formulation, implementation and evaluation
- decision-making and problem-solving

with an understanding of the public policy and organizational environment, the components of which include:

- political and legal institutions and processes
- economic and social institutions and processes
- organization and management concepts and behavior. (p. 3)

NASPAA recognizes that programs may be directed toward different settings, including nonprofit settings. It also notes specializations within these settings, such as social services administration. Of NASPAA's 218 member schools, 31 (14 percent) offer a social services concentration and 49 (22 percent) offer a nonprofit concentration.

The major difference between the MBA and MPA standards is the emphasis of the MPA on "political and legal institutions and processes" and "management of public service organizations," which provides students with an understanding of the public-sector context or how the government works. For the most part, the other components of the curriculum suggest courses that engender the skills needed for effective government management.

Interest in nonprofit management studies is growing in universities across the country, especially among schools of public administration (Dyer & Committee, 1987). Cleary (1990) surveyed NASPAA members and asked them to comment on curricular gaps in their own programs as well as on areas of coverage they perceived as being underemphasized nationally. Of 170 survey respondents, 17.3 percent said that more attention is needed nationally on the study of nonprofit management. Of the 103 survey respondents who answered the question about perceived national underemphasis, 29 percent identified nonprofit management as an area that was being ignored. Nonprofit management topped the chart, followed by ethics and information systems.

MPA programs share many of the same strengths as MBA programs for managing human services organizations. Certainly, MPA graduates, especially those who have completed programs with an emphasis in management, have the potential to assume leadership positions in staff or support departments, such as personnel or finance. Although they may not have as strong a background in accounting as do their business school counterparts, MPA graduates have a superior knowledge of government, political processes, and the civil service, which better prepares them for most management positions in federal, state, and local human services agencies such as public welfare and mental health. Keys and Cupaiuolo (1987) observed that managing public welfare programs requires a working knowledge of budgeting, administrative law, computer science, and quantitative methods for decision making. These are typical fields of study in public administration programs.

In Hoefer's (1993) survey, most respondents believed that an MBA degree was most appropriate for those at the higher management levels, followed closely by the MPA, indicating a perception that these degrees provide the training necessary to move up the career ladder in many of the types of human services organizations in Hoefer's sample. Government agency respondents preferred the MPA at middle levels of management four times more than respondents from private nonprofits.

How well MPA graduates manage the service function in human services agencies may depend on their previous experience or training in human services per se. Presumably, graduates of specialized programs have substantive knowledge of services, as well as generic management skills, and are well qualified to manage programs such as income maintenance and Medicaid. This assumption does not suggest, however, that they are ideally suited to supervise clinical or casework services, which entail a knowledge of psychodynamics and the casework process.

According to Astrid Merget (1986), a former NASPAA president, the MPA ethos can be described as follows:

> What distinguishes an MPA is defined less in academic substance and in practical skill but more in a professional ideology. That ideology affirms the role of government as a proactive translator of policy into action; as an agent for improving social welfare; and as a champion of social justice. Embedded in that ideology is the conviction that politics is a noble profession: politics as the act of deliberation transforms conflict into consensus. (p. 4)

To the extent that Merget's articulation of the MPA ethos is adhered to by the public administration profession and is inculcated in MPA students, the MPA socialization process results in values that should characterize human services delivery systems.

The development of an underlying ethos for MPA programs has been an evolutionary process. Historically, much emphasis was placed on the public administrator serving as an effective manager who operated from a value-neutral perspective and who efficiently implemented policies established by elected executives and legislators. Currently, there seems to be little support for such a one-dimensional view of the public administrator. NASPAA's (1992) standards and mission statement mentions the public service and non-profit sectors as important components of the public administration field.

Apparently, MPA programs are focusing increasingly on nonprofit organizations; thus, their graduates, many of whom work in public human services organizations, can be expected to assume more managerial positions in nonprofit organizations as well.

## MSW DEGREE

### Overview

The importance of graduate social work education for preparing social services managers and administrators has always been limited. The Council on Social Work Education's (CSWE's) annual statistics indicate that only 5.6 percent of all graduate social work students in 1983 were administration majors, and only 9.6 percent were in what social work refers to as "macro" majors, including administration community organization, planning, and social policy (Rubin, 1983). By 1993, however, only 3.1 percent of the MSW students were administration majors, and only 6.0 percent were from the macro majors, including administration (Lennon, 1993). Even if students with minors in administration—those taking one or two administration courses along with the usual array of direct practice courses—are added to this group, only 12.3 percent of graduate school students completed coursework in administration. Clearly, graduate students do not emphasize social work administration.

Furthermore, the prescribed Curriculum Policy Standards for the MSW curriculum put forth by the CSWE minimize the import of social work administration, although content on work with organizations is required in the educational foundation (Minahan, 1987a). Social work administration is not specifically emphasized as a "foundation area." In summary, these CSWE standards do not encourage or mandate social work schools or students to "get ready" for future managerial positions in human services agencies.

It is significant that in 1984 the social work professional organization, NASW, developed a detailed set of standards for the practice of clinical social work, but not for the practice of social work administration (Minahan, 1987b). Presumably, social workers are not expected to practice administration very much during their postgraduate careers.

However, NASW reports that nearly one-third of its more than 150,000 members (predominantly MSWs) consider themselves to be in management positions. Where do they acquire their competency as human services managers? Apparently, most have not found the answers in their graduate social work education; they developed competency as a result of on-the-job training or continuing professional education. In the nonprofit human services sector, the importance of continuing professional education is just beginning to be addressed. Over the past decade one of the authors has trained hundreds of recently promoted human services managers (mostly MSWs from United Way–funded agencies). Almost all reported that they believed that their own bosses had little or no management training and rarely advised them on essential administrative skills. These interviews suggest that most social work majors in nonprofit human services agencies do not choose a social work administrative degree over an MPA or MBA degree for human services administration—they probably do not choose any graduate training for their eventual promotions into management. Nonprofit human services agencies essentially expect their managers to "sink or swim." Social work managers are expected to acquire the knowledge base from their own resources and experiences or to seek outside continuing education once promoted. Public-sector training programs have been more extensive, but here, too, continuing education programs seem to have focused more on advanced direct practice and field-specific skills than on management skills. For example, one child welfare agency administrator in large city recently reported that the agency's 250 managers and administrators had often been offered child welfare courses but rarely received any management skills courses (personal communication with the Administrator, New York City Department of Child Welfare, 1993).

### Utility for human services management

The MSW curriculum continues to stress the one-to-one relationship, which sets it apart from the MBA and MPA degree. Interpersonal skills with clients are stressed in the MSW program. The client's human growth, behavior, and interaction with family and community are the foci for the trained social worker. The worker–client interactions to be learned in graduate schools of social work are clinical and therapeutic in nature. The administrative skills taught (in relatively small measure) focus on managing personnel in their interpersonal remedial interactions with clients. The MBA or the MPA student is trained to seek outcomes of another sort—those that lie in the market, the organization, or the structure of government.

Few MBAs or MPAs have majored in social work administration; in fact, more than 85 percent of graduate students have never taken a social work management or administration course. The MSW curriculum has always been very clinical and appears to be becoming more so. The would-be MSW managers of human services programs seem well prepared to understand the products or services that they will eventually manage. However, they are less adequately prepared to manage workers, budgets, funding sources, contracts, and regulations. Only about 15 percent of MSWs appear to have gained from graduate school the knowledge and skills useful for any eventual promotion into management positions (Cupaiuolo & Miringoff, 1988).

Hoefer's (1993) study supports this position. In response to the question regarding the best degree for entry-level positions, 63 percent responded that no management degree was required, and 22 percent favored the MSW (administrative track). The MSW (administrative track) was viewed as the best degree at the middle level by 27 percent of respondents, followed closely by the MBA (23 percent) and MPA (17 percent) degrees. At the top level, however, the MBA (29 percent) was considered the best degree, followed by the MPA (24 percent) and the MSW (14 percent). The utility of the MSW degree for managerial positions varies directly with how closely connected the position is to the delivery of services; at the highest management levels (that is, those furthest removed from service delivery), the MSW has the least value.

### CONCLUSION

This review of the MBA, MPA, and MSW degrees leads to the conclusion that only MPA programs and their accrediting body (NASPAA) demonstrate interest in nonprofit management and, by extension, in human services organizations. Whereas it would be an exaggeration to imply that the nonprofit sector is getting the same attention in MPA programs as the public sector, it is clear that more MPA students are studying nonprofit management and can be expected to assume more managerial positions in nonprofit organizations.

MBA and MSW programs and their accrediting bodies have not shown a similar interest. Business schools have shown little inclination to include human services management in their curriculum, with the possible exception of managed health care. Schools of social work continue to focus primarily on clinical services, and few of their graduates are likely to have any exposure to management courses.

There is no consensus regarding the "best" degree for human services management. At the service delivery level, the MSW (administrative track) is probably preferable. At higher levels in the organization, and with respect to administrative management functions such as human resources and finance, the MBA and the MPA are probably more desirable. These conclusions are highly tentative, however; prospective employers should look beyond the degree in recruiting for management positions and instead evaluate carefully the qualifications of each applicant. Individual strengths, skills, and experiences might prove more relevant and revealing than any of these degrees.

## REFERENCES

American Assembly of Collegiate Schools of Business. (1994). *Standards for business accreditation.* St. Louis: Author.

Bongiorno, L., & Byrne, J. (1994, October 24). Is there an MBA glut? If you answered no, you pass. *Business Week,* pp. 71–72.

Brooks, J. (1994, December 4). Speak gringo. *New York Times* [Week in Review], p. 4.

Cleary, R. E. (1990, October). *What do public administration master's programs look like?* Unpublished manuscript, National Association of Schools of Public Affairs and Administration, Washington, DC.

Cupaiuolo, A., & Dowling, M. (1983). Are corporate managers really better? *Public Welfare, 41,* 12–17.

Cupaiuolo, A., & Miringoff, M. L. (1988). MBA, MPA, MSW: Is there a degree of choice for human services management? In P. R. Keys & L. Ginsberg (Eds.), *New management in human services* (pp. 44–57). Silver Spring, MD: National Association of Social Workers.

Dyer, D., & Committee. (1987, October). *The nonprofit sector and NASPAA's redefinition of public service.* Unpublished manuscript, National Association of Schools of Public Affairs and Administration, Washington, DC.

Ellwood, J. W. (1985). *A morphology of graduate education for public service in the United States.* Unpublished manuscript, National Association of Schools of Public Affairs and Administration, Washington, DC.

Hoefer, R. (1993). A matter of degree: Job skills for human service administrators. *Administration in Social Work, 17,* 1–20.

Keys, P. R., & Cupaiuolo, A. A. (1987). Rebuilding the relationship between social work and public welfare administration. *Public Administration in Social Work, 2,* 47–58.

Lennon, T. (1993). *Council on Social Work Education statistics.* Alexandria, VA: Council on Social Work Education.

Merget, A. (1986, January). President's report. *Public Enterprise,* p. 4.

Minahan, A. (Ed.-in-Chief). (1987a). Appendix 2: Curriculum policy for the master's degree and baccalaureate degree programs in social work education. *Encyclopedia of social work* (18th ed., Vol. 2, pp. 957–964). Silver Spring, MD: National Association of Social Workers.

Minahan, A. (Ed.-in-Chief). (1987b). Appendix 3: NASW standards for the practice of clinical social work. *Encyclopedia of social work* (18th ed., Vol. 2, pp. 965–970). Silver Spring, MD: National Association of Social Workers.

National Association of Schools of Public Affairs and Administration. (1992). *Standards for professional master's degree programs in public affairs/policy/administration.* Washington, DC: Author.

National Association of Schools of Public Affairs and Administration. (1994). *1994 directory of programs* (Vol. 2, Appendix 2, CSWE curriculum policy). Washington, DC: Author.

National Association of Social Workers. (1984). *NASW standards for the practice of clinical social work.* Silver Spring, MD: Author.

Rubin, A. (1983). *Council on Social Work Education statistics.* Washington, DC: Council on Social Work Education.

# Chapter 4

# The Politics of Human Services Administration

**Burton Gummer and
Richard L. Edwards**

The management of human services organizations can be viewed from at least three perspectives. It can be seen simply as a branch of the general field of management. Human services managers, like government and business managers, must set goals; select the means for accomplishing those goals; acquire funds and physical facilities;

hire people with the necessary skills; design mechanisms for assigning, monitoring, and coordinating work; determine whether the organization is accomplishing what it has set out to do; and introduce changes when needed (Turem, 1986). Human services managers can also be thought of as the directors or, more appropriately, the "peak coordinators" of professional organizations. From this perspective, the manager's primary responsibility is to design and maintain the organizational and administrative structures that will enable the staff to serve their clients as professionally and effectively as possible (Rapp & Poertner, 1992). A third perspective, and the focus of this chapter, is to view the human services agency as a political entity and the human services manager as a political (with a small p) actor (Gummer, 1990). The central tenet of a political perspective on human services organizations is that, like any political system, they are rife with controversies over who "gets what, when, and how" (Lasswell, 1936)—specifically, who will make decisions about the setting of organizational goals and the allocation of organizational resources.

## THE HUMAN SERVICES AGENCY AS A POLITICAL ARENA

The specifics of any administrative practice are determined by the nature of an organization's environment, its institutional setting, its goals, and the ways in which it seeks to accomplish those goals. Human services organizations are characterized by politicized funding, goals with strong value and ideological components, underdeveloped and indeterminate technologies, and administrative and service personnel from diverse backgrounds. Human services agencies, unlike businesses that receive income from the sale of products or services, but like other nonprofit and public sector organizations, are budget driven. Moreover, their budgets are generated by a political process. The politics of funding may be explicit and aboveboard, as in the budgetary processes of state and federal governments (Wildavsky, 1979), or they may be subtle and covert, as is the case with United Way agencies and private foundations (Kramer & Grossman, 1987; Potuchek, 1986). The political nature of funding is related, in turn, to two other characteristics of the human services organization: disputes over agency goals and the underdeveloped nature of service technologies.

## HUMAN SERVICES AND PUBLIC SOCIAL POLICY

Human services agencies pursue goals over which there are serious and widespread ideological disagreements. Some goals, such as distributive justice for poor people, people of color, and other oppressed groups, have been a source of contention since the founding of the republic. As the American system has matured, however, the areas of social life now considered legitimate targets for public intervention have expanded dramatically. These include changing mores regarding sexual orientation, marital relations, gender roles, childrearing, and other lifestyle issues that have their roots in the revolution in personal and family values that began in the 1960s. As the human services system intervenes in issues that once were the exclusive purview of the individual, the family, or, at most, the local community, the amount of controversy over, and resistance to, human services programs has grown. Proponents of both sides of issues such as legalized abortion or condom distribution in the public schools invoke scientific research and professional expertise to bolster their case; however, they use these arguments like a drunk uses a lamppost—for support rather than illumination. The public's response to these issues ultimately is determined by a process in which power and influence, rather than knowledge and expertise, are the deciding factors.

### ENDS AND MEANS

In those rare instances when a consensus is reached and a public policy goal is set, as has been the case of the aim to achieve permanency planning for children in foster care (as mandated by the Adoption Assistance and Child Welfare Act of 1980), the issue becomes one of selecting the best way to achieve the goal. Funders must decide which of the competing proposals for accomplishing the goal are likely to be most effective. Their initial response might be to follow what Potuchek (1986) called the *merit model,* wherein funders evaluate applications for funds "by first assessing the *need* for the services proposed in that application and then evaluating the *effectiveness* of the proposed program for meeting those needs" (pp. 421–422; italics in original).

However, it is very difficult to demonstrate effectiveness in the human services field, largely because of underdevelopment in the technological base of practice. Technologies provide the means for accomplishing goals. For an activity to be worthy of the name "technology," however, there must be a high probability that it will actually achieve the intended results. In this sense, much of human services practice is less a technology than a collection of insights and trial-and-error procedures that suggest ways for approaching problems but do not guarantee a solution in any particular instance. Rein and White (1981) made a distinction between *praxis,* or usual and conventional conduct, and professional *practice:*

> Praxis is what everybody knows how to do and does in a society. Practice consists of a special system of actions unique to and institutionally vested in a professional role. . . . In the "minor professions," where there are no arcane and esoteric skills, praxis and practice are joined. Social workers and teachers do not exercise highly trained and distinctive skills, as do brain surgeons for example. Their profession is constituted by an organization of fairly ordinary human activities. (p. 4)

Lacking reliable, objective criteria for evaluating the potential effectiveness of a particular proposal, funders must use other devices. When people agree about goals but disagree about means, they are likely to use judgment, as opposed to *rational calculation,* as the means of deciding (Thompson & Tuden, 1959). Moreover, to enhance the quality of their judgments, funders set down formal or informal rules that mandate representation by all interested parties; encourage broad dissemination of information, discussion, and debate; and then abide by the will of the majority. In short, they create a political arena for deci-sion making. The politicization of funding decisions can be expected to intensi-fy as competition for declining public—particularly federal—dollars increases among human services agencies and between human services agencies and other recipients of public funds, such as law enforcement or public education.

## INTEREST GROUPS

Another political feature of human services organizations is the existence of many and diverse interest groups, each with a stake in (and many with influence over) agency activities. In general, organizations develop in one of two ways (Meyer, Scott, & Deal, 1981). Technological innovations (such as the silicon chip or fiber optics) may foster the development of rational administrative and organizational structures whose sole purpose is to ensure the precise and efficient production of these items. Alternatively, social processes that redefine certain rules (such as shifting attitudes toward sexual activity among teenagers) may emerge, thus allowing the organizations that conform to those rules to be regarded as rational and legitimate. Social agen-cies usually develop along the latter lines, and, as products of their communi-ties, remain tightly linked to the community's values and resources.

The human services agency's constituencies consist of the general pub-lic; federal, state, and local legislative, funding, and regulatory bodies; founda-tions and other private sector funding bodies; employee unions, professional associations; licensing and accreditation bodies; sources of client referrals; the personnel resource pool; and clients, both as individuals and in organized associations (Martin, 1980). Each group controls or influences, in varying degrees, important resources such as money, skilled personnel, community sanctions, and clients. If a certain group exercises exclusive control over an essential resource (for example, an accreditation body that is responsible sole-ly for determining eligibility for third-party insurance payments), then the agency is placed in a power-dependent relationship and must be responsive to that group's wishes, thus reducing its ability to act independently. Moreover, because the interests of the various constituencies such as the general public, funders, employees, and clients are often different and occasionally antagonis-tic, human services agency managers must develop *goal structures,* a euphe-mism for the melange of contradictory purposes that agencies frequently must pursue to satisfy those constituencies.

The final feature of human services organizations that contributes to their politicization is the mix of professions and occupations involved in their administration and provision of services. Before the 1960s, what are now called human services agencies were referred to as social services agencies.

This may seem like quibbling, but social services agency really meant *social work* agency because the typical social agency was administered and staffed by social workers. Whereas not all of the direct service staff were professionally trained social workers with master's degrees, a considerable number of upper-level administrators were MSWs, and the policies and practices of those organizations were strongly influenced and shaped by the social work profession. However, the antipoverty programs initiated during the Johnson administration viewed social work and social agencies as "part of the problem rather than part of the solution." These programs employed different kinds of service personnel who brought with them alternative organizational forms (the community action agency) and service strategies (welfare rights, legal advocacy). The spate of programs developed since then spurred the development of new service specialties (drug and alcohol counseling, gerontology, rehabilitation of the physically handicapped, child care, and employee assistance) that put an end to social work's hegemony over the field (Mandell, 1983).

A similar development occurred in the management of human services agencies. Public expenditures for health, education, and social services increased from $23.4 billion in 1950 to $492.2 billion in 1980 (Bixby, 1983), of which nearly two-thirds ($314 billion) was spent on social programs alone. As the scope of the welfare state expanded, concern with its proper management became a major issue. Although the social work profession attempted to keep pace with higher demand for trained managers to administer increasingly large and complex agencies (Gummer & Edwards, 1988), the presence of professional social work managers in middle- and upper-management positions declined steadily, beginning in the 1970s (Patti, 1984). Managers with a variety of professional or occupational backgrounds made significant inroads in positions traditionally held by social workers, particularly in the large state and federal human services agencies. In a national survey of the characteristics of commissioners and directors of state departments of social services, mental health, and corrections, Meinert, Ginsberg, and Keys (1993) found that only 20 percent identified themselves as professional social workers. The rest were affiliated with disciplines such as education (17 percent); criminal justice or corrections (16 percent); and smaller percentages identified themselves as public administrators, attorneys, or "health professionals," or as working in nine other professional or occupational fields. "Clearly, no one profession or discipline could lay claim to dominating the CEOs positions" (Meinert et al., 1993, p. 105).

## POLITICS OF HUMAN SERVICES MANAGEMENT

There are a number of reasons for the decline of human services professionals in management positions in the large public social services bureaucracies. Social workers and other human services personnel often came to be considered out of step with an increasingly conservative bent of recent social policy initiatives. Ideology aside, they were often seen as lacking the technical skills and personal traits needed to manage large organizations. They were viewed as preoccupied with consensual decision making and process rather than outcome and as overly identified with the interests of clients at the expense of the interests of society at large. Another reason, and the focus of this chapter, has been the reluctance of many human services managers to engage in organizational politics, with the result that the necessary political skills have not been acquired and important political relationships have not been cultivated.

The aversion of human services professionals (and professionals in general) to organizational politics is largely attributable to the central role that the acquisition and exercise of power plays in the political process. In this sense, professionals are no different from other Americans who view power with suspicion and mistrust; "there is no type of behavior that society regulates more carefully than expressions of power" (McClelland, 1975, p. 22). Americans tend to focus on the negative aspects of power, seeing it primarily as an instrument for destructive purposes:

> We also completely deny the constructive uses of power. . . . [P]ower may be directed toward either oneself or others; it may be oriented toward strengthening oneself or toward influencing others. In our culture we tend to assume that power is only directed toward others. . . . It is difficult for us to consider ways in which power either may be used to assist others or to strengthen ourselves without harming others. (Baum, 1983, pp. 149–150)

Human services managers must acquire a positive attitude toward the use of power. They must learn to view managing organizational politics as a legitimate part of their professional role and to acquire the skills necessary to become effective participants in the political process. For human services managers, this is usually accomplished through the concept of "advocacy" on behalf of clients and programs. When one engages in advocacy, one exercises power on behalf of others. Political theorists distinguish between those who use power to pursue their own interests and those who use power to promote the well-being of the community. Exercising power on behalf of others is an essential quality of leadership and a sign of individual maturity. It is what distinguishes the mere politician from the statesperson, the leader from the "destructive achiever" (Kelly, 1987). Seen from this perspective, power in societies and organizations means efficacy and capacity:

> [It] is analogous in simple terms to physical power: it is the ability to mobilize resources . . . to get things done. The true sign of power, then, is accomplishment—not fear, terror, or tyranny. Where the power is "on," the system can be productive; where the power is "off," the system bogs down. (Kanter, 1979, p. 66)

### Thinking politically

If there is a political worldview, its central assumption would be the inevitability and pervasiveness of conflict in human affairs. Politically oriented managers see political conflict as "the center of management life" and skill at conflict management as "the heart of leadership" (Yates, 1985, p. 7). They assume that people's interests differ and evaluate their actions in terms of the impact they are likely to have on the interests of others. They also know that people's abilities to promote their interests vary with the amount of power and influence they have. Thus, a critical political skill is the ability to understand the various interests represented in a given situation, and the power of different actors to promote their own and to block competing interests.

**Diagnose interests.** The organizational chart provides a starting point for identifying the interests of organizational members. As the saying goes, "Where you stand depends on where you sit." People's organizational interests are heavily influenced by their positions, both hierarchically and functionally. It is safe to assume that people make an effort to protect and enhance their positions and to extol the importance of their work in the organization. On the basis of their analysis of the interests at play, managers should be able to estimate the number of people who will be in favor of, opposed to, or neutral toward their proposals. Specific questions that must be answered include: How much time should one spend consolidating the support of allies versus trying to win over neutrals? Are the objections of those in opposition the kind that can be accommodated by incorporating elements of their interests into the proposal? If not, how much of a threat does the opposition pose to the proposed policy? The answers to these questions require both an understanding of people's interests and an assessment of their power in the organization.

**Assess power.** The organizational chart is a good starting point for assessing power. Although the formal structure does not always reflect the actual distribution of power, it is still the best single indicator of an organization's power structure. In general, people in high organizational positions will have more power than those in lower positions. There are a number of exceptions, but the political manager can operate under the working assumption that an organization's formal structure reflects actual power distribution.

Power may also be assessed by the consequences of its use. An analysis of who benefits, and to what extent, from contested issues gives a clue to the relative power of the parties involved. Such things as budget allocations, assignment of personnel, and other policy choices usually reflect the relative power of organizational members and units. Managers are powerful if they can, for example, intercede favorably on behalf of someone in trouble; get desirable placements or above-average salary increases for subordinates; get approval for expenditures beyond their budgets; get items on the agenda at policy meetings; get regular, frequent, and fast access to top decision makers; and get early information about decisions and policy shifts (Kanter, 1979).

Another approach to assessing the distribution of power is to look at an organizational member's bases of power; these include formal authority, as well as coercive, reward, referent, and expert sources of power. This approach becomes important when there is evidence that the possession of these sources of power is not accurately reflected in the official hierarchy. This situation often occurs in professional organizations like human services agencies where individuals lower in the hierarchy may possess special skills or expertise that enables them to exert influence beyond their official positions (Smith, 1965).

**Control agendas.** The importance of agenda setting in organizational politics has been highlighted by the concept of "nondecisions" as a way of making decisions. This is the idea that "power may be, and often is, exercised by confining the scope of decision-making to relatively 'safe' issues" (Bachrach & Baratz, 1962, p. 948). An important way in which political actors protect their interests is by preventing questions that can adversely affect those interests from being put on the agenda in the first place. Individuals who support the organizational status quo, for example, will want to keep items off agendas, whereas those seeking to introduce changes will be eager to bring issues to the attention of decision makers. From the perspective of the defenders of the status quo, a nondecision is, after all, a decision—namely, a decision to continue doing things in the same way.

One tactic for determining which issues are placed on the organizational agenda is to determine who can attend policy meetings. To bring an issue to the attention of decision makers, someone has to present it and advance it. An individual cannot get into the political game unless he or she can "obtain the *attentive interest* of the relevant decision makers" (Scoble, 1968, p. 10).

Thus, one sure way of preventing an issue from coming up is to exclude the person associated with it from meetings where it can be acted on. Controlling participation in meetings is quite difficult, however, because participation in meetings is the organizational equivalent of enfranchisement, and interested parties exert considerable effort to ensure their presence.

When the manager is unable to keep an issue off the agenda, another tactic is to control the order in which items appear on the agenda. Items at the beginning of an agenda frequently become the vehicle for a discussion of unrelated issues. Meetings are a stage on which the organizational cast can be identified and the organizational drama played out. The first items on the agenda, consequently, are often used by participants to establish their place in the hierarchy by speaking authoritatively and at length about an issue and to show—regardless of the issue's substantive content—how it is related to major organizational concerns. Managers who want to defeat, table, or significantly change an item that is inimical to their interests should encourage the issue's proponents to present it in terms of its broadest ramifications for the organization. An item about adequate parking facilities, for instance, can be escalated to the more general question of the distribution of perquisites within the organization and to the even larger issue of whether the agency subscribes to the principles of distributive justice. Managers can also insist that such items appear early in the meeting so there will be sufficient time for discussion. Items that they want passed, on the other hand, can be presented in as specific and noncontroversial a way as possible and placed near the end of the agenda.

**Control decision alternatives and premises.** A decision can be thought of simply as a choice among alternatives. From this perspective, power rests with the person making the choice. A more complex view of decisions sees decision makers as people who are *presented* with alternatives from which they must choose. In this conception, power is shared between those making the choice and those presenting the alternatives. For example, suppose that a manager of a program for deinstitutionalized psychiatric patients must develop services for maintaining these clients in community residences. One way of doing this is to involve local residents in the creation of a community-sponsored halfway house. This proposal requires a lengthy community organization process and involves sharing decision-making authority with neighborhood residents. A second alternative is to purchase a low-rise apartment house with funds provided jointly by, for example, the state department of mental health and a consortium of business people. This proposal would take much less time to implement, and agency staff would retain control of the program.

### Behaving politically

It is said that inside every politician lurks an amateur psychologist. At a basic level, politicians must understand people's motivations, interests, needs, and goals in order to assess support for and opposition to their positions. This kind of understanding is essential for establishing interpersonal relationships and exercising influence. Networks of relationships are important for obtaining information about developments that can affect one's interests and play a critical role in building coalitions.

**Political behavior as self-awareness.** Although organizational politicians may choose not to disclose their inner feelings to others, they must not keep them from themselves. Self-knowledge in a political context involves understanding the nature and depth of one's commitments to policies, programs, and people. Organizational politics become important when people are unclear about how to act because of a lack of knowledge or because of disagreements over values or ideological issues. An important strength that organizational politicians bring to such situations is their conviction about, and commitment to, a course of action. To be convincing, however, they must know what their convictions are, why they hold them, how far they will go to protect and promote them, and what aspects of their position are negotiable. Managers quickly acquire a reputation for having (or not having) integrity with regard to their stated positions. Managers who eloquently and passionately argue for a policy at a staff meeting and then offer to compromise at the first sign of opposition will lose whatever potential for influence they might have engendered by originally taking a strong stand. The positions that managers take must be carefully thought through and must reflect their actual interests and values.

**Communication skills.** Political managers must be attentive to both the content and the impact of their communications on different audiences. Most public figures live by the rule that one does not say anything to a reporter that one does not want to see in print. The organizational counterpart of this rule is that whatever a manager says to someone sooner or later becomes common knowledge in the organization. Managers are the focus of attention from subordinates, peers, and superiors, as well as interested parties outside the organization. When managers speak, it is assumed that they speak on behalf of the organization or unit. Managers are also assumed to have the power to act on their words; consequently, more importance is attached to their utterances than to those of other, lower-ranked members. Finally, managers are assumed to be privy to important information, so whatever they say, no matter how innocuous, is invested with great meaning. Managers thus are denied the luxury of casual talk and must approach situations with a high degree of premeditation and purposefulness. This is especially true for political managers, because much political communication involves convincing listeners that the course of action being advocated is superior to any other and that their interests will be served by supporting it.

**Building networks.** Networks provide opportunities for organizational members to communicate with people in different divisions within the organization and with people outside it. They are also important tools for informal contacts with superiors and subordinates. Networks can be formal bodies, such as task forces or interagency committees, or informal systems of mutual consultation and influence. They are a major informal communication channel for getting information that cannot be gotten through official means. They are good vehicles for floating "trial balloons" to test the receptivity to a proposal without having to commit oneself formally. For these reasons, networks play an essential role in organizational politics.

Networks are an important element in coalition building. Organizational coalitions tend to be issue specific, with their composition changing as the issues change. Consequently, the manager's general network of relationships cannot be the basis of a coalition for every issue. Whereas some members of the network may be involved in every coalition of interest to a manager, the network as a whole serves an important role as a sounding board for managers to explore who their potential allies and opponents are on a particular issue. Whereas networks sometimes can be a source of political support, they are always a significant source of political information that the manager can later translate into political support.

Networks of relationships in organizations, like friendship networks in general, are built around exchanges of things that people want, ranging from tangible benefits like helping someone get a job or a promotion to intangible items like enhancing a person's self-esteem. Once a network of relationships has been established, managers must not forget that the same amount of effort and skill that went into its creation must be expended on its maintenance. The maintenance work, moreover, has to be done on a routine basis, not just when support is needed. The job of maintaining relationships comes easiest, of course, to those who are naturally gregarious and enjoy the company of others.

## Working politically

Managers engage in political activities to acquire the resources and influence needed to pursue their goals. At the same time, the way that managers carry out their duties has political consequences in terms of increasing or diminishing their influence within the organization. Managers can increase the positive political consequences of their work by carefully adhering to organizational norms, particularly those concerning the proper exercise of power and authority; identifying tasks that their units can do that are considered important to the overall organizational mission; and seeing that their accomplishments and those of their units are accurately and fully conveyed to others within and outside the organization.

**Play by the rules.** Every organization has a "constitution" that sets out rules for acceptable behavior. Constitutions can be formal documents or unwritten collective understandings. Constitutions set forth the rules of the political game delineating who the players are, what plays are fair or foul, and when the game is over and who won.

The overt exercise of power is generally frowned on in human services agencies where people are expected to act solely on the basis of professional or technical grounds. Political managers have to be careful that their actions are seen as properly within the norms of the organization. Actions that are perceived as arbitrary or that disregard accepted procedures will be discredited as dictatorial or as "playing politics." Political managers attempting to manipulate organizational rules to promote their interest and goals must use procedures that have been legitimated within the organization. Politicalization occurs when people cannot agree about the goals that they should pursue in common. In such situations, the way in which a decision is made assumes primary importance. People may not agree with the outcome of a decision, but they will accept it as legitimate and agree to be bound by its terms if the process of reaching it conformed to formal organizational rules and informal norms.

**Perform a useful function.** A function becomes significant when it contributes to dealing with critical uncertainties. The outcome of activity is uncertain when the technology for performing it is underdeveloped and unreliable, when it is subject to external forces beyond management control, or both. Individuals or units that can reduce uncertainties by developing new techniques for dealing with problems, or bring external factors under organizational control, assume influential positions. An organizational function also assumes importance when the people able to perform it are in high demand because they are in short supply. Qualified people are scarce when their skills are the product of technological breakthroughs for which training and educational facilities lag behind, or when supply is purposely restricted by occupational and professional associations to prevent a glut on the market.

**Manage impressions.** Assessing individual or unit competence is a difficult task in any organization because of the difficulty in identifying any one person's contribution to achieving an organizational goal. It is even more difficult in human services agencies, where goals often are poorly defined, ambiguous, and difficult to specify. Consequently, managers must be skilled in controlling the impressions and perceptions that others within and outside the organization have of their (and their unit's) abilities and accomplishments.

The mechanisms used to manage impressions include self-descriptions, accounts, apologies, entitlements and enhancements, flattery, favors, and organizational descriptions (Gardner & Martinko, 1988). Self-descriptions are managers' presentations of such personal characteristics as traits, abilities, behavioral patterns, feelings, and opinions; they can include positive, negative, or neutral information. Accounts are explanations designed to minimize the severity of a difficult situation by justifying the actions the manager took. Apologies seek to convince others that an undesirable event associated with a manager is not a fair representation of the manager's overall abilities. Conversely, entitlements are designed to maximize a manager's apparent responsibility for a good outcome, and enhancements seek to maximize the favorability of the event. Flattery involves complimenting others about their virtues in an effort to make oneself appear perceptive and likable; favors are done in order to gain another's approval. Organizational descriptions are used to legitimize decisions, processes, and policies.

### CHALLENGES

A number of demanding challenges face today's human services organizations. Service providers are under greater pressures than ever to demonstrate the usefulness and effectiveness of their services. These pressures have intensified since the social services became submerged in the larger human services field, with a growing number of providers competing for scarce funds and for service mandates from policymakers who generally are skeptical about the efficacy of social services. At the managerial level, the old business-as-usual practice of selecting managers from senior services workers who have no special preparation for their new roles is no longer acceptable. Human services managers must compete with other professionals for the control of their agencies. Finally, the social policy environment within which human services exist has been and will continue to be an increasingly hostile one.

This chapter has presented ways to manage organizational politics that will decrease the negative consequences of unresolved conflicts and increase the overall effectiveness of an agency and its programs. Unless properly managed, political conflicts within organizations inevitably dissolve into factional disputes, mutual distrust, blame, and feelings of hopelessness and impotence. When successfully managed, these same conflicts and animosities can lead organizational members to a heightened appreciation of each other's goals, values, and interests and to a stronger sense of shared purpose. To accomplish this, human services managers must work at acquiring and using power in their organizations. This should not be done merely for the sake of becoming powerful, but out of a conviction that the acquisition and appropriate use of power is the key to securing human services values and perspectives in their organizations. Managers should provide employees with structured and extensive in-service training on the nature of organizational power, politics, and decision making. To ignore the political realities of human services work is to put one's head in the sand.

## REFERENCES

Adoption Assistance and Child Welfare Act of 1980, P.L. 96-272, 94 Stat. 500.

Bachrach, P., & Baratz, M. S. (1962). Two faces of power. *American Political Science Review, 56,* 947–952.

Baum, H. S. (1983). Autonomy, shame, and doubt: Power in the bureaucratic lives of planners. *Administration & Society, 15*(2), 147–184.

Bixby, A. K. (1983). Social welfare expenditures, fiscal year 1980. *Social Security Bulletin, 46,* 9–17.

Gardner, W. L., & Martinko, M. J. (1988). Impression management: An observational study linking audience characteristics with verbal self-presentations. *Academy of Management Journal, 31*(1), 42–65.

Gummer, B. (1990). *The politics of social administration: Managing organizational politics in social agencies.* Englewood Cliffs, NJ: Prentice Hall.

Gummer, B., & Edwards, R. (1988). The enfeebled middle: Emerging issues in education for social administration. *Administration in Social Work, 12*(3), 13–23.

Kanter, R. M. (1979). Power failure in management circuits. *Harvard Business Review, 57*(2), 65–75.

Kelly, C. M. (1987). The interrelationship of ethics and power in today's organizations. *Organizational Dynamics, 16*(1), 5–18.

Kramer, R. M., & Grossman, B. (1987). Contracting for social services: Process management and resource dependencies. *Social Service Review, 61,* 32–55.

Lasswell, H. D. (1936). *Politics: Who gets what, when, and how.* New York: McGraw-Hill.

Mandell, B. R. (1983). Blurring definitions of social services: Human services versus social work. *Catalyst: A Socialist Journal of the Social Services, 4*(3), 5–21.

Martin, P. Y. (1980). Multiple constituencies, dominant societal values, and the human service administrator: Implications for service delivery. *Administration in Social Work, 4*(2), 15–27.

McClelland, D. C. (1975). *Power: The inner experience.* New York: Irvington.

Meinert, R., Ginsberg, L., & Keys, P. R. (1993). Performance characteristics of CEOs in state departments of social services, mental health, and corrections. *Administration in Social Work, 17*(1), 103–114.

Meyer, J. W., Scott, W. R., & Deal, T. E. (1981). Institutional and technical sources of organizational structure: Explaining the structure of educational organizations. In H. D. Stein (Ed.), *Organizations and the human services: Cross-disciplinary reflections* (pp. 151–179). Philadelphia: Temple University Press.

Patti, R. J. (1984). Who leads the social services? The prospects for social work leadership in an age of political conservatism. *Administration in Social Work, 8*(1), 17–29.

Potuchek, J. L. (1986). The context of social service funding: The funding relationship. *Social Service Review, 60,* 421–436.

Rapp, C. A., & Poertner, J. (1992). *Social administration: A client-centered approach.* New York: Longman.

Rein, M., & White, S. H. (1981). Knowledge for practice. *Social Service Review, 55*(1), 1–41.

Scoble, H. M. (1968). Access to politics. In D. L. Sills (Ed.), *International encyclopedia of the social sciences* (Vol. 1, pp. 10–14). New York: Macmillan.

Smith, D. E. (1965). Front-line organization of the state mental hospital. *Administrative Science Quarterly, 10,* 381–399.

Thompson, J. D., & Tuden, A. (1959). Strategies, structures, and processes of organizational decision. In J. D. Thompson, P. B. Hammond, R. W. Hawkes, B. H. Hunter, & A. Tuden (Eds.), *Comparative studies in administration* (pp. 195–216). Pittsburgh: University of Pittsburgh Press.

Turem, J. S. (1986). Social work administration and modern management technology. *Administration in Social Work, 10*(3), 15–24.

Wildavsky, A. (1979). *The politics of the budgetary process* (3rd ed.). Boston: Little, Brown.

Yates, D., Jr. (1985). *The politics of management: Exploring the inner workings of public and private organizations.* San Francisco: Jossey-Bass.

# Chapter 5

# The Dynamics of Team Management in the Human Services

David I. Siegel

T his chapter uses concepts of group dynamics to illuminate the functioning of teams and work groups in the human services field. It focuses on the functioning of groups of managers and workers in the process of completing the work of organizations or agencies. The discussion may prove useful for human services managers and workers who may be hired to develop teams and work groups.

There is a strong group work tradition in social work and an appreciation of group process as a facilitator of cohesion and task accomplishment. Furthermore, many issues in service groups—leadership, developmental stages, task–process relationships, varying levels of goals, group composition, and structural factors—are similar to those in management teams and work groups. However, neither the social group work literature nor the extensive literature on corporate management teams has been sufficiently used to illuminate team management in the human services, with a few notable exceptions (see, for example, Bargal & Schmid, 1992; Hall, 1985; Norman & Keys, 1992; Weiner, 1990). Norman and Keys and Bargal and Schmid have also suggested that organizational development—the interdisciplinary profession that subsumes team building—has not been widely used in the development of the human services.

It may be that the group work methods developed in the reformist and service tradition of Jane Addams, oriented to disempowered client groups, do not fit well with the productivity, survival, and achievement needs of management, which are often perceived as interfering with client service. It also may be that an emphasis on productivity and related characteristics of the workplace environment distinguish management teams and work groups from traditional group work service groups. In various settings involving different purposes and systems of values, the conceptualization of productivity and achievement changes, so that different models of the use of groups have seemed appropriate.

Groups have purposes, and group work's historical mission has been to help the oppressed overcome inequities and power differences (Lee, 1992). Many leaders saw social work as having a place in industry, especially as a means to help reform movements dealing with inequities stemming from child labor practices, unemployment, and unfair labor practices, particularly against women. However, social work was not considered to be a tool of management. In this context, groups that complete the work of human services organizations must be on guard to ensure that the organization's productivity and survival requirements do not overwhelm client or worker goals.

The first condition for fulfilling this mission is for social work managers to use their knowledge of groups to direct and administer social agencies. In a human services organization, the structure is part of the treatment, and that structure is partially defined by the functioning of its work groups. Therefore, where an organization bases its management on group work norms of participation, group and individual development, empowerment, and mutual aid, it is more likely to succeed in facilitating client self-actualization and goal achievement. Human services managers who do not understand how to facilitate the successful and humanistic functioning of teams and work groups may be left with the rigidity of bureaucracy at the expense of client goal achievement.

Furthermore some of the worst aspects of competitiveness and oppression in capitalist societies are related to certain characteristics of their work

processes. If these processes are overly routinized, with overemphasis on productivity, little attention to employee participation and development, rewards
that foster differential statuses, and lack of respect for diversity, oppression
and violent impulses will increase. Lee (1992) wrote that society is speeding
into a superindustrial era with oppressive technology. It would seem that social
work's mission and that of professions with similar values should include
humanizing these work processes.

The characteristics of the workplace that influence the functioning of
teams and groups in an organization have not been well defined in the social
work literature. Consequently, models relating work groups to the work environment and the appropriate theoretical concepts have yet to be fully developed. Also not adequately understood is the tension between traditional social
work processes, roles, and values and other newer processes and values having
to do with the workplace. As communities gain knowledge of these issues, it
will be possible to use social group work theory, processes, and values to
humanize the work environment.

## CHARACTERISTICS OF THE WORKPLACE

This chapter presents a conceptual framework for the use of
team management and work groups. This framework identifies four characteristics of the workplace environment that influence team and work group functioning and the role of the worker: (1) emphasis on productivity, (2) task
emphasis, (3) the use of time as a limiting and motivating variable, and (4) the
issue of the dual client.

The influence of these environmental factors on team performance is
determined by structural variables such as the type of organization, the management level of the group, and the team's function within the structure. The
function of a team or a work group is defined as including the following: its
part in the work or production process, the support it lends to the work process
(if it is external to it), the role it has in addressing individual worker problems,
and the degree of its responsibility for organizational clients (see Figure 5-1).

### Emphasis on productivity

The performance of teams and work groups is affected by the degree of
emphasis on productivity. This, in turn, is affected by the type of organization
they work for, the management level at which they operate, and the relationship they have to the work process.

**Type of organization.** Organizations can be categorized according to the
degree they emphasize productivity. In an industrial concern, the purpose is to

FIGURE 5-1

# Structural–Functional Variables That Determine the Influence of Workplace Characteristics on Group Functioning

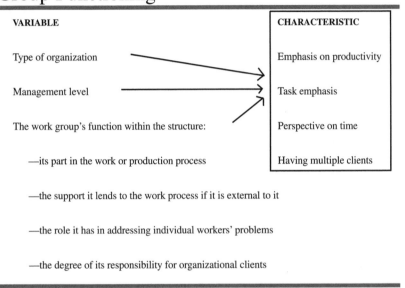

| VARIABLE | CHARACTERISTIC |
|---|---|
| Type of organization | Emphasis on productivity |
| Management level | Task emphasis |
| The work group's function within the structure: | Perspective on time |
| —its part in the work or production process | Having multiple clients |

—the support it lends to the work process if it is external to it

—the role it has in addressing individual workers' problems

—the degree of its responsibility for organizational clients

maximize profits. This is fundamental for organizational survival and for the continued employment of all participants. This is not to say that management is unconcerned with the welfare of its employees. Many theories of successful management emphasize employee participation in decision making. However, the productivity goal influences the purposes of all levels in the organization, puts a premium on task completion, and emphasizes the efficient use of time. Privatization of many human services functions often means having those functions performed by organizations that emphasize the bottom line.

Social services organizations may also emphasize productivity, which can be defined as the emphasis on quantitative outputs, often necessary for survival. This is naturally a task for management groups and usually entails compiling statistics to gauge and justify operations. It should be noted that, in the context of social work, an overemphasis on productivity may interfere with a commitment to strengthening work groups through promotion of inter-personal processes and group development.

Because the mission in these organizations involves client growth and development, it is important that the emphasis on productivity not interfere with time necessary for developmental processes that often constitute the *raison d'être* of these organizations. It can be argued that human services organizations should have a measure of outcome other than productivity. They should use qualitative measures related to achievement of client goals. Indeed, many human services organizations do spend time evaluating qualitative outcomes so that they can improve client service. They may resist pressure to be evaluated on quantitative measures alone. Nonetheless, because it is difficult to measure outcomes related to client service, and many agencies do not want to devote time and energy to this task, quantitative productivity is often given undue emphasis.

Productivity in itself is not evil, and many clients (for example, public housing residents who manage their environment and community businesses) grow and self-actualize by becoming productive. However, an overemphasis on the organization's productivity may change the environment and influence the goals of work groups, such that they lose sight of the original mission of the organization. In other words, productivity can be used to facilitate worker growth, but an overemphasis on organizational productivity can sabotage group process and relatedness.

**Management level.** The emphasis on productivity may well be affected by group management level. Upper management may be the most influenced by productivity concerns, because it may have to demonstrate effectiveness to external constituencies and to justify the survival value of policies. By contrast, at lower levels of management, the workers in human services organizations who are more directly involved with clients and far removed from external pressures therefore may be more oriented to qualitative outcomes.

**The work group's function within the organization's structure.** The degree of emphasis on productivity is also affected by the work group's function within the organization's structure (see Figure 5-1). For example, a group that is an integral part of the work process and whose function is to see the process to completion would be most concerned about output and productivity. Such a group would tend to function on an ongoing basis. A management or interdisciplinary planning team in a human services organization task group or self-managing team in a corporation are examples of this type of ongoing group, in which productivity concerns are usually strong.

Groups that merely support the work process but are not actually part of it, such as time-limited groups involved in team building or process consultation, are less affected by productivity considerations. For other employee groups, such as employee assistance, support, health promotion, and wellness groups, the locus of the problem is defined as being in the individual, and the influence of productivity for these types of groups may be less direct (see Table 5-1).

**Degree and nature of responsibility for clients.** Teams and work groups in human services organizations vary in the degree to which they are responsible for client service. In a mental health clinic, for example, there may be an inter-disciplinary team of professionals (for example, a social worker, psychiatrist, psychologist, occupational therapist, and recreation therapist) who work together to provide direct client service. This kind of group would be influenced by the stress placed on productivity. However, the group's orientation to productivity would also be affected by its approach to working with clients. With some models of practice, such as the therapeutic milieu or community work, the required orientation to interpersonal processes, systems, and a group development perspective may not lend itself easily to quantitative measurements common to an emphasis on productivity. In other models (analytical therapy, cognitive restructuring), the product may lend itself more easily to units of practice that can be measured quantitatively and facilitate an emphasis on productivity. The issue here is that an organization's emphasis on productivity can determine or influence the mode of practice. Furthermore, if a practice mode emphasizing interpersonal processes and group development is used in an organization stressing productivity, tension may result. Ideally the practice mode should be determined by client needs and not the needs of the organization.

In summary, the types of organization, management level, and function of work groups may interact. The emphasis on productivity by management may be different from that of lower-level professionals with responsibility for clients. However, this emphasis will have its effects and must be addressed and negotiated.

### Emphasis on task

The emphasis on productivity reinforces task priorities. This is an interesting issue for human services work because, as the history of social group work and small group theory indicates, it entails a struggle between the relative emphasis to be given to task as opposed to process. In workplace groups, strong forces toward being productive promote an emphasis on task.

Examples of the struggle between task and process include Bales's (1965) seminal work on group theory. Bales postulated that successful groups proceed through different stages of development, alternating between task and socioemotional or process concerns. Groups emphasize task achievement, until the pressure of work builds up and the need for trust and support

# TABLE 5-1
## Organizational Characteristics That Affect Group Functioning and the Role of the Group Worker

| LEVEL OF WORK GROUP | EMPHASIS ON PRODUCTIVITY | TASK EMPHASIS | USE OF TIME AS LIMITING AND MOTIVATING FACTOR | ISSUE OF DUAL CLIENT |
|---|---|---|---|---|
| The group is part of the work or production process itself (work group, self managing team, interdisciplinary team). | Highest—The group may have been assigned to perform a production function. | Highest—Work involves the completion of a task. | The group is ongoing with time for development and integration. There is pressure to complete work quickly. | The interests of the organization are most directly felt, although there may be blending of individuals. |
| The group is time limited and supports the work or production process but is not an ongoing part of the process (team building, quality circles, process consultation). | Moderate—The major purpose may involve improving productivity, but maximizing the use of individual talents and the blending of skills, roles, and behaviors is important. | Moderate—These groups involve working together to solve a problem or further task achievement, but there is attention to procedural process and interpersonal issues. | Time-limited nature usually limits group development and generalizability. The pressure of time can be a motivating factor. | The ultimate purpose still involves productivity, but particular attention is paid to self-actualization through the use of skills and participation in decision making. |
| The group defines the locus of the problem as being in the individual (crisis oriented, short-term employee assistance program groups, health promotion, wellness, and support groups). | Indirect—Assumption is that promoting individual growth and fitness and resolving individual problems will lead to increased productivity. | Moderate—A short-term task orientation is still pervasive, but greater attention is paid to individual problems of living, to interpersonal issues, and to feelings and emotions. | Time limits are consciously used to motivate clients and the worker and hold them to the tasks | The target of change is the individual. The small group is instrumental in achieving individual goals. Service must be justified as aiding productivity. |

becomes acute. After attending to socioemotional needs, members ultimately become satiated and impatient and strive again toward task achievement.

Whereas several models of social group work have stressed the importance of defining a specific task for client goal attainment (see Garvin, Reid, & Epstein, 1976), group workers also believe that group process and mutual aid considerations are crucial for facilitating task achievement. Helen Northen (1976), one of the pioneers of social group work, stated:

> The interdependence of people on one another, a form of mutual aid, contributes a major dynamic for growth and change. The small group is effective in bringing about positive changes if it combines psychological support for efforts to change with adequate stimulation from others to enhance motivation toward the achievement of goals. (p. 117)

Emphasis on productivity and task may lead to a preoccupation with short-term task-centered models of group practice. These may be seen as more efficient and less wasteful of an organization's resources. The danger is that the pressure to complete a task may preclude proper attention to group process and mutual aid. Managers may not understand the importance of group process for task completion, so one of the roles of the social group worker may be to educate managers in this area.

The relative emphasis on task is also influenced by the management level and function of a group within the organization's structure. Upper-management teams that constitute an ongoing part of the work process tend to stress task; time-limited supportive groups (employee development groups, team-building sessions) or groups emphasizing a developmental approach to clients may feel less task-oriented pressure.

### Time as a limiting and motivating factor

**Varying perspectives on time.** Superimposed on the productivity and task emphases of the workplace are varying perspectives on the use of time. Many human services managers and corporate officers have a short time perspective, particularly when their performance is judged by organizational outputs. Consequently, they try to demonstrate their organizational competence by increasing productivity and showing short-term achievement. This, in turn, may result in inadequate long-term planning.

However, the human services managers may also have short time perspectives, when time is measured in financial or quantitative terms and managers must justify their use of time to boards or other constituents. Many human services managers believe with good reason that the major time commitment in their organization should involve work with agency clients, an area of major attention to interpersonal processes and group dynamics. There may not seem to be time left to consider and work with the dynamics of agency teams and work groups. I remember my experience in one of my first jobs as a group worker: The staff was so emotionally concerned about what feedback they received in the weekly employee "T" group that there was little emotional energy left for clients.

A short-term perspective creates a dilemma for the enlightened human services manager or group worker, because most group work models emphasize group development and successively higher stages of integration and effectiveness. Therefore, the organization's perspective on the use of time may be diametrically opposed to that of the social group worker for whom the passage of time may be an ally.

The time perspective of a manager or employee is also affected by the management level and function of a work group to which he or she belongs. High-level management groups may have the shortest time perspectives. However, if the group is ongoing, then there would be a potential for a developmental perspective and an orientation to strategic planning. Groups such as interdisciplinary teams are part of the work process, are ongoing, and potentially have time for development and integration, although management may have productivity concerns (see Table 5-1).

Support groups that are external to the work process (team building, process consultation, quality circles) are generally retained for a specific assignment and function for the short term. Groups in which the locus of the problem is considered to be in the individual worker are under pressure to return productive workers to their jobs as quickly as possible. Thus, they use time limits to motivate workers and hold them to their tasks.

It should be stated that many human services managers have a background in social work practice and appreciate developmental processes. Service groups in their agencies may be allowed to exist for as long as is appropriate for the client. However, this appreciation for development does not always extend to work groups without direct responsibility for client service. Group development of management and work teams and attention to group dynamics may be seen as using time best saved for clients. Furthermore, the use of time must be justified to many constituents, including boards, auditing authorities, funding sources, and the community. Therefore, many human services managers believe that the most effective work group interventions are those that occur in the short term, do not require a great deal of resources, and do not interfere for long with the "real work." I believe this is a tragedy of the human services that can lead to authoritarianism and rigidity and, ultimately, poor client service.

On the other hand, human services managers must be careful not to allow their appreciation of development to lead to a lack of appreciation of the value of time and the importance of getting things done quickly and efficiently. Some managers may be so involved in facilitating agency processes that the agency becomes a launching pad for their careers and the careers of their staffs, and the needs of their clients are lost or become secondary (see Bucher & Stelling, 1969). The best perspective on time by a human services manager may be one that is balanced, with a proper attention to task and outcomes, tempered by an appropriate appreciation of group process and employee group development. This should facilitate the task of reaching client goals, yet not be overdone.

**Value of group development.** Ongoing work groups and teams in the workplace pass through developmental stages, as do traditional social work groups. In reviewing the management literature, Nadler, Hackman, and Lawler (1979) distinguished four stages of development: membership, influence, affection, and growth. Berger (1985) also distinguished four stages, which he defined as preparing for work, challenging authority, getting down to business, and getting close. In a more recent article, Montebello and Buzzotta (1993) mentioned the following stages: cautious affiliation, competitiveness, harmonious cohesiveness, and collaborative teamwork. Brauchle and Wright (1993) defined 10 steps that emphasize the role of trainer in training work teams: establish credibility, allow ventilation, provide an orientation, invest in the process, set group goals, facilitate the group process, establish intragroup procedures, establish intergroup processes, change your roles, and end involvement.

A review of these models suggests that like social work models, they include developing relationships between members, resolving the authority issue between workers (or managers) and members, and achieving similarity of purpose and interest (see Berman-Rossi, 1992). Differences are a matter of degree: Social work models tend to emphasize mutual aid, whereas those from the organizational development or business literature tend to emphasize team task achievements. This reflects social work's orientation toward personal relations gained from work with clients and business's orientation toward products. Many models of development in both sets of literature have their origins in small group theory from the social sciences. According to Berman-Rossi (1992, citing Garland, Jones, & Kolodny, 1965), a particular contribution of social work is the development of life cycle models with typical stages, such as preaffiliation, power and control, intimacy, differentiation, and separation.

**Value of time limits.** It is interesting that short time interventions can sometimes aid functioning. In traditional group work service, the passage of time is an ally: It fosters group development, which leads to individual goal achievement. In work groups, however, the passage of time is not conducive to cost-effectiveness. Setting time limits may therefore be a means of motivating and structuring group members toward task achievement. Effective managers and workers usually respond well to time pressure. There is evidence that many social work agencies and clients can benefit from a focus on task completion within prescribed time limits.

Accordingly, many employee assistance programs have adopted short-term models of practice in which time pressure is used as an aid to treatment. This policy has been adopted partly in response to the need for having employees remain at work more and to pressure these programs to avoid the legal issues involved in long-term treatment:

> Experience in helping people, within time limits, uniting with a client to use the dynamics of time as it holds both client and worker to their purpose, creates a deeply felt commitment, communicated to the client, and quite different from an intellectual grasp of the model. (McBroom, 1984, p. 34)

Wells (1982) wrote that time limitations result "in highly positive pressures on both therapists and client to identify the most pressing problem(s) and to work productively to bring about desired changes" (pp. 9–10).

In summary, team or work group performance can be affected by the time perspective of the organization and manager. Whereas a short-term time perspective is sometimes appropriate, it can interfere with developmental processes. Furthermore, client service models used by professional teams should be determined by client needs, not the organization's time orientation.

### The issue of multiple clients: Group versus individual goals

Because organizational productivity is of concern in the workplace, the team builder may find it difficult to determine who is the client in a work group and whose needs predominate—the organization's or the employee's. For a manager who has primary responsibility for the organization, the dilemma is the extent to which he or she should be concerned for individual needs of workers when organizational survival may be at issue. Whose needs are primary, the organization's, the worker's, or the contracted client's? Also, are the contracted client's needs best represented by management or workers, and how is this evidenced in the group? Human services managers have another crucial concern, that of service responsibility for contracted clients who are not part of the employee work group. According to the *NASW Code of Ethics* (National Association of Social Workers, 1994), their needs are primary. For an occupational social worker hired to do team building or skill development, to what extent do the organization's productivity needs or the agency's survival needs impinge on his or her commitment to individual employees? Another issue for a social worker providing direct service to workers in an employee assistance program is the following: To what extent does having the worker back at work and being productive conflict with a potential need for intensive long-term treatment or hospitalization? Participatory forms of management would seem to be indicated to support social work's ethical responsibility to clients. Managers may have more experience and are concerned that their organization have a positive reputation for service. Line workers work more closely with clients, and therefore, they should have more direct knowledge of their needs.

Another issue is the relative attention paid to group goals versus individual goals. In traditional group work, the individual in the group is assumed to be the client, and the achievement of group goals is seen as instrumental toward the achievement of individual goals. The worker can intervene with the group so that the group will influence the individual (Vinter, 1985). Following this model, the amount of time spent on goal achievement should depend on the needs of the individual.

From the perspective of workplace managers, this flow may be reversed. The achievement of individual goals may be seen as a step toward achieving group goals, and this in turn is a step toward achieving organizational purposes through increased productivity. For example, in a team-building group, understanding members' skills and deficits, teaching new skills, and negotiating roles facilitate team task accomplishment and, subsequently, organizational goals. Ultimately, this flow ought to result in maximum benefit to contracted clients.

In a short-term clinical group (such as an employee assistance program or in an organizational support group such as Caregivers or Alcoholics Anonymous), another type of flow may be evident. As in traditional group work, the goals and purposes of the small group may be instrumental in resolving individual behavioral or emotional difficulties. However, the resolution of individual needs within the group and the small group's existence and purpose still must be justified in terms of contribution to the greater organization. Do they enhance employee productivity, decrease absenteeism, and protect the organization's investment in its workers? The other side of this issue is expressed as follows: Is short-term support in the interest of individual members?

The relationship between group and individual goals, when antagonistic, poses great difficulties in applying group work concepts to work groups. It may involve issues of value as well as theoretical problems. Social workers' basic ethical values will be violated unless the efforts of their work groups ultimately serve individuals and contracted clients.

How do social group workers resolve the dilemma of balancing the interests of organizations, workers, and clients? They do this through constant engagement in a process of negotiating between the legitimate and illegitimate concerns of the organization, workers, and contracted clients. However, because their values emphasize concern for the individual as primary client, they would be wise to promote organizations and theories of organization in which this concern is not overwhelmed by productivity issues and in which the organization's goals and processes are compatible with worker and client goals. The organizations should emphasize a marriage between legitimate organizational goals and individual self-actualization, participation, and achievement.

The function of organizational structure in a human services agency is somewhat different than in other organizations, because the structure and processes of the agency become part of the treatment for clients. This structure is at least partly defined by the functioning of its work groups. If the agency's culture and work groups emphasize growth, development, participation, and pride, this should have a positive impact on clients. This is well known to proponents of the therapeutic milieu or therapeutic community for whom the total environment and the participation of all workers, backed by the strength of group cohesiveness, are part of the therapy.

In his classic article, "Bureaucratic Structure and Personality," Robert Merton (1940) persuasively demonstrated how the organization's structure affects the personality of workers. In particular, where there is little attention to employee growth and development, mutual aid in teams, and an appreciation for group process, social workers will be rigid and mechanical. Therefore, group workers and human services managers have a tremendous responsibility to help humanize organizational processes. The functioning of an organization's work groups determines its structure and ultimately has great impact on the fate of its clients.

Organizational emphasis on productivity may be contrary to models of working with groups that emphasize mutual aid, interpersonal processes, the relationship between process and task, a developmental perspective, and participatory decision making. Therefore, these environmental factors can interfere with the work group's achievement of its goals.

## LEVELS OF WORKPLACE GROUPS

For the purpose of illustrating the effect of the selected variables on social work groups, one may posit different levels of workplace groups. Wegener (1992) identified three categories of employee support groups as part of social work service: (1) groups that are formed to meet developmental needs, (2) groups that are formed in response to work-related needs, and (3) treatment groups. To emphasize the influence of workplace variables, the present analysis focuses on groups formed to carry out organizational work. This is different from but related to Wegener (see Table 5-1).

At the first level are groups that are an ongoing part of the work or production process, usually led by a supervisor or manager from within the organization or agency. This level includes self-managing teams, interdisciplinary teams, and other ongoing work groups. Such groups might include the director, clinical director, administrator, and supervisors of a mental health clinic who meet to set policy, coordinate tasks, develop structure, ensure that clients are seen, and imbue the agency with a sense of identity and mission. They also might include the treatment team at a social services shelter composed of a social caseworker, social group worker, occupational therapist, and recreation therapist who regularly meet and converse about the contribution of each occupation to a philosophy of service as well as a strategy with each client, division of tasks, responsibility for client outcomes, and team accountability and recording.

At the second level are groups usually led by outside consultants that support the work or production process but are not an ongoing part of the work process itself. Their mission might be to resolve specific problems that interfere with the work process, ranging from dealing with interpersonal issues and relationship development to fostering skills development. These groups may be more oriented than ongoing work groups toward addressing individual worker deficits and need for skills or support mechanisms. They include team building and training groups and usually meet in the short term.

At the third level are groups in which the locus of a problem is defined explicitly as residing within an individual. These may include problems relating to fitness and health, substance abuse, family disruption, emotional disturbance, and child rearing. This level would include short-term crisis treatment groups, support groups related to specific individual problems, and groups emphasizing health promotion and wellness. The organizational sanction of these groups rests on the expectation that resolution of individual problems and the provision of skills will ultimately result in greater productivity.

To provide examples of the effects of the workplace variables on groups and social group work, groups at each of the three levels are considered. Key issues here are the relative emphasis given to task versus process and to group versus individual goals. According to Burke (1982), procedural processes relate directly to task accomplishment and include organization, leadership, decision making, and problem solving. Maintenance processes are the activities that help keep the group together as a team and include openness of communication, mutual trust, mutual support, gatekeeping, tolerance of differences, and tension relief.

### Ongoing work groups and self-managing teams

In classical management theory, work groups have been formed as part of the design of the work process, with the primary goals of facilitating maximum productivity and task achievement. From this perspective, groups can be seen as a basic unit of organizational structure, and their composition helps to define jobs and provide the opportunity for rewards.

This tradition can potentially include concern for process and interpersonal issues, but historically the primary emphasis has been on task achievement and productivity. Organizational structure tended to emphasize the efficient use of space, promotion of a smooth work flow, and maintenance of positive economies of scale rather than the promotion of interpersonal relationships and supports. Jobs were designed to create manageable pieces of work and specialized competencies and did not often emphasize the opportunities created for interpersonal rewards. Job rewards were thought of in terms of task achievement, status increases, and promotion opportunities rather than as the inevitable outcome of processes imbued with close interpersonal ties and joint achievement.

In industry, groups were formed for practical reasons, such as economy, creation of a unit of people involved in an issue that can be managed by one person, and physical proximity (Browning, 1977). The responsibilities of ongoing groups, moreover, were usually defined in terms of achieving tasks such as preparing a budget, compiling inventory statistics, solving technical problems, redesigning or modifying production processes, or training fellow members (Simms & Dean, 1985).

Because these groups were considered directly related to production, little attention was paid to procedural processes such as appropriate styles of leadership and means of decision making and problem solving; too often these processes occurred ad hoc with little forethought. The possibilities inherent in ongoing work groups for enhancing cohesion, interpersonal support, and communication were frequently ignored.

Furthermore, many managers do not have the knowledge of group process and structure for more sophisticated analysis of work group effectiveness that could be provided by a social group worker. Successful teams were frequently characterized as involving a blending of individual skills and abilities. From this perspective, Margerison and McCann (1984), for example, identified certain key functions and roles that characterized successful management teams: linking, advising, organizing, controlling, and exploring. They also identified nine other roles that facilitate team performance and suggested that each person is capable of playing up to two or three roles: "Managers must understand the key strengths of their team members and be able to allocate them to work where they can best contribute" (p. 13).

## New theories of management and teamwork

New theories of management, particularly human relations theory, Japanese-style management, and total quality management (TQM), emphasize a broader perspective of on-line work groups. For example, to ensure quality, TQM emphasizes the participation of workers in decision making and responses to customer needs. The literature on teams emphasizes self-managing teams and empowering employees by allowing them to assume greater tasks and make their own decisions.

Although Schilder (1992) indicated that these ideas have their roots in employee involvement strategies such as sensitivity training, quality circles, and "T" groups, they are shown to contribute to improving productivity. He maintained that team direction "involves using the collective brainpower of all employees as a competitive strategy" (p. 69). This means that self-managing teams are still justified in the management literature in terms of their contribution to quality and productivity. Now, however, there is a greater awareness of the importance of interpersonal and procedural processes to productive outcomes.

Jessup (1992) indicated that "the basis for successful teamwork is sharing, sharing one's mission, sharing tasks and experiences and sharing consequences" (p. 65). Jessup also emphasized the importance of an orientation to team development and the importance of the so-called team growth process by citing to B. W. Tuckerman's 1965 formulation of forming, storming, norming, and performing:

> In the forming stage, new groups may have high morale even before they start to address the task at hand. In the storming stage, there may be competition for roles, and there may be recognition of the performance shortcomings that cause discomfort among team members. In the norming stage, teams establish some roles and procedural standards as they begin to accomplish their tasks. In the final stage, performing, both morale and competence are high as teams begin to achieve the performance levels expected. (cited in Jessup, 1992, p. 65)

The social group work literature has a more sophisticated formulation of group development. Berman-Rossi (1992) stated that the "development of the group as a whole is predicted upon the character of two internal processes, that of member to authority and member to member relationships" (p. 240).

Jessup (1992) addressed the dilemma of multiple clients. In her view, a work team must identify

> the expectations of each stakeholder group. For example, top managers are interested in costs, quality, and delivery, and regulatory compliance. Customers care about service, performance and reliability. Family of the team members are concerned about pay, benefits and job security. Team-mates want interesting work, mutual respect, recognition and a sense of accomplishment. (p. 66)

The task of social work managers and work teams is to reconcile the interests of the organization, the workers, and the clients.

Brauchle and Wright (1993) discussed training potential candidates to develop effective work teams: "Trainees need to understand the group process—the way a work group functions—in order to work effectively in teams" (p. 66). The authors presented the nominal group process, a four-step procedure in which participants make individual "silent" lists of group issues, create a master list, collapse and combine list items, and conduct a straw vote to decide which issues are most important. Although this orientation to process is laudatory, it can be developed further through greater understanding of the group as a mutual aid system.

Teamwork "can be more productive, can produce higher quality, and is more cost efficient than solo efforts" (Brauchle & Wright, 1993, p. 59). Part of the reason is that "when tasks that produce an end product are simplified and fragmented, they rob the people who perform the work of self-esteem, a sense of accomplishment and pride in their work" (p. 60). It is more interesting when team members "share a core of functions." Brauchle and Wright also believed that "teamwork is successful partly because of the emphasis it places on people" (p. 60). They cited the Hackman–Oldham model of five character-istics of any job as "a useful guide to designing teams, enriching work and organizing tasks to achieve important business objectives" (p. 60). The five characteristics are

- skill variety: various job activities that call for different skills and talents
- task identity: the extent to which a job is handled from beginning to end, producing an identifiable and complete outcome
- task significance: the extent to which the work has an effect on others or society in general
- autonomy: freedom and discretion in planning, organizing, sched-uling, and performing the work

- feedback: clear and direct information about performance and effectiveness. (p. 60)

Management, self-management, and interdisciplinary teams in human services agencies must also address the issues caused by productivity pressures, the need to complete a task, the pressures of time, and the demands of multiple clients. Managers can facilitate employee growth by creating diverse and interesting tasks, empowering them through permitting independent decision making, and assigning them to membership in cohesive and multiskilled work teams. Managers who are also social workers can use their knowledge of group dynamics to facilitate work group and team outcomes and the accomplishment of client goals by harnessing the power of mutual aid; commonalities of goals, issues, and task; and group development and cohesiveness. They can achieve this within the constraints of time limits and the interests of various constituencies.

### Time-limited groups that support the work process
The second level of groups in organizations are time-limited groups, developed to support the work or production process although they are not really part of the process. Such groups provide a great opportunity for the use of group principles at the workplace. In fact, team-building interventions are similar to social group work in that they emphasize process as well as task. For social group workers, process includes an emphasis on interpersonal and relationship issues.

**Models of team building.** Different models of team building give different emphases to task versus process, to procedural versus interpersonal issues, and to concern for the group versus concern for the individual. In general, there are four primary purposes of team building that help us categorize the major team-building models. Burke (1982) stated them as follows:

1. to set goals or priorities
2. to analyze or allocate the way work is performed according to team members' roles and responsibilities
3. to examine the way the team works on its processes
4. to examine relationships among team members. (p. 268)

In accord with the first purpose, Woodman and Sherwood (1980) stated that "the goal setting model of team development involves, as the name suggests, the setting of objectives by the members of a group and the identification of problems that interfere with the accomplishment of these goals" (p. 167). Under this model, a team-building session might involve members of management and employee groups meeting to reconcile ideas and develop a set of goals.

This type of team building is the most task oriented of all the models, with goal development as a specific task. This model may give some attention to procedural process, providing specific ways for membership participation and a set procedure for follow-up. However, it does not give much emphasis to interpersonal or relationship issues or maintenance processes such as the development of cohesion and support.

In accord with the second purpose of team building, Woodman and Sherwood (1980) stated that "the role model views a group as a set of interacting roles and assumes that group effectiveness can be increased by a better understanding of these roles" (p. 167). Team building typically involves members presenting and discussing each other's perceptions and understandings of their roles and "modifying roles as a function of increased agreement about mutual expectations" (Burke, 1982, p. 275). Again this model tends to concentrate on the task at hand, with procedural issues limited to those involved in clarifying roles. Interpersonal issues regarding who should do more or less and who should change the nature of their role performance do arise. However, considerations of individual needs are limited to how these needs impinge on the roles discussed.

The third model of team building involves examining group procedures, including group norms, leadership style, type of decision-making and problem-solving techniques, communication, and team structure. Procedural processes are emphasized, but maintenance processes, including interpersonal issues of trust and support, are only peripherally considered.

As for the fourth purpose of team building, Woodman and Sherwood (1980) stated that "the interpersonal model is based on the assumption that people who are competent in their interpersonal skills can function more effectively as a team." The goal of intervention with this approach might be to increase mutual trust, interpersonal cooperation, and group cohesiveness by encouraging feedback and open communication. Strategies are developed to deal with interpersonal issues that interfere with the functioning of the team.

This type of model, with its emphasis on interpersonal process, closely approaches traditional social group work. Here, production is not the task of the moment, and the ultimate goal of improving productivity is approached through interpersonal relations and their effect on group performance.

In general at this level of group, which supports the work process, there is somewhat greater freedom to deal with people issues and individual needs and skills. However, the production goals and time perspective of the organization still exert influence.

In moving toward more task-oriented models of team building, organizational development literature may have overreacted to the open feedback emphasis of T-groups. In social group work, task-oriented and socioemotional phases of groups support each other and, with maintenance goals and processes strengthening group cohesion, facilitate task achievement. It is true that organizations must be concerned with task achievement and productivity, but not to the exclusion of interpersonal matters, which ultimately aid group functioning. In fact, the emphasis of social group work education on systems and the various aspects of life that ultimately affect group functioning is recognition of this point. This includes issues such as reward systems, skills training, organizational culture, and management style.

### VALUE ISSUES IN WORK GROUPS

The emphasis on task in the workplace creates a dilemma concerning the role of a group worker. Does the worker's participation in task-centered models or those that emphasize procedure conflict with social work's commitment to the individual? Not necessarily, according to Glasser and Garvin (1976), who discussed the individual as the focus of change: "This principle stresses that the worker focuses on helping each member change either or both his individual behavior or his environment through the group experience. Specified group conditions are created only as they are seen to be helpful in the achievement of individual goals" (p. 77).

Northen (1976) maintained a similar position: "The ultimate value that underlies this approach is that each individual should have opportunities to realize his or her developmental potential in ways that are personally satisfying and socially constructive. Implied in this basic value is simultaneous concern for the dignity and worth of the individual and the integrity of collectives" (p. 120).

How should social group workers react to the potential value conflicts that arise in working with groups in organizations? One way is to see whether one's role helps to make the organization more responsive to individual needs. Argyris, one of the pioneers of the field of organization development, emphasized the relationship between individual personality and organization dynamics. Burke (1982) wrote that Argyris's

> objective was to look for ways in which this relationship could be satisfied: that is that the person and the organization both might compromise so that each could profit from the other . . . the organization must adjust

its value system toward helping its members be more psychologically healthy—less dependent on and controlled by the organization—and the individuals must become more open with their feelings, more willing to trust one another, and more internally committed to the organization's goals. (p. 32)

Thus, group workers can choose to work for organizations whose culture and philosophy emphasize the relationship between organizational achievement and individual autonomy and success. Alternatively, they can help such organizations make changes in this direction.

In their classic book, *In Search of Excellence: Lessons from America's Best-Run Companies,* Peters and Waterman (1982) indicated that the excellent companies they surveyed emphasized respect for the individual through "a plethora of structural devices, systems, styles and values" (pp. 238–239). The orientation toward people is not emphasized in just one intervention (for example, team building, quality circles, T groups) but in the total culture and philosophy of these organizations. Group workers can choose to work in organizations that are people oriented or in settings where their espousal of this position has some effect.

Weisbord (1985), in discussing the theories of Blansfield, identified three issues that determine whether a group that strives to be a team will become one: Am I in or out? Do I have any power or control? Will I have a chance to use or develop the needed skills and resources? Positive answers to these issues will help create a marriage between the goals of the individual and those of the organization, and the social group worker's role is to promote this marriage.

### Groups for personal problems

The last level of work groups to be considered are those in which the locus of the problem is defined as residing in the individual. This type of group most closely resembles group work with clients in social agencies. The main assumption behind the work of these groups is the expectation that by improving individual competence and addressing problems such as substance abuse, workers will become more productive, and absenteeism and benefit costs will decrease. This type of work is becoming more important; as a result of technological growth and changes in the structure of the family, the work world is changing. There is a growth in labor force participation by women, middle-aged people, and elderly people; an increasingly specialized and highly competitive job market; and a shift from blue-collar to white-collar employment opportunities (Gould & McKenzie, 1984). Because of these changes, it is increasingly difficult to maintain a strict separation between employees' work lives and the rest of their lives. Managers have implement-ed employee assistance programs as a means of addressing individual need, to have employees more prepared to work each day and to protect their own investment in the workforce.

**Time limits.** The models of practice followed in employee assistance pro-grams have tended to be short-term or crisis oriented for a variety of reasons, representing a confluence of the interests of organizations and the use of time limits as an aid in treatment. From the organization's perspective, time limits put a premium on maintaining employees on site ready to work. They respond to the unwillingness of many insurance companies to cover long-term treatment (Parad, 1984), decrease the costs of maintaining an employee assistance pro-gram, and provide insulation from the legal accountabilities involved in long-term therapy. From a service perspective, time limits are effective in holding client and worker to their purpose, identifying their most pressing problems, and working productively to bring about change (McBroom, 1984; Wells, 1982).

Time limits in this sense are consistent with the value placed on time in the workplace. They also mean that "tasks, a sequence of actions" (McBroom, 1984, p. 34) are the means of solving problems. This task emphasis is also consistent with management's traditional orientation toward problem solving. In contrast to traditional group work, where the passage of time is considered to permit growth and development, time is a limiting and structuring factor.

**Individual versus group approaches.** It is interesting that most short-term counseling at the work site has been provided in individual sessions, perhaps supplemented by some conjoint work. One reason may be that group therapy is frequently seen as a long-term modality (Donovan, Bennett, & McElroy, 1981). Also, the feeling may be that if treatment is to be brief, a client should at least be seen individually. Many believe that a group cannot be fully effec-tive unless it is given time to develop and integrate.

However, opportunities to make use of existing mutual aid systems are being lost, as workers in the workplace share common problems, a common organizational identity, and common status. This could in turn contribute to group cohesiveness and effectiveness. It is therefore possible that groups would be more efficient.

Organizations have moved further in promoting groups emphasizing skills development (for example, communication, stress reduction) or wellness (smoking cessation, weight reduction). These groups have the advantage of not having to define the worker as a client who is emotionally ill and requiring treatment, which can create resistance.

Because the literature on short-term crisis treatment groups in the workplace is sparse, the experience of the Harvard Community Health Plan with short-term crises is instructive (Donovan et al., 1981). The plan focuses on the present, with "only secondary emphasis on group process," and like Alcoholics Anonymous (AA) "each patient takes a turn telling his or her story" (p. 285). The tone is warm, supportive, and task oriented; the therapists are active and directive and take the lead in clarifying problems.

This type of group shares some characteristics common to other short-term therapies: It is task and problem oriented and time limited, with directive and action-oriented therapies. However, because it incorporates the power of the group as a mutual aid system, it should be possible to conduct this type of group with a freer process of interaction between members and leader–therapists. The leaders can maintain structure and task orientation through focusing and clarifying interventions. Through this interaction, members would become more group oriented and subject to group norms even in the short term. As in individual short-term therapy, the worker–client relationship is still crucial, and attention to group participation and maintenance is of prime importance.

This type of group also shares some dynamics common to self-help groups such as AA, which fosters a universalization and common identity. By telling their story, members keep the consequences of negative or inappropriate behavior in the forefront, and support is provided by positive behavior or striving. Manageable short-term steps are defined and encouraged.

It appears appropriate that a short-term crisis group should address problem situations related to work or common problems of living (inability to work, sleep problems, marital issues, child-rearing crises, reactive depression, and grief). Whereas a short-term crisis group in an employee assistance program may ultimately target the individual, there are still issues related to productivity and to having dual clients (individual and organization). The choice of the short-term model may be partly due to the costs of longer-term models (in terms of benefits, insurance problems, interrupted work). Where problems are severe, workers must find appropriate referral resources that are within their means and are covered by insurance.

A larger issue concerns the group worker's responsibility if the client does not improve. Three general referral patterns to an employee assistance program are common: (1) The client is self-referred; (2) the client is referred by a supervisor or manager who then separates from the process of providing help; and (3) the client is referred by a supervisor who requires some feedback regarding client progress. The first two patterns are comfortable for social work intervention, because the confidentiality of the individual is protected, and there is only a general assumption that individual progress in group will aid the organization. For most situations, group workers in these programs should operate under the first two models, for otherwise the mutuality, openness, and trust necessary for the crisis group to succeed would be impossible, and the primary orientation toward individuals in the group would be sacrificed.

In some situations, however, the third pattern may be appropriate. For instance, where others' health and safety are dependent on an employee's job performance (as is the case with a pilot, air traffic controller, or operator of heavy machinery), there may have to be an up-front understanding that the worker report states of emotional upheaval or substance abuse that threaten others. It is important that this condition of service be discussed in the first session.

Workplace alcoholism programs have been successful partly because the implied threat of loss of job provides the leverage necessary for treatment to succeed. As part of a program of rehabilitation, the worker may have to agree to counseling. In this situation, it is best if work performance, as judged by the supervisor or manager, be the deciding factor regarding job continuance.

### SUMMARY

In this chapter, environmental characteristics of the workplace, which affect the functioning of teams and work groups, have been identified. They include emphasis on productivity, emphasis on task, and the use of time as a limiting and motivating variable. These environmental characteristics are affected by structural–functional variables in the organization, including the type of organization, the management level of the group, and the group's function and purpose within the structure. This last characteristic includes three levels of groups and the nature and degree of a group's responsibility for clients.

Examples of the effect of the three environmental characteristics on team and work group functioning were given by applying them to the three levels of groups: groups that are part of the work and production process, time-limited groups that support the work or production process but are not an ongoing part of the process, and groups in which the locus of the problem is defined as being within the individual. The relationship of these variables to various models of organization and team building were explained, and types of work groups and teams possible in the workplace were described.

### REFERENCES

Bales, R. F. (1965). Adaptive and integrative changes as sources of strain in social systems. In A. P. Hare, E. F. Borgatta, & R. F. Bales (Eds.), *Small groups: Studies in social interaction* (pp. 127–131). New York: Alfred A. Knopf.

Bargal, D., & Schmid, H. (1992). Organizational change and development in human service organizations: A prefatory essay. *Administration in Social Work, 16*(3–4), 1–13.

Berger, M. A. (1985). The technical approach to teamwork. *Training and Development Journal, 39*(3), 53–55.

Berman-Rossi, T. (1992). Empowering groups through understanding stages of group development. *Social Work with Groups, 15*(2–3), 239–255.

Brauchle, P., & Wright, D. (1993). Training work teams. *Training and Development Journal, 47*(3), 65–68.

Browning, L. D. (1977). Diagnosing teams in organizational settings. *Group and Organization Studies, 2*(2), 187–197.

Bucher, R., & Stelling, J. (1969). Characteristics of professional organizations. *Journal of Health and Social Behavior, 10*(1), 3–15.

Burke, W. B. (1982). *Organization development: Principles and practice.* Boston: Little, Brown.

Donovan, J. M., Bennet, M. J., & McElroy, C. M. (1981). The crisis group: Its rationale, format, outcome. In S. H. Budman (Ed.), *Forms of brief therapy.* New York: Guilford Press.

Garland, J., Jones, H., & Kolodny R. (1965). A model for stages of development in social work groups. In S. Bernstein (Ed.), *Exploration in group work: Essays, theory and practice* (pp. 12–53). Boston: Boston University, School of Social Work.

Garvin, C. D., Reid, W., & Epstein, L. (1976). A task centered approach. In R. W. Roberts & H. Northen (Eds.), *Theories of social work with groups* (pp. 238–267). New York: Columbia University Press.

Glasser, P. H., & Garvin, C. D. (1976). An organizational model. In R. W. Roberts & H. Northen (Eds.), *Theories of social work with groups* (pp. 75–115). New York: Columbia University Press.

Gould, G., & McKenzie, C. (1984). The expanding scope of industrial social work. *Social Work Papers, 18,* 1–9.

Hall, J. (1985). Productivity improvement through team building and organizational redevelopment: Evaluating the experiences of a human service agency at the county level. *Public Personnel Management, 14*(4), 409–416.

Jessup, H. (1992). The road to results for teams. *Training and Development Journal, 46*(9), 65–68.

Lee, J. (1992). Jane Addams in Boston: Intersecting time and space. *Social Work with Groups, 15*(2–3), 7–21.

Margerison, C., & McCann, D. (1984). High performing managerial teams. *Organizational Development Journal, 5*(5), 9–13.

McBroom, E. (1984). Differentials of clinical practice at the worksite and in traditional agencies. *Social Work Papers, 18,* 31–38.

Merton, R. (1940). Bureaucratic structure and personality. *Social Forces, 18,* 560–568.

Montebello, A., & Buzzotta, V. (1993). Work teams that work. *Training and Development Journal, 47*(3), 59–64.

Nadler, D., Hackman, R., & Lawler, E. (1979). *Managing organizational behavior.* Boston: Little, Brown.

National Association of Social Workers. (1994). *NASW code of ethics.* Washington, DC: Author.

Norman, A., & Keys, P. (1992). Organization development in public social services—The irresistible force meets the immovable object. *Administration in Social Work, 16*(3–4), 147–165.

Northen, H. (1976). Psychosocial practice in small groups. In R. W. Roberts & H. Northen (Eds.), *Theories of social work with groups* (pp. 116–152). New York: Columbia University Press.

Parad, H. (1984). Time-limited crisis therapy in the workplace: An elective perspective. *Social Work Papers, 18,* 20–30.

Peters, T., & Waterman, R. (1982). *In search of excellence: Lessons from America's best-run companies.* New York: Harper & Row.

Schilder, J. (1992). Work teams boost productivity. *Personnel Journal, 71*(2), 67–71.

Simms, H., Jr., & Dean, J. (1985). Beyond quality circles: Self managing teams. *Personnel, 62*(1), 25–32.

Vinter, R. D. (1985). The essential components of social group work practice. In M. Sundel, P. Glasser, R. Sarri, & R. Vinter (Eds.), *Individual change through small groups* (pp. 9–33). New York: Free Press.

Wegener, N. (1992). Supportive group services in the workplace: The practice and the potential. *Social Work with Groups, 15*(2–3), 207–222.

Weiner, M. (1990). *Human service management: Analysis and application* (2nd ed.). Belmont, CA: Wadsworth.

Weisbord, M. (1985). Team effectiveness training. *Training and Development Journal, 39*(1), 27–29.

Wells, R. A. (1982). *Planned short term treatment.* New York: Free Press.

Woodman, R., & Sherwood, J. (1980). The role of team development in organization effectiveness: A critical review. *Psychological Bulletin, 88,* 166–186.

# Chapter 6

# Creating an "Intelligent Organization" in the Human Services

Edgar Colon

It is a truism that orga-nizations live in an uncertain environment. Environ-mental uncertainty has been a central organizational concept at least since its introduction by Thompson (1967). March and Simon (1958) viewed uncertainty in the decision-making process as a factor in organiza-tional conflict.

Several interrelated factors contribute to environmental uncertainty. Scholars from Bell (1973) to Drucker (1993) have pointed out that the devel-oped West is undergoing a shift from industrialism, dominated by the produc-tion of material objects, to what Drucker has referred to as the "knowledge society," in which the major corporate activity is the production of informa-tion. As Zuboff (1988) has demonstrated, even material production has been taken over by "smart machines" that alter "production worker" tasks to monitoring information produced by fabrication machines on video terminals.

In addition to this transformation of the economy from "smokestack" industries to "high-tech" enterprises, other factors contribute environmental uncertainty. National economies have become global, and the division of labor has increasingly become international. The economic miracles of China and Indonesia, along with the transformation of Japan into a central banker for Asia, have led to an eastward shift of capital, increasing rivalries between the East and West Coasts in the United States. Because of the internationalization of capital and the globalization of competition, corporations have had to become increasingly sensitive to rapidly changing environments.

The concepts of rapid change as a destabilizing factor in social systems was considered by Parsons (1951) in *The Social System*. He asserted that as organizations face rapidly changing environments, the bureaucratic model of organization becomes less effective and gradually gives way to more flexible forms and processes, such as task groups, quality circles, the use of outside consultants, brainstorming, and outsourcing of certain functions.

To adjust to a continually changing environment, organizations have to reform their internal processes and to alter the quality and composition of their resources. First, they may have to alter the structure of their labor force, hiring fewer production workers and more knowledge and technical workers. Second, they may have to alter supervisory and management styles from the authoritarian bureaucratic model to a participatory model as exemplified by the changes instituted in management styles in the "Big Three" American automobile manufacturers. Third, because of the necessity to work as teams and task groups, worker loyalty, morale, empowerment, and loyalty to the company must become more important to the organization. This shift can be seen in corporations' attraction to Ouchi's (1981) *Theory Z* organizational model and their attention to maintaining an organizational culture.

Change, however, is a painful process. Hoffer (1952) wrote, "Even in slight things the experience of the new is rarely without some stirring of foreboding" (p. 3). In his classic analysis of change in an industrial plant, Gouldner (1954) found that many workers were wedded to activities that, if continued, would lead to the plant's doom. Consequently, organizational change means struggle. People who have a vested interest in the status quo may simply be afraid of a loss of job or status.

The purpose of this chapter is to generate a model of the "intelligent organization" as an ideal type for organizational development (OD) in the human services field and apply it to the corporate setting. The proposed OD model contains components that have been demonstrated to work in a variety of contexts; it also embraces humanistic values and promotes improved organizational functioning.

## ORGANIZATIONAL DEVELOPMENT IN HUMAN SERVICES

### Organizational development models

Although the concept of directed organizational change is not new, the idea of a continually evolving, ever-changing, cybernetic organization is relatively new. The cybernetic organization presupposes continuing OD. According to Norman and Keys (1992), there are three models of organizational development:

1. *The laboratory model,* which often uses T group training to develop sensitivities of managers to others, is directed toward opening lines of communication that have been shut down because of mistrust.

2. *The grid model* is one in which managers attend a workshop designed to revamp and devise more effective organizational routines and rituals. The term "managerial grid" comes from the work of Blake and Mouton (1964), who viewed OD as an effort to balance concern for production with concern for people. The grid model focuses on objective evaluations of organizational processes with a view to developing a maximally functioning organization.

3. *The work team model* is one in which data gathered by an outside consultant about the organizational processes are provided to a planning team that meets on a regular basis to evaluate and consider issues raised by the data.

Although these three models have been in existence for at least 20 years, they do not seem to have been used in the reformation or restructuring of human services delivery systems. The unique aspects of human services delivery may account for the lack of OD efforts.

### Organizational development problems in human services

To highlight the difficulty of effecting organizational change and development in human services, Norman and Keys (1992) subtitled an article on the subject "The Irresistible Force Meets the Immovable Object." Bargal and Schmid (1992) attributed this difficulty to the conservative nature of human services organizations as compared with corporations. This nature in turn is due to their dependence on the external environment for legitimacy and resources. Moreover, human services organizations are affected by interorganizational agreements, governing bodies; legislative policies; and the attitudes, needs, and behaviors of clients, all of which make change in such agencies complex and difficult to implement.

Norman and Keys (1992) claimed that there has been little effort to use OD techniques in human services organizations, and they attribute this reticence to two factors: (1) the bureaucratic structure of public domain organizations and (2) the values and philosophy of top management in the human services sector. They contended that if top management were to support change, the staff would follow. Top management, however, tends to value short-term efficiency over long-term effectiveness. Although the potential for significant change exists, Norman and Keys suggested that management usually does not have the will to institute OD.

## Problems with the existing models

According to Hessey and Blanchard (1982), most OD efforts fail. First, because OD must necessarily begin with a management decision taken by an ongoing hierarchy, the decision usually sidesteps consultation with those who may have vested interests in the outcome of OD efforts.

Second, OD focuses on management. Staff personnel, who putatively benefit from OD, are generally excluded from the laboratory and grid models or are relegated to data sources in the work team model. In general, organizations enter into OD only when major symptoms of malaise are evidenced in staff functioning or line-staff relationships. Pfeffer (1981), for example, cited two diagnostic cases, one in which the symptom was high employee turnover and the other in which the symptoms were employee illness, family problems, and burnout.

The present OD models seem to exist in the rarefied atmosphere of the managerial office and do not include the staff in the deliberation process. When management makes a decision to engage in OD, a dialectical process is initiated. On the one hand, they engage in a legitimate activity as leaders of the organization to improve its functioning. This aspect of the decision has the potential to provide greater unity of purpose to the organization. On the other hand, the decision may divide the organization into two groups: the decision makers and those whose lives the decision influences. This aspect of the decision may polarize the organization into conflict groups.

A third reason for the failure of OD efforts is that OD has tended to focus on interpersonal factors, and yet organizational change is an intensely political process and involves technological as well as legal issues (Bennis, 1968). If OD does not deal adequately with relations among superiors and subordinates, compensation structures, and job-related role structures, then the job is incomplete and the venture will fail.

In fact, the chief problem with the extant OD models and their application in human services is their relative blindness to the politics of change.
There is little awareness of the problems of contradictions and unintended
consequences of change. Furthermore, even when OD is precipitated by poor
staff functioning, there seems to be a lack of awareness of the political relationships and conflicts between management and staff.

A bureaucracy, the primary form for human services agencies, was
defined by Weber (1978) as a political structure with a set of well-defined
hierarchical relationships. Accordingly, OD within a bureaucratic structure,
especially one that is staffed by professionals, cannot succeed by being apo-
litical or nonpolitical. In a bureaucracy, managers' primary reference group is
other managers within the organization (Scott, 1961), whereas social workers' primary reference group is the social work profession (Blau & Scott,
1962; Rosenbaum, 1992; Scott, 1961). Numerous studies have indicated that
professional social workers perceive their behavior as primarily influenced
by social work norms and ethics (Billingsley, 1964; Carrigan, 1974; Rosenbaum, 1992). Because managers are organizationally driven and social workers are professionally driven, the potential for conflict over organizational
change is high. Sociologists such as Blau and Scott (1962) and Etzioni
(1964) have indicated that the tensions between professionals and managers
are an ongoing source of organizational conflict. Yet the OD literature has
not addressed this issue.

## TOWARD A MODEL OF GREATER INCLUSION

### Professionals in bureaucracies

Bargal and Schmid (1992) indicated that OD in human services organizations
is complex, because unlike the hierarchical structures in the business sector,
power is located in three domains: the policy or legal domain, including state
and federal statutes; the managerial domain; and the service or professional
domain. They noted that to improve a human services organization's performance, all three domains must be involved. They proposed a multidimensional
model for organizational development. They asserted that staff should be represented in the effort from the very beginning. One prime goal of social work
is client empowerment. From the outset, then, OD in human services organizations should be directed toward staff empowerment. This means that although
OD may be initiated by a management decision, prior to that decision consultation should take place with staff personnel and a consensus about the issues
and the nature of the change should be achieved before proceeding. This recommendation is in line with Bargal and Schmid's suggestion that OD be

conducted from the bottom up rather from the top down and that it involve delegation of authority, responsibility, and partnership.

Bargal and Schmid (1992) also stated that OD should include re-education of leaders and followers. There are two reasons for this. First, if there is a perception of a need for OD, it is likely that there is serious dysfunctioning in the organization. It also means that there is probably a lack of trust between staff and management. Second, management and staff can always benefit from purging bad habits and learning new ways of dealing with each other and adopting new modes of approaching problems.

Central to this learning process is the so-called prefiguring functions, that is, providing a model of future behavior within the organization. OD, then, has two major foci: (1) the here and now and solving existing problems and (2) the future and developing the ability to anticipate problems before they create serious dysfunctioning in the organization. In short, OD should ideally be a transition to the "learning organization."

### The intelligent organization

One of the major advances in organizational theory was the incorporation of the insights of Wiener (1961) on information theory. Wiener posited that a critical factor in the maintenance of an information system was the feedback loop, a control mechanism that allows for adjustments in the decision-making process. Feedback and making organizational adjustments are all the more important where the environmental conditions are changing very rapidly. Argyris (1982) characterized learning as single-looped and double-looped. Single-loop learning involves one-way communication. Whereas one-way communication may be helpful in dealing with technical issues, it may have negative consequences in the form of defensiveness and lack of valid feedback, especially if it is (wrongly) assumed that the person who is telling knows and the person who is being told does not know. Double-loop communication involves a collegial atmosphere in which there is give and take, and efforts are made to synthesize the contributions of all members. Double-loop learning increases organizational effectiveness and the emergence of learning-oriented norms, and it reduces defensiveness.

Mohrman and Cummings (1989) have taken the concept of double-loop learning a step further by introducing the idea of *deutero learning,* or "learning how to learn." As organizations engage in OD, the members learn strategies that either facilitate or inhibit single-loop learning and double-loop learning in an effort to create a more effective learning environment. As organizations engage in deutero learning, they manifest the characteristics of the learning organization.

Senge (1990) suggested several strategies for developing an intelligent solution. One is systems thinking, which refers to the ability to view relationships in their totality. Senge advocated avoidance of cause-and-effect models because of their narrow emphases on linear relationships. They oversimplify relationships and focus on the parts rather than the whole. They also eliminate the feedback loop that is so important in system maintenance. Senge suggested that managers in intelligent organizations look for interrelationships and processes of change rather than cause–effect chains and snapshots.

Thompson (1967) conceived of a maximally functioning organization as one that is environmentally sensitive, but it is also important that an organization's internal structure evolve in a way that maximizes the contributions of its members. Environmental sensitivity is necessary but not sufficient for an intelligent organization. An intelligent organization must also have developed an internal set of structures and functions that maximize the potential contributions of the individuals. It has been empirically established that the major motivating factors among workers besides pay are mainly psychological. They include respectful treatment, interesting work, recognition for a job well done, opportunity for skill development, provision of the opportunity to express ideas about how to do things better to a sympathetic audience, and knowledge about what is happening in the organization (Yankelovich & Immerwahr, 1980). This means that, at some level, all members of an organization must be able to participate in the decision-making process through which organizational change is planned and implemented.

A participatory model does not necessarily mean that everyone participates at the same level of intensity. What is important is that everyone is tied into the information flow up and down the organizational hierarchy. Obviously, OD cannot be conducted through plenary sessions. Task groups must be established to examine various problems and propose solutions. Some constituencies may be represented by a member or a group that collects information for inclusion in the decision-making process and reports back to the consituency on the progress of OD.

As the process of OD unfolds and organization members generate different structures to examine problems and propose solutions, the organization becomes increasingly fluid, and participation increases at every level. Individual members become increasingly involved in the operation of the organization. As this process continues, people interact more and relationships become more intimate.

Increasing intimacy, however, may increase interpersonal conflicts, which may in turn necessitate the institution of mechanisms for negotiation and conflict resolution. When conflicts arise, a mediator may be needed to move the conflict from a negative and distracting problem to a positive issue for the organization in problem solving. Indeed, conflict, as pointed out by Coser (1956), is not necessarily a negative phenomenon. It is through conflict that organizations grow and develop. Conflict necessitates problem solving and generates the application and growth of intelligence. Therefore, it is not to be avoided in the process of OD; rather, it is an opportunity to be seized as an opportunity to engage in problem solving.

Although OD is more inclusive and promises a more rewarding future, it also stirs up conflicts, increases demands, and can lead to emotional exhaustion that is associated with burnout. Therefore, it is imperative that a safety valve be provided in the form of "time-out" activities to ease the stress of change. Otherwise, the change process can be hindered by frustrated participants who might become uncooperative or simply quiet.

Time-out activities can be viewed as rewards for increased and intensified participation. They can take many forms, from time off to a party. They should be developed in the same way as all other decisions—collectively.

In summary, OD in human services should be directed at developing an intelligent organization by fostering rational problem solving through a collaborative model of participatory decision making. The OD model should contain elements that prefigure the methods by which future problems are solved. In other words, OD should become a practicum in inclusionary problem solving. In addition, mechanisms should be instituted for the maintenance of an emotional equilibrium in a stressful work environment. Activities that allow for the release of tensions can be introduced as part of OD. Emotional renewal is as important as organizational renewal.

## OD AND MANAGEMENT TECHNIQUES

### OD and total quality management

Total quality management (TQM) "is a management approach to long-term success through customer satisfaction. TQM is based on the participation of all members of an organization in improving processes, products, services, and the culture they work in" (Bennett, Freierman, & George, 1993, p. 32). This approach arose as a management strategy following World War II as an effort to improve quality in the production of consumer goods. According to Bennett et al., Xerox adopted TQM and trained all of its employees in problem solving and teamwork techniques and encouraged them to form improvement teams around issues of product quality and environmental pollution. TQM is similar to OD in its emphasis on management as an instigator of change and its emphasis on long-term processes. Both TQM and OD emphasize continuous improvement, although TQM seems to be more explicit about long-term strategies for improvement. TQM shares the inclusionary aspects of the model proposed in this chapter.

## BPR and OD

Business process reengineering (BPR) refers to the reformulation of business procedures to make them more efficient and effective. Roberts (1994) reported that the major form of organizational change in the past was the development of organizational procedures that became cumbersome and that technological advances has rendered many procedures obsolete. Therefore, he maintained, a radical rethinking is needed regarding how a company should do business to ensure the delivery of the highest quality product at a reasonable price. Much of process reengineering has to do with eliminating redundant steps in business processes.

BPR focuses on business procedures and is primarily technical in nature. Interpersonal relations and line-staff relationships are not a prominent consideration in BPR. BPR is a technique that is initiated, monitored, and evaluated by management. It presupposes that management can and will shift jobs and procedures around in its effort to satisfy the customer.

### New relationships between management and staff

It is indeed ironic that American managers have had to learn about inclusive methods of management and OD from the Japanese (Boressoff, 1988), whose society is at least as class-based as Britain's and is strongly vertically integrated (Reichauer, 1977). Inclusive, consultative management has increasingly become a goal of American corporations. In efforts to regain or maintain their competitive edge, U.S. companies have realized that they could not achieve this with an alienated workforce.

As many theorists have pointed out, in the information age, increasing numbers of workers manipulate symbols for a living (Bell, 1973; Drucker, 1993). These workers are highly literate and highly skilled professional and technical workers. No longer is management more educated than the workforce. There are fewer class barriers between management and staff, and new partnerships have been forged between them that are necessarily more egalitarian and participatory.

In professions such as social work, nursing, and education, one must have a certain minimum number of years of professional experience to become a manager or an administrator. The increasing professionalism of practitioners in these fields and the emergence of new models of administration has led to the development of more participatory modes of management. For example, in education, shared decision-making models in which faculty members, parents, community members, and even students sit on school policy-making boards have been implemented (Harrison, Killion, & Mitchell, 1989; Louis & Dentler, 1988). Shared decision-making models have been part of a reform movement to make schools more responsive to local environments and to improve educational quality (Sirotnik & Clark, 1988).

## OD IN PUBLIC AND CORPORATE SETTINGS

The concept of OD originated in the private sector and quickly spread to the public sector. In higher education, for example, numerous programs for "faculty renewal" have been instituted (Centra, 1985). OD was practiced in the corporate sector without the benefit of a human services perspective. As OD moved into the public sector, procedures had to be modified to suit the unique characteristics of organizations whose major staffers were professionals. This meant in part that OD efforts had to become more inclusive of staff, a development that was promptly emulated by the private sector. However, there is already a history of inclusiveness that was imported with Japanese corporate models (Ouchi, 1981). TQM has stood for inclusion of all personnel in the process of change. Therefore, an inclusive model should not be a radical change for private sector companies.

### Corporate needs for OD

One of the fundamental premises of contemporary organizational theory states that a properly functioning company must have respect for individuals and their capacity to exercise intelligent decision making (Boressoff, 1988; Peters & Waterman, 1982; Senge, 1990). The model presented in this study is based on that premise. It is also based on the premise that the success of OD depends on the extent of the model's inclusiveness. All employees must have some form of representation and participation in the effort to remake the organization.

Shetty and Buehler (1987) suggested that American firms must develop strategies that ensure their competitive advantage in a global market. To maintain their advantage, Buller (1987) stated:

> It is becoming increasingly evident that high-performing firms recognize that these strategic objectives can only be achieved through a highly skilled and motivated work force. Consequently, these firms view their people as a strategic resource, and they design human resources programs and activities that are explicitly tied to the business strategy. (p. 75)

This means that even if a company is doing well, there can be no place for complacency. Corporations are going to have to evolve strategies of continual renewal to keep pace.

It is incumbent on corporations to maximize their effectiveness through augmenting the potential contributions of their employees and by developing synergistic relationships among them. Shetty and Buehler (1987) provided examples of companies already using human services approaches to organizational change, including J. C. Penney, McDonald's, Eaton, and the Dana Corporation. The four common factors in the programs of these companies are (1) respect for employees, (2) reduction of social distance between managers and employees, (3) increasing participation of employees in organizational improvement efforts, and (4) provision of a system of rewards that is tied to effort and effectiveness.

### Human services professionals and corporate OD practice

Because corporations must continually change, opportunities for OD human services professionals are high in the corporate sector. Indeed, human services professionals bring important special qualities to corporate OD: a systems approach to problems, a focus on process, training in working with groups, skill in diagnosis and problem solving in human relations, and sensitivity to cultural differences.

Central to human services delivery systems is the concept of person-in-environment (Germain & Gitterman, 1980). Social work–trained human services professionals are usually taught to view human behavior as a product of social context. This perspective was expressed by Senge (1990): "When placed in the same system, people however different, tend to produce similar results" (p. 42). The person-in-environment perspective is ideal for OD, because it moves the practitioner away from focusing exclusively on personality and interpersonal relations.

Although the goal of OD in corporate environments is improvement of the product, the improvement is usually achieved indirectly as a consequence of improved processes in developing the product (Goodstein, 1978). Experience in the public sector, where process is more important than product, provides a background in analyzing and attempting to improve organizational functioning and decision making. Corporate executives, because of the necessity to focus on goals, may not be sufficiently aware of the importance of human relations processes in goal attainment. Here again human services professionals can be helpful.

Furthermore, as these professionals well know, a group is much more than a collection of individuals. Groups have qualities and tendencies that are quite distinct from the characteristics of the individual members. In America, with its emphasis on individualism, group properties are often forgotten. The concept of organizational culture was imported from Japan primarily from the writings of Ouchi (1981). Organizational culture is the concept of people sharing common goals, norms, and values. Human services professionals whose backgrounds draw from the social sciences are well aware of the collective properties of the organization and have usually had experience in working with a variety of groups, including families, gangs, committees, work groups, conflict groups, and instructional groups (Walker, 1988). Such experience should be helpful in the corporate sector, where OD often means the development of alternative social groupings directed toward specific problem solving.

Moreover, human services professionals acquire training in diagnosis and problem solving as primary skills both for individuals and groups (Keys & Ginsberg, 1988). Experience in human services diagnosis and problem solving is important in all OD, whether in the public or corporate sector. For human services OD specialists, such skills should generalize well to the corporate sector.

Perhaps one of the greatest advantages a human services OD specialist may have in the corporate sector is the development of sensitivities to cultural differences. Demographic changes throughout the 1990s will result in a workforce composed of 75 percent to 85 percent "minorities," including people of color, white women, and recent immigrants (Lankard, 1990). Women's participation by the year 2000 will account for 47 percent of the workforce; African Americans' participation will account for an additional 12 percent; Hispanics', 10 percent; and Asians', 4 percent (Johnson & Packer, 1987). The increasing multicultural face of the corporate workforce will provide opportunities for culturally sensitive OD interventions. As American organizations move away from a white, Anglo-Saxon, Protestant, male-dominated corporate structure, they will have to develop multicultural sensitivities if they hope to remain competitive in the world market. Social work norms of empowerment and respect for cultural diversity should provide human services–trained OD professionals with special competencies in dealing with corporations that wish to build a cohesive organizational culture on an international basis.

### Multicultural OD in the private sector

Colon (1994) conducted a training program that consisted of four modules demonstrating how diversity can strengthen organizational development in a private child welfare agency. The training modules presented specific learning objectives and learning opportunities to promote and enhance the awareness of workplace diversity issues and the communication and interpersonal skills needed by child welfare managers to address these issues in a meaningful way. On the basis of the concept of valuing differences, they developed an educational process in which managers sorted through their beliefs and assumptions about others and their individual and group differences. The following are the strategies used throughout the training to enhance each manager's multicultural awareness and sensitivity:

1.   Strip away stereotypes.
2.   Learn to listen and probe for the differences in people's assumptions.
3.   Build authentic and significant relationships with people regarded as different.
4.   Enhance personal empowerment.
5.   Explore and identify group differences.

The program promoted the agency managers' ability to be open to personal growth and development and to value human differences, thereby moving them toward the development of manager–worker relations that are empowered, interdependent, and synergistic. The educational process included examining critical incidents around issues related to multicultural sensitivity.

The first session presented an overview of the issues of cultural diversity in the workplace. The second session consisted of a panel of four experts on issues related to African Americans, Hispanics, women, and gay men and lesbians in the workplace. In the third session, the trainer led a discussion on issues of cross-cultural communication between employees and managers. In the fourth session the trainer described strategies and approaches to assist participants in managing the diversity within their work site. Although the program was designed for the training of managers, staff members were included to provide feedback on managers' communicative behaviors. Such a model might prove beneficial in corporate environments.

As corporations enlarge the pool of candidates for managerial positions, the background of the managerial stratum is going to diversify. As the numbers of women and people of color increase in corporate management, issues of gender and ethnic–racial equity and treatment are bound to emerge. The ability of companies to solve problems of human relations may well be their key to survival in the global economy.

## CONCLUSION

In this article a model of the intelligent organization has been proposed as the goal of OD. The intelligent organization is one that can quickly adapt to a changing environment without enduring debilitating internal conflicts. Because the structure of the intelligent organization changes with changes in its context and in the talents of its personnel, the organizational model can only be outlined in terms of principles and processes.

The first principle is the inclusion of all people in the organization in the process of change. Everyone must have access to the decision-making process. Inclusion is necessary for informational and political reasons. For decisions to be functional, information sources must be maximized. To minimize intraorganizational conflict, consensus should be sought on actions related to the process of problem solving.

The second principle is sensitivity to the environment. The intelligent organization must be aware of and respond to the needs and demands of the task environment. OD should include representatives from the task environment or at least information provided by significant members of the task environment. In the corporate sector, the task environment includes customers who make decisions on the basis of competing claims among providers. Sensitivity in the corporate sector may be measured in terms of such criteria as market size, history, and trade barriers. In the nonprofit sector, the task environment includes clients who may have less in the way of choices, such as parents of public school children, but lack of sensitivity may lead to a loss of legitimacy and conflict with those to whom services are supposed to be provided.

OD is driven by a desire to make an organization fully functioning. To do this, organizations must activate the potential of organization members, communicate respect for them, open lines of communication, and maintain feedback loops. Intelligence, whether for the individuals or the organization, can be defined as the ability to solve problems. The intelligent organization is one that is designed to solve problems with a minimum of dysfunctional conflict and unintended consequences (Senge, 1990).

The intelligent organization is flexible. Structure adapts to the tasks at hand. Personnel are assigned to given tasks on the basis of skills and talents. In addition, people with certain skills are teamed up with others as a means to reproduce skills throughout the organization and intertemporally.

The intelligent organization maintains functional internal processes. Procedures that are dysfunctional or that interfere with the smooth functioning of the organization are examined and alternatives are proposed. The proposals lead to experimentation and evaluation.

The intelligent organization is one in which there is worker involvement and commitment. When all workers are engaged in the process of continual renewal, they have a stake in the organization. Management must realize that such involvement increases commitment and job satisfaction but also makes more demands on the individual worker and can lead to emotional exhaustion and burnout. Therefore, rewards and time-out activities are important for worker commitment. The intelligent organization understands that work life is one aspect of a person's total being. Friends and family may well take precedence over work commitments. This fact must be acknowledged and supported within the organizational culture.

The sensibilities that human services professionals bring to OD are unique and important. Human services professionals bring a humanistic orientation to organizational change and a systems perspective of the person-in-environment that allows for an examination of the larger picture. They also bring experience working with people in groups and insights into cultural differences. The well-trained human services professional who has developed skills in diagnosis and problem solving in human relations should be able to provide OD know-how to organizations in the nonprofit and corporate sectors. Because all organizations must develop high-functioning systems, and human services–oriented OD professionals can be indispensable in accomplishing this task, it is incumbent on the profession to train more social workers in OD.

### REFERENCES

Argyris, C. (1982). *Reasoning, learning, and action.* San Francisco: Jossey-Bass.

Bargal, D., & Schmid, H. (1992). Organizational change and development in human service organizations: A prefatory essay. *Administration in Social Work, 16,* 1–13.

Bell, D. (1973). *The coming of post-industrial society.* New York: Basic Books.

Bennett, S. J., Freierman, R., & George, S. (1993). *Corporate realities and environmental truths.* New York: John Wiley & Sons.

Bennis, W. (1968). Editorial. *Journal of Applied Behavioral Science, 4*(2), 228.

Billingsley, A. (1964). Bureaucratic and professional orientation patterns in social casework. *Social Service Review, 38,* 400–407.

Blake, R. R., & Mouton, J. (1964). *The managerial grid.* Houston: Gulf Publishing.

Blau, P., & Scott, R. (1962). *Formal organizations.* San Francisco: Chandler.

Boressoff, T. (1988). Modern management in day care and early childhood education. In P. R. Keys & L. H. Ginsberg (Eds.), *New management in human services* (pp. 235–258). Silver Spring, MD: National Association of Social Workers.

Buller, P. F. (1987). Human resources contributions to competitive strategy: An overview. In Y. K. Shetty & V. M. Buehler (Eds.), *Human resource strategic management* (pp. 75–78). New York: Elsevier–North Holland.

Carrigan, Z. (1974). *The effect of professional role position on the definition and perception of interdisciplinary social work practice in a health setting.* Washington, DC: Catholic University of America.

Centra, J. (1985). Maintaining faculty vitality through faculty development. In S. M. Clark & D. R. Lewis (Eds.), *Faculty development in higher education* (pp. 141–156). New York: Teachers College Press.

Colon, E. (1994). *The effects of a multicultural awareness program on the interpersonal relations and communication behaviors of child welfare managers.* Unpublished doctoral dissertation, City University of New York, Graduate Center.

Coser, L. (1956). *The functions of social conflict.* New York: Free Press.

Drucker, P. F. (1993). *Post-capitalist society.* New York: Harper Business.

Etzioni, A. (1964). *Modern organizations.* Englewood Cliffs, NJ: Prentice Hall.

Germain, C., & Gitterman, A. (1980). *The life model of social work practice.* New York: Columbia University Press.

Goodstein, L. D. (1978). *Consulting with human service systems.* Reading, MA: Addison-Wesley Press.

Gouldner, W. A. (1954). *Patterns of industrial bureaucracy.* New York: Free Press.

Harrison, C. R., Killion, J. P., & Mitchell, J. E. (1989). Site-based management: The realities of implementation. *Educational Leadership, 1,* 55–58.

Hessey, P., & Blanchard, K. (1982). *Management of organizational behavior utilizing human resources* (4th ed.). Englewood Cliffs, NJ: Prentice Hall.

Hoffer, E. (1952). *The ordeal of change.* New York: Harper & Row.

Keys, P. R., & Ginsberg, L. (1988). *New management in human services.* Silver Spring, MD: National Association of Social Workers.

Johnson B. W., & Packer, H. A. (1987). *Workforce 2000.* Indianapolis: Hudson Institute.

Lankard, B. A. (1990). The multicultural work force: Trends and issues. (ERIC Document Reproduction No. ED 321153)

Louis, K. S., & Dentler, R. A. (1988). Knowledge use and school improvement. *Curriculum Inquiry, 18*(1), 33–61.

March, J. G., & Simon, H. A. (1958). *Organizations.* New York: John Wiley & Sons.

Mohrman, S. A., & Cummings, T. G. (1989). *Self-designing organizations: Learning how to create high performance.* Reading, MA: Addison-Wesley.

Norman, A. J., & Keys, P. R. (1992). Organization development in public social services—The irresistible force meets the immovable object. *Administration in Social Work, 16,* 147–165.

Ouchi, W. G. (1981). *Theory Z.* New York: Avon Books.

Parsons, T. (1951). *The social system.* New York: Free Press.

Peters, T. J., & Waterman, R. H., Jr. (1982). *In search of excellence: Lessons from America's best-run companies.* New York: Warner Books.

Pfeffer, J. (1981). *Power in organizations.* Marshfield, MA: Pitman.

Reichauer, E. O. (1977). *The Japanese.* Cambridge, MA: Belknap Press.

Roberts, L. (1994). *Process reengineering.* Milwaukee: ASQC Quality Press.

Rosenbaum, G. (1992). *Role conflict and job satisfaction of master's level social workers who practice in the acute care hospital setting.* Unpublished doctoral dissertation, Adelphi University, Garden City, NY.

Scott, R. (1961). Professional employees in a bureaucratic structure: Social workers. In A. Etzioni (Ed.), *A comparative analysis of complex organizations* (pp. 82–140). New York: Free Press.

Senge, P. M. (1990). *The fifth discipline: The art & practice of the learning organization.* Garden City, NY: Doubleday.

Shetty, Y. K., & Buehler, V. M. (1987). Strategies for gaining competitive advantage: An introduction. In Y. K. Shetty & V. M. Buehler (Eds.), *Human resource strategic management* (pp. 3–11). New York: Elsevier–North Holland.

Sirotnik, K. A., & Clark, R. W. (1988, May). School-centered decision making and renewal. *Phi Delta Kappan,* 660–664.

Thompson, J. A. (1967). *Organizations in action.* New York: McGraw-Hill.

Walker, J. (1988). The place of social group work in organizations. In P. R. Keys & L. Ginsberg (Eds.), *New management in human services* (pp. 102–115). Silver Spring, MD: National Association of Social Workers.

Weber, M. (1978). Economy and society. In G. Roth & C. Wittich (Eds.), *Industrial society* (Vol. 2). Berkeley: University of California Press.

Wiener, N. (1961). *Cybernetics: Or control and communication in the animal and the machine* (2nd ed.). Cambridge, MA: MIT Press.

Yankelovich, D., & Immerwahr, J. (1980). *Putting the work ethic to work.* New York: Gallup Organization.

Zuboff, S. (1988). *In the age of the smart machine.* New York: Basic Books.

# Chapter 7

# Managing the New Multicultural Workplace

Yvonne Asamoah

anaging

the multicultural workplace in the year 2000 and beyond presents challenges and opportunities for human services. The new diversity is an inescapable part of America's "demographic destiny" or "demographic reality" (Gardenswartz & Rowe, 1993). The Hudson Institute's report (Johnston & Packer, 1987)

shocked corporate America into the realization that the workforce is no longer predominately white or predominately male. The new demographic reality forced managers and employees alike to shift from denial of the new diversity to managing it (Havassy, 1990; Loden & Rosener, 1991; Thomson, 1989). Human services managers are sometimes slow to repond to cutting edge organizational and management issues. However, they must begin to think seriously about diversity (or lack of it) in their environments and its effects on organizational operations and service delivery.

The statistics depicting changes in the tapestry of the American workforce are compelling and reflect a major societal shift. The most significant increases are occurring and will continue to occur in the year 2000 and beyond among women, people of color, immigrants, and older populations.

By the year 2000, women will make up an estimated 47 percent of the workforce and will constitute 60 percent of the new entrants to the workforce. They are also moving rapidly into careers and positions in organizations traditionally held by men. An increase in the number of people of color has rendered the term "minority" meaningless. Estimates suggest that by 2000, people of color will constitute 29 percent of the workforce.

The immigrant population is growing faster than it ever has since World War I and in many major cities accounts for a substantial portion of the workforce. These newcomers represent a variety of cultures, languages, and skills. The workforce is also slowly getting older. A more mature workforce presents compelling and immediate challenges to organizations (Gardenswartz & Rowe, 1993; Johnston & Packer, 1987).

The needs, demands, and talents of women, people of color, immigrants, and older people can no longer be ignored or trivialized. Managers must consider not only the different cultures (in the broadest sense of the word) that these new populations bring to the workplace but also the way in which the demographically new labor force will affect the organization's culture. As Jamieson and O'Mara (1991) stated, the "one size fits all" mentality must give way to thinking that accommodates and promotes flexibility. The change in mentality will require a fundamental shift in attitude by management and employees.

Although the mix of cultures, genders, lifestyles, and values can be stimulating and potentially beneficial to the organization, it can also lead to conflict. Solving the resulting conflicts and problems often is beyond the competence of even the best-intentioned managers, who may not have the knowledge or skills to understand or handle them. The challenge of managing the new diversity is formidable, but the stakes are very high (Gardenswartz & Rowe, 1993).

Bennet (1986) made an interesting observation about the way individual and collective experiences have failed to prepare society for the level of intercultural sensitivity essential for working in and managing a multicultural work environment:

> Intercultural sensitivity is not natural. Cross-cultural contact often has been accompanied by bloodshed, oppression or genocide. . . . Today, the failure to exercise intercultural sensitivity is not simply bad business or bad morality—it is self-destructive. (p. 27)

A first step on the road to valuing differences in the workplace, including cultural differences, is to understand the dimensions of diversity. Loden and Rosener (1991) suggested that two dimensions of diversity must be considered—primary and secondary. The primary dimensions include age, ethnicity, gender, physical ability or disability, and sexual orientation. Because these factors are unalterable, they are extremely powerful in their effects on others. Secondary dimensions of diversity include factors such as geographic location, income, marital status, parental status, religious beliefs, and work experience and are significant in shaping individual personalities. They are also alterable.

Skin color, gender, and age generally trigger split-second assessments and reactions that influence present and future encounters (see, for example, Elsea, 1988). Cultural variables such as time orientation, personal space, eye contact, and facial expression also exert strong influence on one's reactions to others and one's assessment of others' intentions and expectations. Although alterable, these variables may be extremely resistant to change and, thus, as powerful in influencing encounters in the workplace as primary dimensions of diversity.

### RECOGNIZING DIVERSITY–RELATED PROBLEMS

Two kinds of diversity-related problems may occur within an organization: (1) problems that stem from the increasing diversity of the workforce and management's failure to recognize the significance of this change and its effects on the organization and other employees and (2) problems that arise because the organization lacks diversity at all levels, resulting in significant differences between the diverse clientele and the people who deliver and manage the services.

Fortunately, recognizable symptoms of real and potential diversity-related problems can serve as warning signals to managers and supervisors. These include:

- lack of a diverse staff at all levels in the organization
- communication difficulties because of language barriers and working style differences
- difficulty in recruiting and retaining members of different racial, ethnic, and cultural groups
- open or subtle conflict between groups or between individuals from different groups
- ostracism of individuals who are different from the norm
- barriers in promotion (perceived or real) for diverse employees
- frustrations and irritations resulting from cultural differences
- perceptions that people are not valued for their unique contributions

- misunderstandings, mistakes, and productivity problems because employees do not understand directions, requirements, or expectations
- an increase in grievances by members of diverse groups
- lack of smooth social interaction between members of diverse groups; formation of cliques on the basis of some definable ethnic, cultural, racial, or language difference
- EEOC suits or complaints about discrimination in promotions, pay, and performance reviews
- ethnic, racial, or gender slurs or jokes
- resistance to working with or negative comments about another group on the basis of racial, ethnic, cultural, gender, religious, sexual orientation, or physical ability differences
- complaints about staff speaking other languages in the workplace. (Gardenswartz & Rowe, 1993).

This list represents some of the symptoms that are easily observable or even measurable (for example, turnover rate, frequency of complaints, number of lawsuits, diversity or lack thereof at various organizational levels). Other, more subtle but no less harmful symptoms may not immediately appear to be related to diversity—for example, low morale, "hall gossip," working to the rule, absenteeism, frequent tardiness, rise of an informal structure that undermines the formal structure (including leadership positions), splitting of staff, and the rise of an organizational "culture" that has negative effects on service delivery. Management and staff often do not recognize an organizational "culture" that forms around diversity issues and that can negatively affect service delivery. Unfortunately, clients often recognize these symptoms and respond negatively to them.

An astute, diversity-sensitive manager ought to recognize both the subtle and overt symptoms as signs of trouble that require solutions. However, some symptoms are more complex than they appear, are misunderstood, or are underestimated, primarily symptoms related to communication and career development.

### Communication

In a diverse organization, communication problems can lead to low productivity or even a breakdown in the production process. Problematic situations include

1. failing to understand that communication barriers and breakdowns between members of different cultures can cause anxiety, disorientation, depression, sleep disorders, and identity problems—the same symptoms identified in "culture shock"
2. interpreting certain individual behaviors in the context of one's own culture and value system, thereby missing the mark—ethnocentrism

3.  wrongly assuming that an employee's accent indicates an inability to comprehend and use English effectively
4.  wrongly assuming that meanings attached to nonverbal communication, like gestures and facial expressions, are universal
5.  failing to recognize that praise for individual accomplishment is not a motivating factor for all cultural groups; in fact, some employees may be embarrassed if personal achievements are singled out, because they place value on group and team behavior
6.  failing to recognize that many employees will not initiate tasks without specific instructions because such action is considered a challenge to authority and, thus, a lack of respect
7.  failing to recognize that physical distance between speakers has important meaning and varies across cultures (in some cultures closeness of contact with people in authority is prohibited because it shows disrespect; employees who believe this may appear resistant in an organization that values openness and immediate feedback and that has an open door policy for employees.)
8.  misinterpreting body language
9.  failing to recognize that some cultures rely on implied meanings of messages and are not as explicit or direct as North American culture
10. assuming that smiling and nodding imply understanding when they may cover up embarrassment or be an attempt to please
11. lacking awareness of the ways in which cultural differences lead to misinterpretations of messages
12. assuming that employees speaking a foreign language are talking about oneself
13. assuming that equal opportunity and affirmative action are synonymous with cultural diversity (equal opportunity and affirmative action are equity issues, and it is possible for an organization to score high marks in these areas and still not manage diversity effectively. [See Talico, Inc., 1992, for details on intercultural communication.])

An important aspect of managing diversity is the ability to "take the stand of the other" and realize that ways of processing information and relating to people in authority are not universal. So many misunderstandings occur because managers do not recognize critical factors in intercultural communication patterns and differential interpretations (Harris & Moran, 1987; Jamieson & O'Mara, 1991; Kim & Gudykunst, 1988; Talico, Inc., 1992).

Cultural sensitivity is essential in considering the structure and wording of memorandums and deciding whether an oral or written communication is most appropriate in a given situation. Cultural sensitivity is also important in conducting performance reviews and entrance or exit interviews, in supervisory sessions, and in managing conflicts. Gardenswartz and Rowe (1993) suggested, for example, that employees may resist performance evaluations for cultural reasons but may never communicate their objections. For example, evaluations, as constructed in U.S. organizations may be a totally foreign experience for which employees have not been prepared. Discomfort might also arise because the evaluator is racially and culturally different from the person being evaluated, so issues of fairness may surface. Managers must try to understand the various sources of discomfort to minimize misunderstanding and resistance.

Conflicts often reflect communication problems. Perception of conflict differs across cultures; some people will view conflict as something to be avoided at all costs because harmony and smooth relationships are valued. Perception of "loss of face" is a very important determinant of how employees respond to conflict. Some people may see walking away from a confrontation as a sign of weakness or defeat, but this behavior may be perceived as honorable by others. Managers must be sensitive to these nuances and must expedite resolution of conflicts before they fester and become more unwieldy.

Managers of diverse environments must also communicate creatively with employees whose learning styles, language proficiencies, and relational patterns differ from the norm. This may be frustrating and time-consuming, but to do less could spell disaster.

### Promotion and career development

According to Morrison (1992), "managing diversity" means sharing control with people who are different. To manage diversity effectively, it is essential that diversity issues are considered at both the leadership level and the direct service delivery level:

> Affirmative action practices should not be limited to recruitment; they should also be used to achieve the goals of multiculturalism that involve developing the potential of all people so that they are able and willing to contribute at the highest possible levels. (p. 9)

A critical element in the notion of sharing control is the career development of employees. Creative managers will find ways in which their organizations can meet the career development and mentoring needs of their employees. Career development and mentoring are critical factors in the promotion and advancement opportunities of people of color, women, and people with disabilities (Agosta, 1994; Asamoah, Haffey, & Hodges, 1992; Cameron, 1989; McCabe, 1991; Willie, 1987; Wright, King, Berg, & Creecy, 1987). The "glass ceiling" does not apply only to women. Many employees will choose an organization because they perceive that it will facilitate career development. When employee aspirations in this area are ignored, however, employees will be disenchanted and may become a liability to the organization.

## INCREASING SENSITIVITY AND VALUING DIFFERENCES

One of the most significant barriers to effectively managing diversity is failure of top management to recognize that problems exist. Some managers adopt a "hear no evil, see no evil" stance or assume that because they have made an effort to recruit and hire a diverse staff, they have done enough. Morrison (1992) analyzed diversity and leadership issues on the basis of data from the Guidelines on Leadership Diversity (GOLD) Project, and she noted that many managers assume that no news is good news. "Assumptions abound because some topics having to do with differential treatment are still considered taboo in organizations" (p. 165).

Diversity issues are sensitive and often painful, and many employees and managers perceive (unfortunately, rightly so) that it is risky to address them. Risks of backlash, as perceived by employees, range from fear of differential treatment and ostracism to outright dismissal. Management reluctance to deal with these issues stems from a fear of stirring up employees who may then make new demands or expose the organization to negative publicity.

Morrison (1992) underscored the importance of frequently gathering data about diversity and monitoring progress toward achieving it. Data must be gathered from many sources and must include perceptions as well as "hard" data such as numbers of people of color and women at different levels in the organization, promotion patterns, differential turnover, and so on. "Substituting data for assumptions helps prevent situations in which solutions go in search of problems" (p. 166).

There are many ways to conduct a "diversity audit" to determine what problems exist and which ones require immediate attention, including surveys, interviews, focus groups, experiential exercises, and use of outside consultants. Ready-made inventories are also available. They are easy to administer and score and can serve as a basis for raising awareness and stimulating discussion (see, for example, Gardenswartz & Rowe, 1993; Morrison, 1992; Talico, Inc., 1992). These inventories and other experiential exercises may be used by outside consultants to good effect, especially if they are perceived as "neutral."

However, care must be taken in deciding what information is needed, who will collect it, how it will be collected, and how it will be used. It would be a mistake for an organization to put employees through the exercise of divulging sensitive information on multicultural issues and then do nothing about what has been revealed. This could lead to rebellion. Managers must be prepared to consider seriously and to act on information gathered through a diversity audit and to hold themselves accountable for monitoring progress. In other words, management must make a commitment to take diversity issues seriously once employees' views have been formally solicited.

There is a growing body of literature that is helpful in both identifying diversity-related problems and effecting solutions (see, for example, Austin, 1989; Block, 1987; Epstein & Mohn, 1992; Havassy, 1990; Jamieson & O'Mara, 1991; Loden & Rosener, 1991; McNeely, 1987, 1989; Morrison, 1992; Pinderhughes, 1989; Synder, 1987; Thomson, 1989; Tsui, Egan, & O'Reilly, 1992; Wick & Leon, 1993). Jamieson and O'Mara have written a particularly useful chapter on resources available for gaining the diversity advantage.

Assessing organizational readiness to tackle diversity issues is important. Although using psychoanalytic frameworks for analyzing organizations is controversial, knowledge of the existing mental state of the organization would provide a clue about what other factors may adversely affect a diverse workforce (see, for example, Cohen & Cohen, 1993; Kets de Vries, 1991; Kets de Vries & Miller, 1989). Dysfunctional organizations face a tougher challenge in managing diversity. For example, if an organization is already paranoid, manic, or intoxicated, the self-analysis required in a diversity audit may send it off the deep end (Cohen & Cohen, 1993).

Development of "personal action plans" by employees is a useful experiential exercise after diversity issues have been identified through a diversity audit. As a group, staff are asked to develop their own personal action plans to help the agency identify and solve diversity issues and to identify and handle their own personal difficulties with diversity. These plans can either be written and shared with the group (anonymously) or collected, summarized, and presented to the group. The former is more effective, because public commitment to change is a more effective way to ensure future action.

One of the first steps toward managing diversity and valuing differences is recognizing the differences that "really make a difference" and in what ways. There are individual differences and group differences, and not all of them have equal significance. Individual strengths are often overlooked because they may not be immediately apparent or are not a part of the job description. For example, one employee identified "a sense of humor" as a primary strength in an agency serving homeless people during an experiential exercise on valuing differences. Her colleagues and supervisor were surprised that she considered this a strength. Everyone benefited when she described how she used humor in the supervisory process to help her staff manage the stress and potential burnout involved in working with this population.

Making use of employee self-identified strengths increases employees' feeling of being valued and appreciated. The entire organization also benefits. The more diverse the organization, the greater the potential for tapping into strengths that might not be present in a less heterogeneous environment.

Similarly, it is important to recognize how employees identify themselves and what that identity may mean to them. It is important for colleagues to know, for example, that a person who looks African American and speaks English with no accent may consider her primary identity to be Latina. There are many other such examples.

In what ways does the organization affirm or disaffirm the identities employees bring? In what ways does the organization show respect or disrespect for employees whose primary identity is not mainstream or is devalued by the larger society? What does the organization do to ensure that employees are comfortable no matter how they identify themselves? How can the organization positively use each employee's identity either in enriching the organizational climate or in improving culturally sensitive service delivery?

Managers can positively manage diversity within an organization in numerous ways,

1. by recognizing the value of flex management; flex management is a mindset that reflects "a deep appreciation of individual differences and the understanding that equality does not mean sameness" (Morrison, 1992, p. 35). Employees have different lifestyles and responsibilities. Flex management allows employees to have a wider range of options in terms of how they meet work requirements. This issue is critical as more women with children enter the workforce.

2. by recognizing the cultural relevance of "boundaries" in an organization; not all employees want to get totally "wrapped up" in their work, and they may resent "pitching in" to do all kinds of jobs outside their job description or working overtime without compensation "for the good of the organization." Grassroots organizations with charismatic leaders operating with low overhead expenses often fall into this trap. Although employees may be enthusiastic and dedicated to the goals of the organization, they are not married to it (see Hanks & Sussman, 1990).

3. by recognizing the value of diverse feedback.

4. by providing opportunities on the job for all employees to learn about other cultures and appreciate the richness of a diverse staff.

5. by recognizing that problems in the organization may be structural; if this is the case, more training is not the solution. Although identified

problems may stem from management's failure to manage diversity, multicultural training may not be the first step to take. When an organization has major structural problems, diversity issues get magnified and the wrong problems get targeted for solution.

6.  by recognizing that the agency must create a safe environment for candid discussion of diversity issues.
7.  by recognizing that any diversity training must be done according to plan over a period of time with adequate evaluation and follow-up; training should include all staff at all levels and should be scheduled in a way that makes this possible.
8.  by valuing differences as resources and including respect for difference as part of the organizational language.
9.  by distributing an annual diversity progress report to everyone.
10. by setting up a "diversity advisory committee" made up of staff at all levels to monitor diversity progress and advise management accordingly.

## THE EFFECTS OF DIVERSITY ON SERVICE DELIVERY

The relationship between diversity and service delivery is particularly critical in human services organizations. The significance of the issues might best be captured by posing four questions:

1.  What is the racial/ethnic/cultural/gender/sexual orientation and physical abilities composition of the clientele served?
2.  Within these broad categories, what is the spectrum of diversity that exists?
3.  What is the nature of the diversity of the staff who are delivering services to this clientele, and do they present a picture of "credibility" to the clientele served?
4.  How do issues of diversity within the organization affect service delivery to any clientele, but particularly to clientele who themselves are different from those who deliver or manage the services?

Since the 1980s, the cultural competency of people who deliver health, mental health, and general social services has received increased attention (Atkinson, Morten, & Sue, 1989; Boyd-Franklin, 1989; Devore & Schlesinger, 1987; Fukuyama, 1990; Hassenfeld & Chesler, 1989; Mandell, 1983; Pinder-hughes, 1989). Less attention has been focused on the agencies that are responsible for hiring and other administrative duties. Cross (1988) drew attention to this deficit and urged managers to pay more attention to the "cultural competency" of the agency as a whole. Cross suggested looking at cultural competence as "a set of congruent behaviors, attitudes and policies that come together in a system, agency or professional and enable that system, agency or professional to work effectively in cross-cultural situations" (p. 1). Attitudes, policies, and practices are located on a continuum ranging from cultural destructiveness to advanced cultural competence. In between these extremes lie cultural incapacity, cultural blindness, and basic cultural competence.

Culturally competent agencies are characterized by acceptance and respect for difference, continuing self-assessment about culture, expansion of cultural knowledge, hiring unbiased employees, seeking consultations from communities of color, and examining what it is not capable of delivering to a diverse clientele. Advanced cultural competency in an organization is characterized by holding culture in high esteem. Such an agency moves beyond basic competence to proficiency. Its activities include adding to the knowledge base of culturally competent practice through research, developing new therapeutic approaches, disseminating results of demonstration projects, using specialists in culturally competent practice, and advocating for cultural competency throughout the entire human services system. A culturally proficient agency will not overlook the composition of its board of directors in relationship to the clientele served (Widmer, 1987).

This continuum model can be effectively used in a diversity audit. Employees can be asked to place their organization on a point along this continuum. The results may be extremely revealing (and surprising) for management; they can form the basis for introductory discussions on diversity issues.

### CONCLUSION

Increased diversity in the workplace of the year 2000 is inevitable. However, it is not sufficient for managers simply to value diversity and let matters fall where they may. Learning to *manage* diversity will be a skill required of all new managers in the human services in the year 2000 and beyond. As Morrison (1992) rightly noted, "developing diversity is a struggle" (p. 266). Making it work positively for the organization is a challenge. Fortunately, there are many lessons to learn from organizations that have taken the challenge seriously and have designed effective programs (Jamieson & O'Mara, 1991; Morrison, 1992; Wick & Leon, 1993). As Morrison (1992) wrote,

> These leading-edge organizations and their leaders have not had an easy time of it. They have made plenty of mistakes along the way, but they persist in recovering from them. What happens after risking and failing in trying to solve diversity issues is no different from any other type of risk—you pick yourself up and go on. That's what leaders do. (p. 267)

Solutions for the problems of managing diversity are not immediately at hand. Finding the most effective management technique is a long-term and continuous process. There is no excuse, however, not to act. Commitment on the part of management is the first step. Discovering ways that management techniques can empower and affirm employees is critical to maximizing the energies and contributions a diverse staff can make to effective service delivery.

## REFERENCES

Agosta, D. (1994). *Women, organizing, and diversity: A workbook and guide to the video* (The Women Organizer's Video). New York: Hunter College School of Social Work, Education Center for Community Organizing.

Asamoah, Y., Haffey, M., & Hodges, M. (1992). Training minority managers in the field of aging—A collaborative model for professionalization and improvement of services to the elderly. *Journal of Gerontological Social Work, 18*, 73–84.

Atkinson, D. R., Morten, G., & Sue, D. W. (1989). *Counseling American minorities* (3rd ed.). Dubuque, IA: William C. Brown.

Austin, D. (1989). The human service executive. *Administration in Social Work, 13*(Special Issue), 13–36.

Bennet, M. J. (1986). Toward ethnorelativism: A developmental model of intercultural sensitivity. In M. Paige (Ed.), Cross-cultural orientation: New conceptualizations and applications. New York: University Press of America.

Block, P. (1987). *The empowered manager: Positive political skills at work.* San Francisco: Jossey-Bass.

Boyd-Franklin, N. (1989). *Black families in therapy: A multisystems approach.* New York: Guilford Press.

Cameron, R. W. (1989). *The minority manager's handbook.* New York: Warner Books.

Cohen, W., & Cohen, N. (1993). *The paranoid corporation and 8 other ways your company can be crazy.* New York: Amacom.

Cross, T. L. (1988). Services to minority populations: Cultural competency continuum. *Focal Point, 3,* 1–4.

Devore, W., & Schlesinger, E. (1987). *Ethnic sensitive social work practice.* St. Louis: C. V. Mosby.

Elsea, J. (1988). *The 4 minute sell.* New York: Simon & Schuster.

Epstein, M., & Mohn, S. L. (1992). Planning for pluralism: A report on a Chicago agency's efforts on behalf of immigrants and refugees. *Journal of Multicultural Social Work, 2,* 199–123.

Fukuyama, M. A. (1990). Taking a universal approach to multicultural counseling. *Counselor Education and Supervision, 30,* 6–17.

Gardenswartz, L., & Rowe, A. (1993). *Managing diversity: A complete desk reference and planning guide.* San Diego: Pfeiffer & Co.

Hanks, R. S., & Sussman, M. B. (1990). Where does family end and corporation begin: The consequences of rapid transformation. *Marriage and Family Review, 15* (Special Issue), 1–13.

Harris, R., & Moran, R. T. (1987). *Managing cultural differences* (2nd ed.). Houston: Gulf Publishing.

Hassenfeld, Y., & Chesler, M.A. (1989). Client empowerment in the human services: Personal and professional agenda. *Journal of Applied Behavioral Sciences, 25*(Special Issue), 499–521.

Havassy, H. M. (1990). Effective second-story bureaucrats: Mastering the paradox of diversity. *Social Work, 35,* 103–109.

Jamieson, D., & O'Mara, J. (1991). *Managing workforce 2000: Gaining the diversity advantage.* San Francisco: Jossey-Bass.

Johnston, W. B., & Packer, A. E. (1987). *Workforce 2000: Work and workers for the 21st century.* Indianapolis: Hudson Institute.

Kets de Vries, M.F.R. (1991). *Organizations on the couch: Clinical prespectives on organizational behavior and change.* San Francisco: Jossey-Bass.

Kets de Vries, M.F.R., & Miller, D. (1989). *The neurotic organization.* San Francisco: Jossey-Bass.

Kim, Y. Y., & Gudykunst, W. B. (1988). *Theories in intercultural communication.* Newbury Park, CA: Sage Publications.

Loden, M., & Rosener, J. B. (1991). *Workforce America! Managing employee diversity as a vital resource.* Homewood, IL: Business One Irwin.

Mandell, B.R. (1983). Blurring definitions of social services: Human services vs. social work. *Catalyst: A Socialist Journal of the Social Sciences, 4,* 6–21.

McCabe, J. (1991, August). Women in the executive suite. *Black Enterprise*, p. 43.

McNeely, R. L. (1987). Predictors of job satisfaction among three racial/ethnic groups of professional female human service workers. *Journal of Sociology & Social Welfare, 14,* 115–136.

McNeely, R. L. (1989). Race and job satisfaction in human service employment. *Administration in Social Work, 13,* 75–94.

Morrison, A. M. (1992). *The new leaders: Guidelines on leadership diversity in America.* San Francisco: Jossey-Bass.

Pinderhughes, E. (1989). *Understanding race, ethnicity, & power: The key to efficacy in clinical practice.* New York: Free Press.

Synder, P. J. (1987). Organizational behavior in the cross-cultural delivery of services: A case example of an agency serving the deaf. *Human Organization, 46,* 113–119.

Talico, Inc. (1992). *Intercultural Communication Inventory.* Jacksonville Beach, FL: Author.

Thomson, J. S. (1989). Assessing staff diversity to build a stronger organization—Valuing our differences. *Life-Long Learning: An Omnibus of Practice and Research, 12,* 28–31.

Tsui, A. S., Egan, T. D., & O'Reilly, C. A., III. (1992). Being different: Relational demography and organizational attachment. *Administrative Science Quarterly, 37,* 549–579.

Wick, W. C., & Leon, L. S. (1993). *The learning edge.* New York: McGraw-Hill.

Widmer, C. (1987). Minority participation on Boards of Directors of human service agencies: Some evidence and suggestions. *Journal of Voluntary Action Research, 16,* 33–44.

Willie, C. V. (1987). *Effective education—A minority policy perspective.* Westport, CT: Greenwood Press.

Wright, R., Jr., King, S. W., Berg, W. E., & Creecy, R. F. (1987). Job satisfaction among black female managers: A causal approach. *Human Relations, 40,* 489–506

# Chapter 8

# Women and Social Work Management

Lynne M. Healy, Catherine M. Havens, and Barbara A. Pine

T

he topic of women in social work management has generated great interest and considerable heat over the past several decades. Social work is overwhelmingly a profession of women, but men still hold a disproportionately large share of management positions. Although recent gains have been made in the numbers of women securing leader-

ship positions, these have only partially recouped earlier losses, leaving women in fewer positions of power today than in the 1950s. Yet, there is some evidence that female managers make significant and perhaps unique contributions to leadership roles. Moreover, new approaches to management that emphasize participation, power sharing, and teamwork with smaller, more autonomous work units are highly consistent with feminist leadership styles.

The authors hold up the "gender lens" to social work management, providing an up-to-date picture of women in social work administration. What is their current status? What are their special contributions to management, particularly to social agencies? What are the social, organizational, and personal barriers to their professional advancement? The chapter discusses the differences between equality and equity and the competing paradigms of viewing women in management from an equality versus a complementary contributions perspective. Elements of a feminist management style are presented and, through discussion and case illustrations, women's potential for leadership success in social work is affirmed.

## WHAT IS THE STATUS OF WOMEN IN
## SOCIAL WORK MANAGEMENT?

Social work is largely a women's profession. In 1993, 77.6 percent of the 134,240 members of the National Association of Social Workers (NASW) were women (Gibelman & Schervish, 1993b). Yet, every study conducted on women's status in the profession in the past few decades has documented that women remain disadvantaged in their share of leadership positions, in salary, and in more subtle areas such as tasks and job status.

Of particular relevance to this chapter is that women are greatly underrepresented in social work management positions. Gibelman and Schervish's (1993b) analysis of NASW membership data revealed that 25.6 percent of male members are in management, compared with only 12.9 percent of female members. They concluded that a glass ceiling limiting women's career advancement exists in social work (Gibelman & Schervish, 1993a). A North Carolina study found that 33 percent of men were in administration, compared with 11 percent of women (York, Henley, & Gamble, 1987). Szakacs (1977) studied gender of chief executive officers (CEOs) in social agencies and concluded that "if the present trend continues, there will be no women in social work leadership positions by 1984" (p. 12). She based this dire prediction on her analysis of the numbers of women in chief executive positions in member agencies of the Child Welfare League of America (CWLA), the Family Service Association of America (FSAA), federally funded mental health clinics, and schools of social work. For example, the proportion of female-led CWLA agencies fell from 36 percent in 1966 to 19 percent in 1976; the drop in FSAA was even more dramatic, from 60 percent in 1957 to 20 percent in 1976. In 1976, 15 percent of social work schools had female deans. The current figures show improvement, but not parity. In 1990–91, 37.3 percent of CWLA agencies were led by women, an improvement back to 1966 levels (CWLA, 1990); by 1994, women had regained CEO positions in 38.8 percent of FSAA agencies (FSAA, 1994). The most dramatic improvement has been in schools of social work; in 1994, 45 percent of schools had female deans or acting deans

(42 percent of permanent deans are female; Council on Social Work Education, 1994).

A closer analysis of women's status in management shows more subtle forms of discrimination that follow women throughout their careers. In a recent study of career paths of men and women social work graduates of the University of Chicago, Lambert (1993) found that men and women were equally likely to be hired as top administrators in their first job after graduation. "Within three years, however, significantly more men than women are top administrators; this difference between men and women increases over the course of their careers" (p. 11). In addition, Lambert found that among those holding top administrative jobs, tasks differed by gender. At every career stage, more men than women managed budgets, and the budgets they managed were larger. Finding gender differences in other functions as well, she concluded that "men have more control over budgets, they are more involved in managing the organization and in managing relationships with funders, boards of directors, and other governing agencies. These differences in the organizational power of men and women show up in their first jobs and continue over the course of their careers" (p. 17). Kravetz and Austin (1984) also found that female administrators felt they were given less responsibility and autonomy in their positions than male administrators of similar rank.

Women are disadvantaged in their access to administrative positions and even in the administrative tasks they are assigned. Moreover, Kravetz and Austin (1984) found additional evidence that women's challenges in administration go beyond access to top positions. Close to two-thirds of the women studied reported that stereotypical attitudes of others—superiors, subordinates, colleagues, board members, and funders—continually made their jobs more difficult, especially in interactions with superiors, behaviors of subordinates, and their own access to professional networks. In short, women in this women's profession are far from achieving equity in social work management careers. The following section discusses some of the reasons for this.

### WHY ARE WOMEN UNDERREPRESENTED IN SOCIAL WORK MANAGEMENT?

Women aspiring to of leadership roles in social agency management face two types of barriers, external and internal.

### External barriers

Formal and informal external barriers exist within the environment. They are manifested in agency policies and practices in the organizational structure, and in attitudes and behaviors. The most overt of these external barriers is gender discrimination in hiring, promotion, and salary.

Although the Equal Pay Act of 1963 and Title VII of the Civil Rights Act of 1964 made gender discrimination illegal, problems still exist. These are most evident in the wage gap between men and women. As recently as 1987, women earned only 64 cents for every dollar earned by men (Mason, 1992). The statistics on women in social work management cited earlier confirm the effects of discrimination in hiring and promotion. Moreover, numerous studies document a large and persistent wage gap between male and female social workers, including those in management positions (Gibelman & Schervish, 1993b; Hesselbrock, 1992; Strobino & McCoy, 1992; York et al., 1987).

Antidiscrimination policies have limitations. In a gender-segregated workforce, it is difficult for women to prove that their jobs are equal to higher-paying jobs held mostly by men, as required for protection under the Equal Pay Act. The concept of comparable worth has not been a widely applied solution to this problem. Moreover, the legal concepts of equal pay and equal opportunity often do not address all forms of discrimination that women experience (Dean, 1991). Many women face discrimination on the basis of race, immigrant status, age, or sexual identity. Thus, a complex array of stereotypes combining gender, racial, and cultural factors results in dual discrimination for these women.

Sexual harassment, too, can act as a potent barrier to women's advancement. Statistics indicate that anywhere from 42 percent to 90 percent of working women experience some form of harassment during their employment history (Hill, 1992). Social work is far from a safe haven. Studies show that as women rise in organizations, they face harassment from new sources, including funders, board members, and other executives (Kravetz & Austin, 1984; Maypole, 1986). Seeking legal redress can be costly and humiliating; a litigious employee often pays a price in terms of limited career development.

Women's opportunities within an organization can also be hampered by task assignments, position descriptions, personnel practices, relationships among peers and subordinates, and communication networks (Calkin, 1983; Haynes, 1989; Kravetz & Austin, 1984). There is also substantial evidence that an organization's values and culture can constitute informal barriers to women's advancement. Channeling women into positions that offer little visibility, mobility, or influence is an example of this, as are gender differences in job qualifications, task description and assignment, and mechanisms for evaluating performance (Haynes, 1989). Although not technically illegal, such barriers clearly violate professional ethics.

Lack of access to the organization's informal network is another form of subtle discrimination. For example, decisions may be made in informal settings where women are not present. Women can be excluded by simply being left out of meeting breaks or premeeting sessions where preliminary "deals" are made and vital contacts initiated (Fagenson, 1993). When women are excluded in these ways, they have less access to their superiors and ultimately to the resources needed for the high performance and morale of their departments (Trempe, Rigny, & Haccoun, 1985).

Lack of access to the organization's network has other disadvantages as well. Role modeling and mentoring are well-documented mechanisms for advancement and achievement in organizations. A key strategy for upward mobility of both men and women, mentoring is likely to be even more important for women given their relative disadvantage in career advancement (York, Henley, & Gamble, 1988). Yet, women may not be chosen as protégés for several reasons; they hesitate to proclaim their self-worth, refrain from actively seeking a mentor, and fear that a mentor relationship may be perceived as a sexual one if the mentor is male (Gerrard, Oliver, & Williams, 1976; Haynes, 1989; Kram, 1985). Additionally, very few women are available to be mentors or role models for other women. A survey of 2,000 female managers noted that as the women advanced to upper management, they did not have female mentors to offer support (Noe, 1988).

### Internal barriers

A second set of barriers affecting women's representation in management ranks is internal: aspirations, behaviors, and attitudes attributed to women that are viewed as inhibiting career advancement and job performance (Haynes, 1989; Kravetz & Jones, 1982).

Among the most talked about barriers to women's career advancement is the conflict between family and work responsibilities. In her study of two-career parents, Hochschild (1989) found that women bear the lion's share of family responsibilities, including caring for children and older family members and running the household. This skewed distribution of labor, combined with limited time, the emotional pull of parenthood, and a woman's perception of what it means to be a good mother, may contribute to her personal sense of conflicting responsibilities. Proposals for differentiated career ladders for workers with family responsibilities (Schwartz, 1989) were quickly dubbed the "mommy track" by the media an indication of the widely held view of women as primary caregivers. Moreover, very few organizations have progressive and flexible "family friendly" personnel policies, and too many of them view child and family care as a woman's, not a parent's (mother's and father's) responsibility, which accounts for the failure to provide sufficient support in either case.

Other behaviors have also been cited as reasons for women's lack of advancement. Although the trait theory of leadership has long been discredited by theoreticians (Hersey & Blanchard, 1982), belief in it seems to persist in management practice. A set of characteristics linked to the socialization of males—including competitiveness, aggressive behavior, analytical thinking, nonemotional attitude, and comfort in hierarchical structures—continues in subtle and not so subtle ways to be regarded as essential for successful managers. In contrast, characteristics attributed to women such as expressiveness, passivity, sensitivity, and being feelings oriented (Bardwick & Douvan, 1971; Broverman & Broverman, 1970; Chodorow, 1971) have, at least in the past, been seen as less well suited to leadership roles (Brager & Michael, 1969; Kadushin, 1976). Recent studies have shown that women continue to be perceived by some as limited in the toughness, stability, creativity, and judgment required to meet the demands of high-level management positions (Odewahn & Ezell, 1992). Within this trait framework, female socialization is discussed as a handicap. To increase their chances of representation among executive ranks, women are encouraged to be more assertive, directive, decisive, task oriented, nonemotional, and analytic, and less oriented toward relationship— in other words, to adopt the attitudes and behaviors associated with traditional (that is, male) management styles. Popular literature, including such books as *The Managerial Woman* (Hennig & Jardim, 1977), *Games Mother Never Taught You* (Harragan, 1977), and *The Women's Dress for Success Book* (Molloy, 1977), illustrates this approach to career advancement in management, as do the myriad training courses for women that promise to teach them how to "fit into" management roles.

Another insidious obstacle to women's progress is the literature (including recent books on social work management) that presents what is *wrong* with women's ways of behaving and relating. One passage from a recent book on social work management noted that "women must be competent, credible, confident, and visible. They must be cooperative enough to be accessible, but competitive enough to keep an appropriate distance, while maintaining their femininity and being careful not to evoke damaging perceptions of impropriety" (Benshoff, 1991, p. 176). Benshoff clearly suggested that women seeking success in administrative positions must adapt: "The female manager must quickly learn to be comfortable with her own authority. She must learn how to set limits without sounding angry; she must learn to express anger without sounding aggressive; and she must learn how to delegate, hold others accountable, and take charge without alienating" (p. 180).

Although an adaptation strategy has offered women managers some measure of success, this approach appears to have limited relevance for both the individual woman and the organization. Careers are reaching a plateau, the glass ceiling seems unbreakable, and some women are opting out of organizational management. The demands and strains of managerial roles are intense and may be particularly frustrating to those who have been required to deny much of their identity and many of their potentially useful skills. Furthermore, women may have unique contributions to make to management, contributions that are particularly relevant for human services administration (Odewahn & Ezell, 1992). Women are increasingly questioning the assumption that there is only one way to be a manager. Organizations can reward women's styles and socialization by openly acknowledging the diversity of styles essential to effective leadership (Haynes, 1989).

### EQUITY VERSUS COMPLEMENTARY CONTRIBUTIONS

Within the past decade, the social work profession has shown a strong desire to achieve equality for women in the workplace and, perhaps more so, in volunteer professional leadership. The *NASW Code of Ethics* (1994) specifically makes all social workers responsible for promoting equity and preventing discrimination by gender. Therefore, for a profession with a clear commitment to equality, equal access and equal representation are values worth pursuing. Recently, other reasons have emerged from an emphasis on gender difference rather than the earlier presumptions of gender similarity. Equity's new companion is an increasing emphasis on valuing the differences between men and women, calling for increased numbers of women in management to improve social agencies and, perhaps, to make both management and the work environment more congruent with the goals and values of the social work profession.

There are two major models of the role of women as leaders or managers. Adler and Izraeli (1988) identified these as the equity model and the complementary contribution model. The equity model assumes that given access, women will meet existing norms, as established by men. The complementary contribution model assumes a difference and emphasizes the importance of recognizing different styles and the value of different contributions. From the equity perspective, no changes in program, policy, workplace climate, or other factors would be expected when an agency is led by a woman. In contrast, the complementary perspective argues that, at least where their contributions are supported, women will bring unique perspectives, resulting in better, more "complete" organizational outcomes.

Expanding on this dichotomy, due Billing and Alvesson (1987) presented a model composed of four alternative rationales for increasing women's representation in leadership positions. Two represent the equity perspective, and two represent the complementary contribution perspective. The first rationale (equity) is that women should be encouraged to seek leadership positions because talent is equally distributed in the population; therefore, fairness requires equal access as a right. The second rationale (meritocracy) is that access must be open to ensure selection of the very best talent from the whole population, for the greater social good. The third and fourth rationales for women as managers stress their difference: The third presents the notion of unique contributions emanating from women's different experiences and socialization, whereas the fourth presents a view of women as holders of radically different values that will force changes in organizations. Although the complementary contributions model for assessing potential for success is often ridiculed when discussing gender, this is precisely the viewpoint underpinning the substantial literature and emphasis on success in managing diversity and multiculturalism.

## DO WOMEN MANAGE DIFFERENTLY?

Empirical studies on whether women manage differently from men have yielded mixed and conflicting results. As expressed in the title of their article, "Men and Women as Managers: A Significant Case of No Significant Difference," Donnell and Hall (1980) reported that studies comparing men and women as managers have not found significant differences. Powell's (1990) review of research on managerial behavior also supported the "no differences" view. In a 1987 study of bureaucracies at the state and federal levels, Bayes (1987) found no gender differences in the styles of high-ranking managers. Noting that women made up 20 percent or fewer of high-ranking managers in all agencies studied, she concluded that "having a token position in a public bureaucracy clearly quells women's 'different voice' if that in fact exists" (p. 33).

Other studies, however, have found gender differences. For example, national opinion polls in the United States show clear and persistent gender differences in policy preferences. The greatest difference is on the issues of use of force and violence, where women are much more likely to oppose the use of force both domestically and in foreign policy, which affects their opinions on gun control, defense spending, and capital punishment. Women have also been found more likely to support "compassion issues"—such as poverty programs, student loan programs, government-funded health care—and regulation and protection issues such as speed limits, seat belt laws, and bans on cigarette advertising (Shapiro & Mahajan, 1986).

Do gender differences on policy extend to human services management? Affirmative evidence was found in a recent study of state government department heads, in which commissioners were asked their opinions on a range of statewide policy issues, including abortion, gay rights, family leave, the death penalty, and taxes (Havens & Healy, 1991b). Among a generally liberal group, in a Democratic administration, the female leaders were far more supportive of gay rights and far less likely to believe that family leave legislation would hurt businesses and state agencies than their male counterparts. Other gender differences were found on topics such as abortion but fell short of statistical significance.

Other studies have found gender differences in work attitudes and perceptions. Neuse (1978) studied middle- and upper-level public administrators in Texas and found gender-related differences in work values. Women ranked more highly the chance to be of service to people, the chance to use their skills creatively, the opportunity to work with highly qualified and motivated people, and satisfaction in doing a job well. Values ranked highly by men were the chance to work for state government, the opportunity to meet important people, and prestige. Values ranked equally by men and women included advancement, salary, benefits, and the freedom to think and act independently (Neuse, 1978). It is particularly interesting that the men in Neuse's study indicated a higher sense of responsibility to agency hierarchy (the director or the governor), whereas the women ranked higher the sense of responsibility to their profession and to the groups served by the agency. If this difference holds for human services administrators, it would suggest that commitment to clients and to professional values, rather than hierarchical responsibilities, may differ by gender.

In their study of women social work administrators in the New York metropolitan area, Chernesky and Bombyk (1988) found that female administrators believe that they manage differently from men. Close to 66 percent of respondents in their study believed they actually did different things than male managers did, and 78 percent thought they held different values or perspectives. Among the differences reported were more concern for workers, including more investment in their careers; special appreciation of the dual responsibilities of women workers; more use of collaborative styles and increased staff participation; and attention to the quality of the work environment. Differences in the ways women perceive their behavior have been supported by other research. The challenge is to determine whether perceptions and actual behavior match.

Another study raises the prospect of the symbolic impact of women in leadership positions, which comes not only from what the women do but from what others may do in response to their presence. Saltzstein (1986) found that city employment of women increased in cities with women mayors. This was attributed only in part to deliberate mayoral action; more often it resulted from changed behavior of hiring managers and women applying for work in response to the presence of a female leader.

The study of state departmental leaders by Havens and Healy (1991a) involved in-depth interviews of 36 leaders, 21 of whom were commissioners or deputy commissioners in the state's human services agencies (13 women and eight men), and 15 of whom were in the nonhuman services side of government (five women and eight men). Questioned on a broad range of topics related to gender differences in leadership, these leaders identified a number of perceived differences in priorities and management style. The commissioners were unanimous in stating that having more women in leadership changes the policy agenda, bringing new issues forward. Among the issues named were those that might be expected to concern women such as affirmative action, child care, and family issues. However, the issue agenda also included areas such as human rights, privacy in corrections, objective job evaluation, and consumer legislation. As in Chernesky's (1986) study, the women in this study believed that they had changed the work environments of their agencies; almost 79 percent reported changes such as increased sensitivity to family issues, permitting increased flexibility in schedules, and a "nicer, more civilized climate" (Havens & Healy, 1991a).

If anything is clear from the many studies on gender and leadership, it is that little is, in fact, clear and that there is much conflicting evidence on the topic of gender difference. In addition, it remains difficult to separate perceptions of differences from documented behavioral differences. Such a separation may be artificial and not particularly useful for advancing social work management.

What is useful is an examination of new management approaches that emerge from the positive differences either perceived or practiced by female managers in many of the studies cited. Perhaps there is a natural "goodness of fit" between what has been termed a feminist leadership style and social work values in action. The following section describes key elements of a feminist leadership style and the confluent forces demanding new management approaches. Then, case examples illustrate the harmonious integration of these elements in the management of social agencies.

## WHAT SHOULD WOMEN MANAGERS DEVELOP AS THEIR MANAGEMENT STYLE?

New management approaches emphasizing the value of participation, shared decision making, and empowerment are increasingly viewed as essential for successful management in today's turbulent environment. Organizations seeking their employees' best efforts must establish these as their operating values (Kantor, 1989; Lee, 1994). Ironically, these approaches and their underlying values, now seen as mainstream, were central to what had been termed an alternative and feminist management system (Weil, 1988). Whether new or old, these values and their application in the workplace are very much in keeping with social work values (Edwards & Gummer, 1988; Hooyman & Cunningham, 1986).

### Feminist leadership style

Several authors have delineated elements of a feminist approach to management. Weil (1988) defined a system based on this approach as being characterized by nonhierarchical relations, with an empowerment focus, involving a strong emphasis on process and mutual planning and problem solving, carried out by flexible teams whose leadership is based on expertise suitable for the task at hand. Similarly, Chernesky (1986) noted that in a feminist or alternative agency, expertise is not correlated with hierarchical position; rather, individuals at all levels teach and learn, with workers assuming responsibility for evaluating the quality of their own work. This is similar to the feminist working environment cited by Perlmutter (1990), in which the value of every staff member's contribution and his or her participation in decision making is recognized. Hooyman and Cunningham (1986) delineated six key elements of a feminist leadership style: valuing women's perspectives; emphasizing the big picture; reconceptualizing power; democratic structuring; valuing process equally with product; and an orientation to fundamental structural change.

Several of these elements deserve additional comment. The subject of power is central to any discussion of management, and no issue has been more problematic for women in their exercise of leadership. Because power was seen as inherently unfeminine, it is not surprising that considerable attention has been paid to new models of power. The feminist conception of power is described as *power to* rather than *power over* (French, 1985). *Power over* supports the command and control notions of hierarchical leadership; by holding a superior position, one has the authority to command. *Power to* views power as expansive, not finite; it can therefore be shared with other members of a group or organization, including subordinates. Whereas power is still viewed as important to task accomplishment, power sharing is preferred as a means of expanding the abilities of the organization through enhanced participation. Participation and sharing power with others in the organization are illustrated in a case example later in this chapter.

This alternative view of power, which places high value on the maintenance of working relationships, emphasizes consensus as a model for resolving conflict. At least four major strategies for conflict resolution can be identified. One is the competitive or "win–lose" approach; favored for its quick results, win–lose can result in long-term tensions between the winners and losers. Loden (1985) reported that most men preferred a competitive approach; when winning was unlikely, men preferred avoidance as a means of dealing with conflict. Female managers, however, expressed a preference for collaboration and consensus building to resolve conflicts. When time or the degree of opposition did not allow consensus, women's second choice was accommodation, an approach that preserves relationships even at the expense of goal achievement. Each strategy has drawbacks, but the feminist preference for consensus, when used selectively, is an important contribution to new management approaches in social agencies.

## New management approaches

Multiple and confluent forces are driving the trend toward more democratic, participatory approaches in the workplace, especially in social agencies. The turbulent environment of today's social agency requires organizational flexibility to facilitate building consensus about the values and goals of the organization. The high stress of many social work jobs and the potentially alienating qualities of some social agencies can be relieved only by designers willing to humanize the workplace. Social work interventions aimed at empowerment and partnerships with clients will not work if staff are not empowered as professionals (Weil, 1988). The increased pressure on social agencies to demonstrate program effectiveness, increasingly with fewer and fewer resources, requires regular staff participation in assessing and improving the quality of their work. Finally, demographic shifts affecting both staff and clients in social agencies have underscored the importance of valuing diversity and using differences effectively to improve both services and workplace climate. These shifts, led by female workforce participation, also underscore the importance of fully using the talents of women workers. The congruence of elements of feminist leadership with demands of the new management environment is clear. Hierarchical, rigidly structured organizations whose leaders do not share power with staff will not be able to navigate their turbulent environments. Democracy and teamwork are now the order of the day. Demographic shifts, particularly in women's labor force participation rates, underscore the value of women's perspectives in humanizing the workplace and creating more "family friendly" policies and practices. Attention to both process *and* product, as stressed in feminist models, requires competence in human relations and a range of interpersonal skills. It should be noted that participatory strategies are much more demanding than command and control approaches. They require special skills, a personal sense of competence, an openness to criticism, and perseverance (Peace, 1991). The authors conceded that women do not hold a monopoly on the values inherent in a feminist leadership style, neither do all female managers adhere to these values.

## NEW SOCIAL WORK MANAGEMENT STYLE IN ACTION

The case examples that follow have been drawn from the real-life experiences of social work managers. They are "action shots" of women who have successfully integrated the values and skills of a feminist leadership style with those of social work to effectively manage complex situations.

### Power-sharing and participation

The following case illustrates a social work manager's success in involving staff and others in assessing program strengths and weaknesses and in developing a plan for needed changes. It is a good example of the kinds of program decisions that are best made using a participatory approach. The example also illustrates the concept of a learning organization—one that creates and acquires new knowledge to improve performance (Garvin, 1991).

**Case example.** Recently, faced with the requirements of a consent decree and other forces for change, the deputy commissioner of a mid-sized state child welfare agency decided to undertake an assessment of her agency's efforts to reunify families separated by foster placement. She knew from past experience that line staff were the best source of information about how things worked (or did not work) in the day-to-day casework with families and children. She also knew that any of the resulting recommendations for improving the direct service aspects of the program would need to come from staff who would implement the changes. Finally, she knew that the sanction and support of top-level managers would also be required, especially for broader, systems changes.

As a first step, the deputy commissioner organized a leadership group of eight top-level managers to plan the project. This group was also charged with providing any needed supports for the work group that would actually carry out the assessment, ensuring that the work was carried out in a timely way, receiving the work group's report and recommendations, and prioritizing and planning for needed changes. Inherent in this strategy was the idea that the leadership group would be a voice of support and encouragement for, and information about, the project throughout the agency.

The second group consisted of direct service staff in foster care and child protection, supervisors, foster parents, training academy staff, staff from community agencies providing contract services, court personnel, and birth parents. With leadership to the work group provided by a coordinator, these volunteers met for a series of all-day sessions to review various aspects of their program, including relations with other organizations such as the courts. The result of their efforts was a comprehensive set of recommendations for program improvements that ranged from the simple to the more complex.

As a final activity of the assessment process, the deputy commissioner and the leadership group planned a day-long meeting with the members of the work group and other key people in the agency, including the commissioner. This event served three overall purposes: first, to celebrate the work of the two groups and acknowledge their contribution to the agency; second, to share the results of the efforts; and third, to begin the process of planning for change.

In discussing her experience, the deputy commissioner noted other benefits that she felt her agency derived from this sharing of power with others. These included the affirmation of the commitment staff feels toward the families and children the agency serves; the conviction that line staff and foster parents can be "trusted" to make good decisions; the opportunities of group members (most of them female) to develop and exhibit leadership skills; the improved relations that result when people from different groups come together—for example, caseworkers and court personnel; and the enthusiasm staff expressed about the opportunity to be involved in this way, as well as their general enthusiasm for the work, despite the many challenges of public child welfare work. This last is important, since burnout clearly is a major concern of managers in large public agencies.

This administrator was quick to say, however, that participatory approaches have their limitations in large bureaucracies. Sometimes they are simply too cumbersome and time-consuming to use; at other times, they are inappropriate.

### Staff empowerment and career development

In studies of women's approach to management, power sharing and staff empowerment are almost always mentioned as preferred elements of management style. In addition, many women in management express an interest in assisting other women in moving up and list demonstration of concern for staff as a special aspect of their management style. The following case example illustrates these strategies.

**Case example.** Two female managers in an information and referral agency instituted, with staff participation, a job enrichment and staff career development approach to task assignment. In this agency, the job descriptions of line staff specified telephone information and referral casework with clients and associated record keeping as the sole staff duties. The overall work of the agency, however, included extensive outreach and public speaking to social agencies, civic groups, and United Way volunteers. In addition, the agency was responsible for periodically providing the community with an updated social services resource directory. Rather than define these latter activities, as is typically done, as exclusively management functions, all casework staff were given opportunities and encouragement to take on a limited number of public presentations about the information and referral service. Staff also became involved in helping to update the resource directory.

There were many positive outcomes of the expanded job descriptions. Caseworkers felt increased ownership of and pride in the program. An unexpected outcome was that through their contact with agencies and potential service users, the casework practice improved. The participatory approach extended to other aspects of the program. Staff became involved in helping to plan staff meetings and staff development sessions and took on some of the tasks related to updating resource information. On a personal level, staff self-confidence grew and staff were empowered to plan their careers, mostly in social services. A number of staff members left to assume jobs that were considerable promotions in responsibility and salary; others went back to school to pursue graduate degrees.

An apparent drawback of the staff empowerment approach was staff turnover. Under the new system, the average staff tenure was about three years, after which many moved on to further develop their careers. An alternative view, however, redefines this as positive. In social services, entry-level jobs should often be just that. Success is to keep staff long enough to be able to provide competent service, but not long enough to become stagnated at the entry level. That so many female staff were launched into promotional opportunities through their experiences in the information and referral program can be claimed as a major success of the empowerment–job enlargement strategy.

### Conflict resolution and consensus decision making

Agencies face many difficult decisions, some of which involve controversial issues or issues about which participants have deep convictions. The following case illustrates the management strategies involved in decision making in such a situation.

**Case example.** The all-female board of a woman- and girl-serving agency was faced with making a decision that threatened the harmony of the board.

The agency, fortunate to have a significant endowment, was faced with a decision of whether to divest its investment portfolio of South African holdings. The board members who proposed divestiture thought that the decision would be quick and easy; after all, the agency had the eradication of racism as its most important mission. Instead, the decision took many months and caused considerable conflict.

The unique composition of the board may have contributed to the intensity of the conflict; one-third of the members were African American; one-third were Hispanic, and one-third were white. These women represented a wide spectrum of political and social views; some were from the business community and others worked in social services. The divestiture discussion soon degenerated into accusations. The more liberal members accused those from the business sector of being more concerned about the bottom line than about racism; black women from the business community accused whites of being more concerned about racism 10,000 miles away than at home. Fortunately, board members recognized that their board was in trouble and that the way in which this decision was made would have important ramifications for future board functioning.

The board then made several important decisions. One was to delay making a decision on divestiture. Another was to launch an educational process to obtain information both about apartheid and its impact and about the impact of divestiture on investment value and return. A most important decision was the decision *not* to take a vote on the issue, even though at various points in the process, the prodivestiture side probably had enough votes to claim a simple majority.

As part of the educational process, members of two sister agencies came to share their divestiture experiences with the board. One agency had spent several months educating itself before a consensus decision was reached. The other, after some similar contentious discussions, took a quick vote that resulted in a small majority favoring divestiture. Although the decision did not damage the agency's financial standing, some board members resigned, whereas others withdrew into inactivity. Relationships among board members and even staff took years to restore to productive levels. This negative experience underscores the value of consensus decision making.

After almost six months of an educational process, a decision was reached by consensus. This was possible because during the educational sessions, held prior to each board meeting, members from both sides of the issue attended and participated in the discussions of both social issues and finances. All agreed later that it was a valuable learning process. More importantly, the educational effort permitted mending of relationships. The board decided through a discussion and eventual consensus to divest. Most significantly, this process resulted in strengthened board decision making for future issues, most of which are reached by vote, not by consensus.

The role of the agency executive was interesting. Under the agency structure, the executive functions as a voting member of the board. Initially, she raised some concerns about the financial impacts of divestiture. Quickly seeing the threat posed by the conflict outlined above, she modified her role to that of quiet facilitator of the educational process. Although this might have been viewed through a traditional management lens as ineffective management, it represents higher-level self-assurance and confidence in the board. Board members recognized this and, again, working relationships for the future were positively affected. The executive then proceeded to replicate the educational process with staff, enhancing agency cohesion around this important policy issue. For issues of this importance, all agreed that consensus decision making is worth the investment of time and relationship building.

### An alignment of values

One responsibility of a social work manager is ensuring alignment between the values espoused in the agency's mission and purpose and the operation of that agency. In the following case illustration, the social worker had to undertake a range of fundamental structural, operational, and program changes to bring her organization into alignment. This case further illustrates the importance of valuing a women's perspective in making needed improvements, especially when the clients served are primarily women, as in this case involving a women's prison.

**Case example.** A social worker who had worked her way up the management ladder to become warden of a women's prison took the opportunity to make a number of fundamental changes in what she had considered to be inhumane policies. As her first activity, she worked with management and corrections staff to draft a new mission statement for the facility. The motto of the facility became "changing society one life at a time" and the mission was redirected from punishment of offenders to their reintegration into society. The new organizational principles of providing a safe, caring, secure, and humane environment were expressed in redesigned cells with attractive furniture; in on-grounds garden apartments where women could spend weekend visits with their children; in visiting areas that were made comfortable and attractive and afforded some privacy for family visits; and in the refurnished dining room with small, comfortable seating arrangements and tables decorated with linens and flowers. The citizenship principles were reflected in program enhancements that included vocational training and nontraditional occupations. Training sessions of particular interest to these women such as dealing with sexual and physical violence as well as parenting skills and improving self-esteem, were provided. To ensure that everyone was committed to the new mission and goals of the facility, the warden organized training programs for staff at all levels in the organization.

To be sure, such fundamental change, however beneficial, has its costs. The radical shift away from punishment drew much political fire from conservatives. When an election put the warden's critics into power in the state's government, she was forced to resign. However, the extent of the changes she helped to create have so radically reformed the prison that most of the changes will likely remain as a legacy to her tenure as warden.

### WHERE DO WE GO FROM HERE?

This update on the status of women in social work management suggests numerous directions for enhancing the ability of women to contribute to leadership of the profession.

The first step must be continuing work to eradicate gender discrimination. Research studies and personal testimonies from women in the field all confirm that discrimination continues to exist. Special effort should be made to eliminate dual discrimination against women of color, immigrant women, lesbians, and those labeled too old or too young.

Beyond elimination of discrimination, views will differ regarding the exact meaning of equality. It will be necessary to address the tension between the concept of equality and different notions of women and management and to sort out the contradiction arising from the denial of gender difference on the one hand and the embrace of difference in managing racial and ethnic diversity on the other. We believe that the approach that values differences should be extended to all. This approach accepts and appreciates differences that result from gender as well as from culture and does not use such differences to deny legal or procedural equality.

Many of the barriers to women's advancement and success in management arise from organizational structures and approaches that conflict with the values and goals of social work. Improving women's access to and comfort level in management jobs requires redesign of agency policies and changes in the organizational culture defining appropriate management behavior. Examples of required changes include the adoption of "family friendly" workplace policies; assumption of power sharing as a norm, leading to increased involvement of staff and clients in agency decisions; openness to diverse contributions; and acceptance of a range of administrative strategies as situationally appropriate. Other structural changes might include setting targets for hiring or promoting women to management positions, an approach that has been successful in increasing female and racial/ethnic membership on boards and committees in the profession; establishing policies, procedures, and training to prevent discrimination and sexual harassment; and encouraging the development of mutual support and mentoring relationships for women.

The implications for social work education are clear. Courses in social work management should cover knowledge of and skills for implementing affirmative action programs and new personnel initiatives such as parental leave and flextime. Students should be given opportunities in the classroom and practicum to develop competence in the range of techniques used in participatory management approaches. Students should be helped to gain career development skills, including building a support network, using mentors, and long-range career planning. In one social work graduate program, students who took an elective course on women in administration reported that career planning had been especially helpful in clarifying interests and goals and setting priorities as they pursued management careers following graduation (Healy, Havens, & Chin, 1990). Finally, all students should be guided toward an examination of their own potential for leadership that integrates the skills, knowledge, and values of the social work profession.

Encouragement and further definition of a management style that is based on the values of the profession, the basic tenets of feminism, and the best new approaches to leadership is particularly relevant to the field of social work. The social agency of the future will face even stiffer competition for funds, clients, and qualified staff. A management style that stresses empowerment is not only congruent with the professional values of determination and change; it also offers the best prospect for shaping organizational climates to suit better service delivery. Creation of positive work environments will increasingly be necessary for human services agencies, not only to prevent the productivity loss of worker alienation but to stem the flight of social workers into private practice, a fact often attributed to the negative aspects of agency practice.

Moreover, if social agencies are to be led by social workers, agencies must try harder to recruit and promote women to top positions. The demographics of the profession are clear: Women are in the majority; the talent pool for leadership is overwhelmingly female. Thus, the competing perspectives on women in management converge. The high proportion of women in social work underscores the meritocracy argument calling for inclusion of women to ensure access to the best talent for leadership; ethical imperatives of the profession support the equity rationale of striving for fairness; and the complementary contributions perspective offers the prospect of positive changes in agency policy and practice through incorporating the best of the feminist model. All three perspectives call for increased attention to promoting the advance of women in social work management.

## REFERENCES

Adler, N. J., & Izraeli, D. N. (1988). Women in management worldwide. In N. J. Adler & D. N. Izraeli (Eds.), *Women in management worldwide* (pp. 1–16). Armonk, NY: M. E. Sharpe.

Bardwick, J. M., & Douvan, E. (1971). Ambivalence: The socialization of women. In V. Gornick & B. Morgan (Eds.), *Women in sexist society* (pp. 147–159). New York: Basic Books.

Bayes, J. (1987). *Do female managers in public bureaucracies manage with a different voice? Studies of bureaucracies in the United States and the State of California.* Paper presented at the American Political Science Association Convention, Chicago.

Benshoff, D. (1991). Getting there and staying there: Women as managers. In R. Edwards & J. A. Yankey (Eds.), *Skills for effective human services management* (pp. 171–185). Silver Spring, MD: National Association of Social Workers.

Brager, G., & Michael, J. A. (1969). The sex distribution in social work: Causes and consequences. *Social Casework, 50,* 595–601.

Broverman, I. K., & Broverman, D. M. (1970). Sex role stereotypes and clinical judgements of mental health. *Journal of Consulting and Clinical Psychology, 34,* 1–7.

Calkin, C. L. (1983). *Women administrators: A profile of their advancement.* Paper presented at the Annual Meeting of the Profession of the National Association of Social Workers, Washington, DC.

Chernesky, R. (1986). A new model of supervision. In N. Van Den Berg & L. B. Cooper (Eds.), *Feminist visions for social work* (pp. 128–148). Silver Spring, MD: National Association of Social Workers.

Chernesky, R. H., & Bombyk, M. J. (1988). Women's ways and effective management. *Affilia, 3*(1), 48–61.

Child Welfare League of America. (1990). *1990–91 Directory of member agencies.* Washington, DC: Author.

Chodorow, N. (1971). Being and doing: A cross-cultural examination of the socialization of males and females. In V. Gornick & B. Maron (Eds.), *Women in sexist society* (pp. 173–197). New York: Basic Books.

Civil Rights Act of 1964, P.L. 88-352, 78 Stat. 241.

Council on Social Work Education. (1994). *Directory of colleges and universities with accredited social work degree programs.* Alexandria, VA: Author.

Dean, V. (1991). Women in the workplace. In C. Lefcourt (Ed.), *Women and the law* (pp. 2-1–3-53). New York: Clark Boardman & Callaghan.

Donnell, S. M., & Hall, J. (1980). Men and women as managers: A significant case of no significant difference. *Organizational Dynamics, 8,* 60–70.

due Billing, Y. D., & Alvesson, M. (1987, July). *Women power and leadership.* Paper presented at the Third International Interdisciplinary Congress on Women, Dublin.

Edwards, R. L., & Gummer, B. (1988). Management of social services: Current perspectives and future trends. In P. R. Keys & L. H. Ginsberg (Eds.), *New management in the human services* (pp. 1–27). Silver Spring, MD: National Association of Social Workers.

Equal Pay Act of 1963, 29 U.S.C.A. §206.

Fagenson, E. (1993). *Women in management: Trends, issues, and challenges in managerial diversity.* Newbury Park, CA: Sage Publications.

Family Service Association of America. (1994). *Directory of member agencies in the United States and Canada.* Milwaukee: Author.

French, M. (1985). *Beyond power.* New York: Ballantine Books.

Garvin, D. A. (1991). Building a learning organization. *Harvard Business Review, 69*(6), 78–91.

Gerrard, M., Oliver, J. S., & Williams, M. (Eds.). (1976). Women in management. In *Proceedings of the conference: Women and men, colleagues in management.* Austin: University of Texas.

Gibelman, M., & Schervish, P. (1993a). The glass ceiling in social work: Is it shatterproof? *Affilia, 8*(4), 442–455.

Gibelman, M., & Schervish, P. (1993b). *Who we are: The social work labor force as reflected in the NASW membership.* Washington, DC: NASW Press.

Harragan, B. L. (1977). *Games mother never taught you.* New York: Warner Books.

Havens, C., & Healy, L. (1991a). Cabinet level appointees in Connecticut: Women making a difference. In D. Dodson (Ed.), *Gender and policymaking: Studies of women in office* (pp. 21–30). New Brunswick, NJ: Center for the Study of Women and Politics.

Havens, C., & Healy, L. (1991b). Do women make a difference? *Journal of State Government, 64*(2), 63–67.

Haynes, K. S. (1989). *Women managers in human services.* New York: Springer.

Healy, L. M., Havens, C. M., & Chin, A. (1990). Preparing women for human service administration: Building on experience. *Administration in Social Work, 14*(2), 79–93.

Hennig, M., & Jardim, A. (1977). *The managerial woman.* Garden City, NY: Anchor.

Hersey, P., & Blanchard, K. (1982). *Management of organizational behavior* (4th ed.). Englewood Cliffs, NJ: Prentice Hall.

Hesselbrock, M. (1992). *Salary differential based on gender in the membership of the Connecticut chapter of the National Association of Social Workers.* Unpublished manuscript.

Hill, A. (1992). *The nature of the beast.* Panel presentation on sexual harassment and policy making at the National Forum for Women Registrars, San Diego, CA.

Hochschild, A. (1989). *The second shift: Working parents and the revolution at home.* New York. Viking Press.

Hooyman, N. R., & Cunningham, R. (1986). An alternative administrative style. In N. Van Den Bergh & L. B. Cooper (Eds.), *Feminist visions for social work* (pp. 163–186). Silver Spring, MD: National Association of Social Workers.

Kadushin, A. (1976). Men in a women's profession. *Social Work, 21*, 441–447.

Kantor, R. M. (1989). Foreword. In L. J. Spence (Ed.), *Winning through participation: Meeting the challenge of corporate change with the technology of participation* (pp. xi–xiv). Dubuque, IA: Kendall/Hunt.

Kram, K. (1985). *Mentoring at work: Developmental relationships in organizational life.* Glenview, IL: Scott, Foresman.

Kravetz, D., & Austin, C. D. (1984). Women's issues in social service administration: The views and experiences of women administrators. *Administration in Social Work, 8*(4), 25–38.

Kravetz, D., & Jones, L. E. (1982). Career orientations of female social work students: An examination of sex differences. *Journal of Education for Social Work, 18*(3), 77–84.

Lambert, S. J. (1993, March). *Examining the career paths of men and women social workers.* Paper presented at the Annual Program Meeting of the Council on Social Work Education, New York.

Lee, C. (1994). The feminization of management. *Training 31*(11), 25–31.

Loden, M. (1985). *Feminine leadership.* New York: Times Books.

Mason, M. A. (1992). Standing still in the workplace: Women in social work and other female-dominated occupations. *Affilia, 7*(3), 23–43.

Maypole, D. (1986). Sexual harassment of social workers at work: Injustice within? *Social Work, 31,* 29–34.

Molloy, J. (1977). *The women's dress for success book.* New York: Warner Books.

National Association of Social Workers. (1994). *NASW code of ethics.* Washington, DC : Author.

Neuse, S. M. (1978). Professionalism and authority: Women in public service. *Public Administration Review, 38,* 436–441.

Noe, R. (1988). Women and mentoring: A review and research agenda. *Academy of Management Review, 13*(1), 65–78.

Odewahn, C. A., & Ezell, H. F. (1992). Attitudes towards women managers in human service agencies: Are they changing? *Administration in Social Work, 16*(2), 45–60.

Peace, W. H. (1991). The hard work of being a soft manager. *Harvard Business Review, 69*(6), 40–47.

Perlmutter, F. D. (1990). *Changing hats: From social work practice to administration.* Silver Spring, MD: National Association of Social Workers.

Powell, G. N. (1990). One more time: Do female and male managers differ? *Academy of Management Executives, 4*(3), 68–75.

Saltzstein, G. H. (1986). Female mayors and women in municipal jobs. *American Journal of Political Sciences, 39,* 140–164.

Schwartz, F. (1989). Management women and the new facts of life. *Harvard Business Review, 67*(1), 65–76.

Shapiro, R. Y., & Mahajan, H. (1986). Gender differences in policy preferences: A summary of trends from the 1960's to the 1980's. *Public Opinion Quarterly, 50,* 42–61.

Strobino, J., & McCoy, M. (1992). Recruitment, retention and promotion: Management issues related to salary equity. In L. M. Healy & B. P. Pine (Eds.), *Managers' choices: Compelling issues in the new decision environment* (pp. 27–43). Boca Raton, FL: National Network for Social Work Managers.

Szakacs, J. (1977, April). Survey indicates social work women losing ground in leadership. *NASW News*, p. 12.

Trempe, J., Rigny, A., & Haccoun, R. (1985). Subordinate satisfaction with male and female managers: Role of perceived supervisory influence. *Journal of Applied Psychology, 70,* 44–47.

Weil, M. (1988). Creating an alternative work culture in a public service setting: The Los Angeles sexual abuse program. In F. Perlmutter (Ed.), *Administration in alternative service settings* (pp. 69–82). Binghamton, NY: Haworth Press.

York, R. O., Henley, H. C., & Gamble, D. N. (1987). Sexual discrimination in social work: Is it salary or advancement? *Social Work, 32,* 336–339.

York, R., Henley, H. C., & Gamble, D. N. (1988). The power of positive mentors: Variables associated with women's interest in social work administration. *Journal of Social Work Education, 24,* 242–250.

# Mentoring and Networking in Human Services

**Michael J. Kelly and Kaitlin A. Post**

This chapter concerns two related management ideas—mentoring and networking. They are important because they are very effective, cost-efficient ways of changing how an organization operates and relates to the environment. They are related because they both use human relationships as agents of change. When an organization combines mentoring and networking, it becomes flexible and forward looking.

## WHAT IS MENTORING?

Mentoring is a relationship of growth, development, and sharing between two individuals. Over the course of time, the protégé (junior partner) grows from a novice to a peer who shares skills, knowledge, and interests with the mentor. The relationship is one of interaction between two individuals who bring different skills or knowledge and then learn from each other.

Mentoring comes in two forms: natural and formal. In natural mentoring, people pair up on their own and the organization does little except provide a supportive environment for career development activities. Many believe that this is the only true form of mentoring (Kram, 1983). The method has been avidly studied as a means of enabling women to succeed in the male-dominated business culture.

Formal mentoring is a program established by an organization to meet some of its developmental needs. In formal programs, the organization decides who will be mentors and protégés and how they will be paired. This is a relationship between two organizational roles. Some people believe that a good supervisor is a mentor, but formal mentoring goes beyond the supervisory relationship.

Traditionally, human services agencies have not placed a great deal of emphasis on human resource development. Most small agencies have only a few staff members who routinely take care of their own professional development. This same model of self-development is also practiced in larger agencies. The business community has always been concerned with competition and the need to develop quality, flexibility, and a competitive edge. Therefore, businesses invest a great deal of time, money, and effort in the attempt to improve staff quality and skills. Some businesses follow a self-replacement model, whereby individuals are not promoted until they have developed their own successors.

Mentoring is a very powerful, cost-effective human resource development tool. It provides a quick way to socialize new employees into the cultural norms of the organization, which helps reduce the high costs of employee turnover experienced by so many human services agencies. Buonocore (1987) suggested an "employee assimilation system" as one solution to employee turnover problems. Mentoring is also a good method for incorporating cultural diversity into the system. It improves communication within the organization because it provides feedback between two individuals on a regular basis. Indeed, the future belongs to organizations that are flexible and focused on quality, and mentoring is one way to infuse that philosophy throughout an organization.

Mentoring dates back to Greek mythology, where Mentor was the friend and tutor of Odysseus. A system of apprenticeship was used in ancient Babylon, Egypt, Greece, Rome, and modern Europe. Apprentices learned from experienced crafters and paid for the privilege by working for a specific number of years after their apprenticeship. The most talented of the young crafters were usually singled out to work under the direct tutelage of the master crafter and thereby received more assistance, advice, and support. For the purposes of this chapter, the following organizational definition of mentoring is used: It is a relationship between two individuals, one being more experienced than the other in terms of age, work history, or tenure with the organization, in which the senior partner provides advice, assistance, or opportunities to the other in excess of those provided in the normal supervisory or evaluative functions of the organization.

### Purpose

Mentoring is as variable as the individuals who are involved in the relationship. The depth of the relationship depends on the comfort level of both parties and the length of the relationship. It can range from something as simple as an occasional "parental" chat to an intense relationship that involves every aspect of professional life. However, there are basic, consistently described mentor functions: socialization, technological assistance, career advancement, and emotional support.

Socialization is one of the most important functions. It provides assistance in understanding the organization's culture. Culture, the sometimes bewildering array of unwritten and unspoken norms and values, must be assimilated before "membership" in an organization is granted. Buonocore (1987), for example, believed that socialization is so important that it should be a formal part of the orientation for new hires to reduce turnover. Socialization may also include networking with persons or groups outside the organization (Macaulay, 1986).

In technological matters mentors help build protégés' technical skills and provide opportunities for them to demonstrate their skills. This may be accomplished through direct teaching or through challenging assignments. The desire of protégés to develop competence and demonstrate specific skills is often complemented by the mentors' need to teach and become more of a generalist.

Career advancement is another very important function of the mentoring relationship. It may include information about opportunities, letters of reference, or sponsorship for advancement to a particular position. It is also a way to inform protégés that they have come of age. It is a recognition of achievement.

Emotional support encompasses acceptance, supportive criticism, and encouragement. It is a separate activity, but it is also interwoven with the other functions. Bowen (1985) included emotional support as part of his definition of mentoring; he described a relationship that requires a strong emotional commitment from both parties. The degree of emotional support will depend on the closeness and length of the relationship.

Mentoring relationships occur when both parties recognize some common interest and choose to pursue it. The relationship may begin with one party approaching the other, perhaps very tentatively, to explore the possibility of a closer relationship. Another way it can begin is through an active search by a protégé for mentor. Having a mentor may well be the surest and fastest way up the career ladder (Roche, 1979; Scandura, 1992; Wilbur, 1987).

Organizations adopt formal mentoring programs for a variety of reasons, the most important being the desire to effect change through the expansion of skill. The organizational benefits of mentoring are discussed in the next section. The basic components of a formal mentoring program include matching, creating relationship time, evaluation, and organizational sanction. Matching may be a voluntary process, or upper management may choose to assign individuals to the program. Either way, mentors and protégés are identified and paired. Next the mentors and protégés must have time together to develop a relationship. This time may be spent working on a specific project or exchanging information about careers and the organization. After the program has been in place for a length of time, it is evaluated for results and effectiveness. The most important step in a formal mentoring program is organizational sanction. This means that the organization comes to accept mentoring as an effective means of meeting its needs and encourages or requires individuals to participate in the program.

## Benefits

Mentoring has been around for a very long time, but only during the last 20 years has the phenomenon been studied. Why is mentoring popular? Several studies have found that mentoring in either the natural or formal form benefits the protégé, the mentor, and the organization. However, it has a cost: It takes time, commitment, and a lot of work.

Protégé benefits are specialized training, self-confidence, acceptance within the organization, and career advancement (Noe, 1988; Olian, Carroll, Giannantonio, & Feren, 1988; Vance, 1982; Wright & Wright, 1987). Studies have found that protégés earn more money and derive more pleasure from their work than people who have not been mentored (Riley & Wrench, 1985; Roche, 1979; Whitely, Dougherty, & Dreher, 1991). Another study found that protégés benefited from collaborative work with mentors (Wright & Wright, 1987). The mentor may model cultural norms, give challenging assignments, provide introduction to important social networks, and sponsor promotions (Macaulay, 1986). Although mentoring can create problems for the protégé—overdependence, jealousy of coworkers, and perceptions of romantic involvement (Burke, McKeen, & McKenna, 1993; Ragins & Cotton, 1991; Richey, Gambrill, & Blythe, 1988; Wright & Wright, 1987)—the studies indicate that the benefits outweigh the potential drawbacks, especially if the individuals exercise some caution in their choices.

The mentor benefits from the relationship as well. One of the greatest reported rewards is the personal satisfaction derived from watching the protégé develop abilities, self-confidence, and career opportunities. Mentors also benefit from professional development and the protégé's technical skills and new ideas (Wright & Wright, 1987). Mentors frequently use their protégés as a "sounding board" for new ideas and possibilities. The protégé's enthusiasm, more recent education, and fresh viewpoint may stimulate the mentor's creativity and generate new ideas or solutions to old problems. In some organizations, mentoring is recognized as an effective means for management development, and managers are rewarded for developing the management potential of other employees. As with protégés, there are potential negatives for the mentors. In cross-gender mentoring, the mentor may suffer from perceptions of romantic or sexual involvement, abuse of power, or the possibility of sexual harassment charges.

The organization can experience many benefits from either natural or formal mentoring relationships. In the case of formal mentoring, the program can be focused on a particular problem or series of problems. For instance, some organizations use mentoring programs to help reduce turnover by assigning mentors to new hires to facilitate the socialization process (Collin & Scott, 1978). The truly interesting aspect of mentoring, however, is its utility in working on a single problem from several perspectives. In the case of turnover, for example, a company may use mentoring to influence organizational knowledge that will reduce the stress level of new hires (Buonocore, 1987), to socialize new hires into the cultural norms more quickly (Collin & Scott, 1978), or to retrain employees after a merger (Zey, 1988).

Studies have reported numerous benefits to the organization, including reduced employee turnover; supplements to management training programs; provision of informal training in technical and people skills; enhanced organizational values, culture, and expectations; and attraction and retention of new hires in a tight labor market. Additional benefits include fulfillment of affirmative action goals, incorporation of people of color into the organizational structure, increased innovation and communication, higher productivity, and increased employee satisfaction (Collin & Scott, 1978; Fagenson, 1988; Zey, 1985, 1988). Studies have not reported any negative consequences for organizations with mentoring programs.

## WHAT IS NETWORKING?

Networking is the process of developing relationships with other people or groups outside the organization for the purpose of exchanging information about such issues as future regulations, the nature of services provided, additional services needed by a client population, or plans for expanded service. Information from outside the organization is valuable to planning and anticipating future needs and opportunities.

Networking has been around for a very long time. The original network was probably developed when cavemen first discovered that some individuals were better hunters or gatherers than they were and that if they were to share, everybody would be better off. Here, we focus on networking in the organizational setting and define the term as follows: *Networking* is a relationship between one individual and another individual, group, or organization that provides a reciprocal benefit in terms of information, advice, knowledge, or collaboration.

According to this definition, it would be possible for an individual to "network" with someone from a different organization to obtain a "mentor." Mentoring and networking are two closely related concepts based on relationships that are mutually beneficial. The benefit derived may explain why people have been mentoring and networking without any outside interference for hundreds of years.

Networking is an everyday activity in the business world, where information is the most valuable commodity. Business professionals are constantly seeking information regarding future regulations, competitors' plans, opportunities to collaborate, and potential new markets. It is the only way they can survive. In a recent unpublished study we conducted, we found that members of the business community routinely subscribed to journals related directly to their type of business, journals bearing on their professional role, and publications related to the general business and political environment. In contrast, individuals from human services agencies reported reading only the materials circulated by the organization.

Networking is accomplished in a number of ways to satisfy different goals. It includes studying information available from journals and other publications related to the specific service area. It also includes developing relationships with people or groups in organizations that are in the same field, are involved in serving clients, or have an impact on the organization's operation. By networking with other organizations one can develop an early warning system so that change can be addressed in a proactive manner. Networking also provides an opportunity to influence public perception of an organization. Most important, networking provides one with information about opportunities that might otherwise be missed.

Networking is one benefit that protégés may receive from a mentoring relationship. The mentor may arrange for the protégé to attend professional conferences (Wright, & Wright, 1987) or provide an introduction into important social networks inside and outside the organization. The mentor may also introduce the protégé to community leaders. Through networking, the mentor may help the protégé identify opportunities for career advancement. In addition, mentors can show protégés how they use networking as a natural part of performing their functions.

## HOW TO MANAGE A FORMAL MENTORING–NETWORKING PROGRAM

Networking and mentoring are very similar because they are both based on information exchanged between individuals. Both processes allow for the infusion of new ideas, perspectives, and possibilities for all parties. Because of these similarities, the two processes work very well together. The program design that is discussed next, a mentor–network program, incorporates career development, socialization, and environmental scanning all in one package. This section discusses how to design, implement, and evaluate a formal mentoring program with networking.

### Implementation

The first step in designing a mentoring project is for the organization to decide what it is trying to accomplish. Does it want to cut costs by reducing employee turnover? A good solution might be a mentoring program designed to socialize new hires. Is the organization having difficulties with communication and "turf" wars? A mentoring program that pairs mentors and protégés across functional or program lines could increase cooperation and appreciation between units. The objectives of the program are also important in the evaluation process.

The design of the program should include the nature of the commitment from mentors, protégés, and supervisors. Someone in the organization, preferably the manager, should be assigned to oversee the program. The time spent developing the mentoring relationship will mean that sometimes the protégé or the mentor will not be available for other assignments. Limits should be set on the amount of work time that will be assigned to the mentoring program. The expectation that mentors and protégés will work together in addition to their regular shifts should be clearly spelled out for all parties. If extra work assignments, meetings, or travel are part of the program, these should be clearly explained to all parties.

The organization must decide whether participation is voluntary or mandatory. Either way, it is important to include a way for participants to drop out without penalty. Any formal program must recognize that it is essentially forcing a relationship on two unacquainted individuals. There will be cases where the match does not work. There are other reasons that participants might wish to withdraw, such as a promotion of the mentor or changes in the family situation of either party. Whatever the reason for withdrawal, a plan that allows participants to drop out or be reassigned will minimize problems as the program continues.

The evaluation procedure should be designed before the program is started. It is best if a preprogram measure is used to allow comparative data analysis. Measures should be taken again during and after the program. A delayed measure of six months to a year after the program ends can gauge how well the program is achieving its objectives. Depending on the size of the organization, the measures can be as in-depth as a personal interview or a more easily administered written survey. A combination of personal interview and survey might provide the greatest amount of detailed information.

The optimum time to inform the entire organization about the program is after the program is designed but before participants are selected. A mentoring program by its nature will cause anxiety among some of the personnel. Some of the common fears include interpreting selection as a protégé as an indication of poor work performance or future promotions, or interpreting nonselection as mentors as exclusions from upward career mobility. Therefore, the information that is circulated should be very clear about the program objectives, the nature of the commitment expected of the participants, the selection process that will be used, and the limits of the program.

The objectives chosen for the program will also define the participant pool. If new and recent hires are targeted to increase retention, then the protégés will be known, but mentors will have to be selected. There are a number of things to consider at this point. The number of participants is important and will be determined by the size of the organization. In smaller organizations, a mentor might be assigned each time a new employee is hired. In a large organization, however, it might be necessary to assign mentors only to a certain percentage of new hires or only to positions that have a consistent history of turnover.

Mentors must be selected carefully. They should be two or three position levels higher than protégés and not in the direct line of supervision. Positioning is important from two perspectives. If the mentors are too high in the organization, the protégés will not feel comfortable discussing or working on issues related to their positions. If the mentors are at the same level as the protégés' supervisors, power issues can become a problem between mentors and the supervisor. According to several studies, cross-gender mentoring carries the highest level of real or perceived risk for both the mentor and the protégé. The culture and opportunities within the organization will have to determine the issue of cross-gender mentoring.

After the mentors and protégés have been selected, they must be "matched." The individuals who decide the matches should consider first the objectives of the program, then work experience, gender, age differences, management or leadership styles, and personal interests. The greater the knowledge of the participants, the greater the likelihood that the matches will be successful. Whenever possible, the mentors and protégés should be given two or three potential matches to choose between. Once the matches are decided, the participants should be notified.

It is very difficult for two people who are not acquainted to join together in what is largely a speculative venture. Holding a start-up meeting can greatly speed the process of relationship building. The meeting is an opportunity for mentors and protégés to get acquainted. The meeting should include a review of program expectations and allow time for questions to be discussed. It may be necessary to preempt possible reservations of the group by making some comments about potential drawbacks of participation. The meeting can also be an opportunity for the mentors and protégés to become acquainted with other working pairs that can serve as a support group in case any problems occur. The start-up meeting is an excellent time to make the necessary arrangements for the next evaluation component.

After the mentors and protégés have been introduced and instructed to begin, there is very little for the organization to do. The relationships must find their own ground and begin to grow. However, feedback throughout the program is very important. An informal chat in the hallway or an occasional phone call can help identify problems early and allow for any necessary corrections.

### Evaluation

The evaluation should include two basic components. First, how well did the program achieve the organizational objectives established at the beginning of the program? It should be clear that if the program was developed to increase participation by people of color in administrative functions but participation did not increase, the program was not a success. Second, what is the satisfaction level of the program participants? If the program achieved the organizational objectives, then it would be desirable to continue the program for several years. Participant satisfaction can have a major impact on the willingness of others to participate in future programs. If the program was successful in both areas, then it could be incorporated into the structure of the organization. New protégés and mentors could be matched at regular intervals as more experienced pairs graduate. Former protégés usually make excellent mentors because of their fresh experiences in the program.

A mentoring relationship is unfair in the sense that one person cannot treat all people equally. However, it is eminently fair in that anyone who wants a mentor can have one; they just have to look and be open to possibilities. A mentor does not have to belong to the same organization as the protégé. In fact, some of the best mentoring relationships are those that include an outside influence. The different perspective allows a greater depth and breadth to the relationship, and the relationship is less likely to end because of a transfer or a promotion.

A mentoring relationship may change over time. The change may be abrupt, as in the case of a physical move to another part of the country or a change of employment by either party. Or it may be a gradual change as the protégé develops in abilities, skills, and knowledge. The relationship may slowly shift from one of mentor helping protégé to one of colleague helping colleague. Darling (1985) used the term "peer mentoring" to describe the change to a relationship between colleagues. Many mentors and protégés continue to maintain contact many years after the mentoring relationship has ended.

## REFERENCES

Bowen, D. D. (1985). Were men meant to mentor women? *Training and Development Journal, 39,* 30–34.

Buonocore, A. J. (1987). Reducing turnover of new hires. *Management Solutions, 32,* 5–10.

Burke, R., McKeen, C., & McKenna, C. (1993). Correlates of mentoring in organizations: The mentor's perspective. *Psychological Reports, 72,* 883–896.

Collin, E. G., & Scott, P. (1978). Everyone who makes it has a mentor. *Harvard Business Review, 56,* 89–101.

Darling, L. A. (1985). Endings in mentor relationships. *Journal of Nursing Administration, 15,* 40–41.

Fagenson, E. A. (1988). The power of a mentor. *Group and Organization Studies, 13,* 182–194.

Kram, K. E. (1983). Phases of the mentor relationship. *Academy of Management Journal, 26,* 608–625.

Macaulay, S. (1986). The judge as mentor: A personal memoir. *Journal of Legal Education, 36,* 144–149.

Noe, R. (1988). An investigation of the determinants of successful assigned mentoring relationships. *Personnel Psychology, 41,* 457–479.

Olian, J., Carroll, S., Giannantonio, C., & Feren, D. (1988). What do protégés look for in a mentor? Results of three experimental studies. *Journal of Vocational Behavior, 33,* 15–37.

Ragins, B., & Cotton, J. (1991). Easier said than done: Gender differences in perceived barriers to gaining a mentor. *Academy of Management Journal, 34,* 939–951.

Richey, C., Gambrill, E., & Blythe, B. (1988). Mentor relationships among women in academe. *Affilia, 3*(1), 34–47.

Riley, S., & Wrench, D. (1985). Mentoring among women lawyers. *Journal of Applied Social Psychology, 15,* 374–386.

Roche, G. R. (1979). Much ado about mentors. *Harvard Business Review, 57,* 14–28.

Scandura, T. A. (1992). Mentorship and career mobility: An empirical investigation. *Journal of Organization Behavior, 13,* 169–174.

Vance, C. N. (1982). The mentor connection. *Journal of Nursing Administration, 12,* 7–13.

Whitely, W., Dougherty, T., & Dreher, G. (1991). Relationship of career mentoring and socioeconomic origin to managers' and professionals' career progress. *Academy of Management Journal, 34,* 331–351.

Wilbur, J. (1987). Does mentoring breed success? *Training and Development Journal, 41,* 38–41.

Wright, C. A., & Wright, S. D. (1987). The role of mentors in the career development of young professionals. *Family Relations, 36,* 204–208.

Zey, M. G. (1985). Mentor programs: Making the right moves. *Personnel Journal, 64,* 53–57.

Zey, M. G. (1988). A mentor for all reasons. *Personnel Journal, 67,* 49–51.

# Chapter 10

# Japanese Quality Management Techniques

**Paul R. Keys**

merican hu-

man services agencies confront numerous management

problems that impede effective delivery of services to

clients. One model that might help to overcome many of

these difficulties is derived from management techniques

used by Japanese public and private social welfare agen-

cies. Useful Japanese processes include traditional

and formal participatory management practices, lifelong training, and participation by service workers in most agency decisions. Benefits of these practices

*This chapter is based on an exploratory study by the author of management practices in Japanese public and nonprofit human services organizations. The study was supported by the Japan–U.S. GARIOA/Fulbright Commission/Fulbright Program. At the time, the author was a GARIOA/Fulbright Senior Research Scholar of the Faculty of Integrated Arts and Social Sciences, Department of Social Welfare, Japan Women's University, Tokyo. This article is taken from that research:* "A Study of Japanese Management Applications to American Public and Nonprofit Health and Human Services Organizations."

include improved communications, a high quality of client services, and high employee agreement with the principles and values of the service agency. Keys (1988) examined the use of Japanese management practices and found that their selective use in American human services agencies can make an important contribution to more effective management. However, more research is needed to determine the proper uses and the appropriate tools in this vital area.

## ANALYSIS OF THE PROBLEM

There are serious agency management problems in contemporary human services organizations. Some of these problems are especially prevalent in large, public agencies; others are more apparent in nonprofit agencies. The chief problem areas include:

- poor staff morale, resulting in absenteeism, tardiness, favoritism, apathy, and high staff turnover (Turnover approaches 100 percent in units of some large, public, child welfare agencies.)
- fragmentation of effort, duplication of services, and low productivity in deliverable service to clients.

A close examination of these problems reveals that the underlying causes have to do with the following interrelated areas:

- lack of creativity and fear of innovation on the part of managers and directors
- lack of information and insufficient communication channels among management, staff, and field workers
- limited staff involvement in agency decision making
- lack of training and too narrow an understanding by many employees of their roles in the organization. (This in turn results from narrowly defined job descriptions that inhibit inventive solutions to social service problems across department lines; narrow job descriptions cause staff to treat client and organizational problems alike as a series of separate, isolated, issues; holistic, comprehensive approaches are, therefore, inhibited.)

One of my own observations illustrates some of these issues. An executive director of a large and well-respected residential treatment facility attempted to maintain an extremely tight rein on her managers and employees. She attempted to "prevent problems from occurring." But this management style did not allow top managers to make decisions without prior approval. The executive director supervised an extremely talented group of associate directors and department heads. Fearing her disapproval, however, they did not experiment with new, and perhaps controversial, treatment approaches. They mostly carried out her directions to the letter with little dialogue. Because of the centralized authoritarian management climate, there was much currying of favor, and continual conflict among various factions within the staff. Morale was poor. Unfavorable information was withheld from management by supervisors, although this information would have facilitated more-effective problem solving and decision making. Client services suffered. Staff began to unionize for protection.

In my experience, these problems are quite common in some larger nonprofit agencies. Frequently staff have the opinion that top management do not recognize problems of line workers "in the trenches" or do not care about them. Such organizational problems in the administration of human services organizations must be resolved.

The lack of proper staff orientation and training creates other problems are created that affect client service delivery. Too often staff receive only minimal agency-sponsored training and development. Lack of training can indirectly affect clients through high turnover. The most innovative, sensitive, caring, and effective staff are often the first to leave under adverse conditions. Failure to address management and training issues can quickly lead to alienation, staff burnout, absenteeism, and tardiness as staff believe that management do not listen or care.

In large agencies, other problems include a lack of information, which impedes the staff's ability to do assigned work. Too little information leads to less staff ownership and involvement in plans, policies, and decisions. It furthers an "us versus them" mentality. Lack of information, commitment, and poor morale leads to a narrowly focused understanding by staff of their role in operating the organization. An inevitable result is that clients suffer from unsatisfactory services.

Inadequate funding may be the source of many service difficulties, but lack of commitment by staff aggravates an already poor situation. Given the existing management attitudes just described, staff commitment to problem solving and delivery of quality services becomes almost nonexistent. Moreover, there is little team spirit in such organizations.

Are there solutions in the international social welfare arena to these issues and problems? My research on Japanese management practices suggests that there are. Japanese management, training, and human resources techniques emphasize motivation, innovation, quality, and full staff participation in decision making and problem solving. They also emphasize continual, comprehensive, and intensive employee training in the principles, values, and beliefs of the organization. Moreover, they emphasize employee group processes, teamwork concepts, and mobility assignments to remove artificial barriers to comprehensive client services.

This article is the result of an exploratory research study of Japanese social welfare management practices. It examines management ideas and practices used in Japanese social welfare agencies that may be useful to American nonprofit agencies.

## JAPANESE MANAGEMENT PRACTICES

Many management practices used by Japanese social welfare agencies directly address American social agency management problems. Among these are the following (Keys, 1991):

1. *Flexible job descriptions.* Japanese business and human services organizations allow a great deal of latitude across individual and organizational lines. This flexibility allows adaptability in job duties and responsibilities as well as quick response to client service needs. Although agencies may have extremely rigid boundaries among units, they use very general and flexible job descriptions to avoid limiting the problem-solving abilities of employees. Flexible responsibilities encourage proactive response to problems across organizational lines wherever they occur in an agency. Flexibility avoids the "not in my job description" syndrome often heard in American human services agencies, where employees refuse to concern themselves with problems not specifically assigned.

2. *Use of* Nemawashi *informal decision-making processes. Nemawashi* is a Japanese word that means "cultivating the roots." It is emblematic of Japanese participatory management processes. It consists of informal discussions and compromises that precede formal meetings and pave the way for a consensus that everyone in the agency can actively support. Not all employees are consulted in advance, but the process does lay the groundwork for securing support from key staff persons. Consequently, key persons are allowed to participate and to suggest changes in discussions of matters that affect them. In Japanese circles, the process of formal recognition and consultation may be more important than the actual content of the process. Consultation is proof of the respect and importance given the participant in the organization. *Nemawashi* is similar to preselling or "private negotiation" in the United States. In Western management, however, a decision may take place without prior discussion or participation of those affected. Often, management "just decides" the matter for the entire organization.

Employees in American public social services agencies often work under strict top-down, authoritarian managements. These allow little room for discussion, participation, or bottom-up suggestions. Employees, however, are fully aware of the "roadblocks" and "monkey wrenches" that they can throw into a system to block action where they disagree or have no voice. *Nemawashi* helps management avoid such situations.

3. *The* Ringi *decision-making process.* A typical Japanese organization circulates a *Ringi-sho*—a written memo—which serves as a communications device and as evidence of prior discussion and distribution of a decision. Although the real decision may be made in another forum (for example, through *nemawashi*), those at the top initiate the *ringi* process to promote their ideas and program directions. Lower-level employees may then prove the details or workability of the idea. Members of the organization affected by the decision read and place their personal seal (called a *hanko,* a small rubber signature stamp) on the *ringi* document. The *ringi* is evidence of staff consensus to top management decisions. Ratification can be quick, automatic, and relatively free from later conflict. Carrying out a decision can be similarly swift and relatively free of employee ill will and potential sabotage.

"Top Management sits" is a notion often used to describe the *ringi* process. It means that, frequently, top management wait until line staff have reached a consensus before formally adopting a position. The *ringi* process communicates impending decisions to all who may be affected, thus allowing for necessary changes and securing enough cooperation to take almost immediate action. In Western management circles, the most frequent objection to Japanese management processes is that they "take too much time." This objection ignores the (often long) delays caused in Western systems by employee discontent with decisions. Resistance to top-down directives may continue for months or years where consensus has not been created by management.

4. *Promotion of the* wa. This process is roughly equivalent to the American concept of creating or maintaining morale. *Wa,* meaning "unity," is a by-product of many Japanese social welfare organizational practices designed to foster group consensus and harmony in the workplace. The Japanese call the product of these processes and activities "maintaining the *wa.*" Among devices used are various comprehensive, lifelong, training strategies (described below).

The chief goal of Japanese training strategies is not only to impart knowledge but to allow employees to get to know each other on a personal level and to impart the values and philosophy of the organization to the employee. Such training is designed to avoid workplace conflicts, foster teamwork, and create an informal support system for each employee.

5. *Job reassignment and rotation.* Contemporary thinking in Japan is that any employee may be retrained to do any job. Accordingly, there are fewer and lower boundaries between and among jobs than in America. In

Japan, systematic training policies familiarize employees with one another's jobs. These policies take the form of job rotation or job reassignments.

*Jinji-idó* describes the process of planned and routine rotation and reassignment of employees to various jobs. *Amakudari* and *shukko* are specific types of reassignments and job rotations. In Japanese social welfare, *amakudari* is the process by which a manager is retired from a social welfare–related government agency, often the funding source, to take a major management position in a public or nongovernmental social agency. The employee generally retires and does not usually return to the former agency. That manager is said to "descend from heaven" and is called an *amakudari* employee.

A *shukko* employee rotates to an affiliated organization. *Shukko* employees may later return to the former organization. Job rotation in large social welfare agencies is usually a sign of eventual promotion of an employee.

An American counterpart to these practices would be for a secretary of a state public welfare agency to require all top state managers (including himself) to spend one week per year as interns at a county social service department, for training and familiarization with local agency concerns and problems. "Loaned" employees would work on service and client issues, including direct client contact. Such a practice would be analogous to the Japanese *shukko* process.

An example of a similar American practice would be for a director of a local job training agency to require each department head to trade places annually with another department head in the same agency. This, too, would foster teamwork and joint problem solving during the rest of the year. Each director would better understand the problems and needs of other directors.

6. *Extensive training.* Comprehensive and lifelong training is another feature of Japanese agencies and business organizations. Such training takes many forms and combines social and formal features. The chief executive begins the training process with a formal recognition ceremony for new employees that includes a speech. Within a few weeks, a welcoming party, called a *kangei-kai,* is given for newcomers to meet other employees. A *kangei-kai* is more than a social event; it is a ceremony designed to show the new arrivals that they are now a part of the "family." It begins with formal and personal introductions to the people with whom they will work. Typically, in Japan, this affiliation is for life (though in actuality it is until retirement). The same is true of social welfare organizations.

In some organizations, an overnight social excursion and retreat called a *gasshuku* follows the newcomer's *kangei-kai*. The *gasshuku* gives new employees an in-depth orientation to the organization, including organizational values, ways of operation, history, and traditions. Not all social welfare organizations sponsor a *gasshuku,* but intensive training and some overnight training retreats are very common.

Later in the year, there may be another overnight social excursion, called a *shain-ryokó. Shain-ryokó* is an annual event that traditionally includes sight-seeing, a banquet, and much social interaction.

Some nonprofit Japanese agencies have adopted the Japanese business practice of the morning pep talk (*chórei*). This is a daily discussion of the *shaze* or *shakun.* The *shaze* refers to values and the *shakun* to the principles by which the organization operates. These activities are not the "morning exercises" depicted in American movies of Japanese corporations. In social welfare agencies, the gathering is often a serious discussion of client treatment principles. The discussion or lecture may include examples of the values and philosophy of the agency in operation. For example, if independence and self-sufficiency are the desired service goals, examples of how employees should meet the goals would be briefly discussed. *Chórei* is a communications device for imparting agency information. It can also be a means of spurring employees on.

7. *Total quality control (TQC)–total quality management (TQM).* Total quality control is the literal translation of the Japanese term for total quality management now popular in American business, government agencies, and some nonprofit organizations. American management theorists have added some features that distinguish TQM from the purely Japanese system. They now refer to it as continuous quality improvement or business process improvement. TQC is a business technique that is not used by Japanese social welfare organizations.

A "quality circle" (QC) is a group or team process designed to improve work procedures and reduce problems. (With the advent of TQM and business process improvement, these are now often called "multifunctional" or "cross-functional teams.") This process entails periodic staff meetings that involve examining and suggesting work improvements to their superiors. Line workers rather than supervisors or managers usually chair these meetings. Usually, a prior commitment is given by top management to examine QC suggestions and to implement those that are appropriate. The QC team receives feedback regarding the implementation of its suggestions based on employee opinion.

In an American social welfare agency, TQM would involve many of the Japanese management and training principles with the addition of agreed-upon, statistically measurable goals. It would include various levels of line and management employee teams (called "functional job improvement teams," or QC teams) to figure out the needs of the organization and how to respond to them. Such teams would also monitor achievement of agreed-upon quality goals. Development of an organizationwide plan with regular reports and statistical monitoring devices is among the many techniques used for TQM.

Unions in Japanese organizations usually provide strong support for management techniques. Japanese unions are weak compared with their U.S. counterparts. Unions are organized along company lines (company unions) rather than by industry as they are in the United States. Alston (1986) discussed the role of Japanese unions in depth.

### IMPLEMENTATION IN JAPAN AND IN THE UNITED STATES

Japanese social welfare agencies use many principles and practices of business organizations, albeit with subtle changes designed to meet unique social welfare agency needs. For example, Japanese agencies report extensive use of the *ringi* process and *nemawashi* and some use of lifetime employment practices. Training practices discussed previously are similarly popular with Japanese agencies. Use of welcoming parties, formal new staff orientation ceremonies, overnight retreats, and the like are routine. Moreover, these orientations and training practices seem to be quite popular with staff because they are enjoyable, social, and partylike.

Japanese agencies also use various forms of *chorei* (morning lectures) each day. Some directors give a five-minute talk to staff on the mission and service philosophy of the agency. Other directors discuss their philosophy of client relations in detail. Still others use the occasion for mutual discussion of staff issues or as a time to discuss general agency issues.

Japanese human services managers change these practices to accommodate the differences between their agencies and businesses. For example, adoption of some management practices will depend on agency size. Typically, large public agencies will routinely transfer or rotate managers, but smaller nongovernment agencies may not have enough staff for this type of training. QC is not popular in Japanese agencies. There are, however, some inconclusive reports of QC experiments in hospital settings.

In the American context, objection may be raised to the use of Japanese principles and practices because of cultural differences. It is clear, however, from their successful use in purely American businesses that *some* principles, such as training and participatory management, have universal appeal and can be effectively used in any workplace. Participatory management processes outlined in this chapter differ little from similar, purely American techniques and processes. The popular book by Peters and Austin (1985), *A Passion for Excellence: The Leadership Difference,* promoted these practices in the United States. Other authors have proposed similar participatory management principles for efficient and effective organizations.

Not all principles and practices of Japanese management are appropriate for American social welfare agencies. Some principles are effective, including the use of more general job descriptions, the *ringi* process, use of participatory management styles, and use of informal consensus-building processes (*nemawashi*) (Alston, 1986; Ouchi, 1982). Comprehensive training practices, including job rotation, can reduce some American social welfare agency issues, such as poor morale, employee resistance to change, high turnover, and limited staff involvement in suggesting improvements. Consensus or morale-building practices such as those that maintain the *wa* are also workable. Indeed, there is some association between use of *nemawashi* and job retention and use of *kangei-kai* welcoming parties and improved employee morale and job satisfaction.

## CONCLUSION

American human services agencies face many managerial obstacles that impede effective delivery of services to clients. These are well documented in the social work literature. New approaches are needed to overcome these barriers to services delivery in both public and private agencies. Japanese participatory management, human resources, and training concepts address many of these matters and can be useful to managers in child and family services and, more generally, in social services agencies in the United States.

Traditional management techniques used by Japanese social welfare agencies to foster harmony and participation in the workplace may be useful devices for innovative American agency executives. Although not universally applicable, these ideas and techniques do hold promise for helping resolve specific agency management issues in the United States.

## REFERENCES

Alston, J. P. (1986). *The American Samurai: Blending American and Japanese managerial practices.* New York: Walter de Gruyter.

Keys, P. R. (1988). New management in action: A case study. In P. R. Keys & L. H. Ginsberg (Eds.), *New management in human services* (pp. 133–166). Silver Spring, MD: National Association of Social Workers.

Keys, P. R. (1991). *An exploratory study of Japanese management practices of benefit to American human services organizations.* Tokyo: Japan–U.S. Educational Commission Fulbright Program.

Ouchi, W. (1982). *Theory Z.* Reading, MA: Addison-Wesley.

Peters, T., & Austin, N. (1985). *A passion for excellence: The leadership difference.* New York: Random House.

# Chapter 11

# Total Quality Management in Health Care Settings

## *A Preliminary Framework for Successful Implementation*

Erin    Morrissey    and
Abraham    Wandersman

T he health care in-
dustry faces the challenges of finding a means to contain rising costs, excessive waiting times, and allegedly
high error rates (Berwick, Godfrey, & Roessner, 1990).
To meet these challenges, many organizations have
begun to implement a system of continuous quality
improvement, such as total quality management

(TQM). TQM is also referred to as total quality leadership to underscore the importance of the involvement of all levels of the organization, not just management (personal communication with L. Solow, consultant, September 7, 1994). TQM is described as a "strategic integrated management system for achieving customer satisfaction" (Federal Quality Institute, 1990, cited in Rago & Reid, 1991, p. 253). When TQM principles are applied to health care processes, the increase in quality service can bring both a reduction in costs and an increase in employee motivation (Anderson & Daigh, 1991).

This chapter provides an organizing framework for the successful implementation of TQM in hospital settings. To do so, it will be necessary to lay the foundation for the framework, beginning with a brief review of the standards of care set by the Joint Commission on Accreditation of Healthcare Organizations (JCAHO). The main principles of TQM and some barriers to TQM implementation in health care are also discussed, and a framework for the application of TQM to hospitals is presented that identifies the fundamental components of successful TQM implementation.

## THE QUALITY MOVEMENT IN HEALTH CARE

Although TQM has only recently begun to be implemented in hospital settings, the importance of setting standards for quality has long been recognized in health care organizations. At the Third Clinical Congress of Surgeons of North America in 1912, it was decided that some system of standardization of both hospital equipment and care should be developed that would ensure delivery of quality service. To this end, the American College of Surgeons (ACS) published *The Minimum Standard* in 1917, which outlined the criteria for the evaluation of medical care. In 1918 the ACS initiated a voluntary accreditation program called the Hospital Standardization Program (HSP), which recognized those institutions that met the specified standards (Shanahan, 1983).

By the 1950s the HSP had grown considerably, and the cost of operation was too burdensome for the ACS. In 1951 the Joint Commission of Accreditation of Hospitals was established by the joint efforts of the ACS, the American College of Physicians, the American Hospital Association, the American Medical Association, and later, the American Dental Association. Over the next 40 years JCAHO continued to raise standards of quality and to improve evaluation techniques (see Table 11-1).

In 1953 the hospital commission published the *Standards for Hospital Accreditation,* which was a revised and expanded version of *The Minimum Standard.* However, from 1953 through 1975, the standards outlined the expectations of quality only in general terms and did not provide specific

TABLE 11-1

# Evolution of Health Care Quality Standards and Quality Evaluation Approaches

| TIME PERIOD | QUALITY STANDARD PROGRAM | EVALUATION APPROACH |
|---|---|---|
| 1917–1952 | Minimum standard | Medical record review |
| 1953–1975 | Standards for hospital accreditation | Morbidity and mortality review |
| 1975–1978 | Quality of professional services | Retrospective medical audits |
| 1979–1991 | Quality assurance | Ongoing organizationwide 10-step evaluation process |
| 1992–present | Quality assessment and improvement | Integrated system of continuous quality improvement |

guidelines to use in the assessment and improvement of quality (JCAHO, 1991). During this time, hospital reviews tended to focus on specific cases of unacceptable practice and used such indicators as morbidity and mortality data. In 1975 the Joint Commission raised the standards from "minimal essential" to "optimal achievable" and published them as the *Quality of Professional Services* (QPS; Shanahan, 1983). This set of standards implied that an end level of optimum quality exists. Quality service, then, would be defined as consistently performing at this optimum level. The standard also required that the optimal care should be documented, generally through "retrospective, outcome-focused, time-limited audits of care" (JCAHO, 1991). However, health care professionals realized that medical audit requirements were too limiting and did not allow for more meaningful evaluations of staff and patient perceptions of the quality of service (JCAHO, 1991).

In 1979 the Joint Commission eliminated the QPS section and the numerical requirements for audit, replacing them with new standards for hospitals based on quality assurance (QA; Shanahan, 1983). Whereas the QPS standards were problem focused and emphasized individual and departmental accountability, the new QA standards emphasized a coordinated, organizationwide system (JCAHO, 1991). However, a lack of methodology made the design and implementation of a hospitalwide effort an overwhelming challenge in many hospitals. In 1985 a set of standards for a systematic ongoing monitoring and evaluation process was published, which outlined a 10-step process of quality assurance. Many hospitals ran into difficulties implementing the 10 steps, citing such issues as inadequate indicators of quality, deficient interdepartmental activities, and the perception that quality assurance was performed only to appease the Joint Commission (JCAHO, 1991).

A solution to these problems was soon discovered outside the field of health care, in the total quality movement that had long been successful in Japan and had recently been growing in American industry. In 1987 the National Demonstration Project on Quality Improvement in Health Care showed a high rate of success in improving quality and lowering costs, thus indicating that both the philosophy and the tools of quality improvement are effective in the health care industry (Berwick et al., 1990; JCAHO, 1991). With such a promising new system, JCAHO formed the Organizational and Managerial Indicators Task Force, chaired by Bill Dowling, to begin planning its new approach to quality improvement. The task force involved a number of administrators, most notably Paul Batalden, who challenged the members of the committee to think in terms of continuous quality improvement (CQI) and who influenced the Joint Commission's decision to adopt a CQI/TQM approach to quality (personal communication with Professor A. D. Kaluzny, University of North Carolina at Chapel Hill, August 8, 1994). JCAHO introduced the Agenda for Change, which included multiyear initiatives for quality improvement and in 1992 renamed the quality assurance chapter of the *Accreditation Manual for Hospitals* "Quality Assessment and Improvement" (JCHAO, 1991). Currently, JCAHO accreditation standards require the implementation of TQM, or a similar quality-focused program, designed to promote continuous improvement in hospital performance and quality.

### PROMISES AND PRINCIPLES OF TQM

The basic premise of TQM in hospitals is that an improvement in quality service can effect an improvement in customer satisfaction, employee relations, and motivation as well as a reduction in costs (Anderson & Daigh, 1991; Melum & Sinioris, 1992). However, the implementation of TQM principles requires a revised management philosophy and a change in organizational culture that will foster employee involvement and commitment to continuously search for ways to improve the organization's processes and services.

There have been a number of influential contributors to the TQM movement (Crosby, 1984; Deming, 1986; J. M. Juran, 1989), each of whom has identified essential tenets of TQM implementation (Table 11-2). According to TQM, organizations are advised to focus their efforts on customer satisfaction, identify problem areas by measuring both work processes and outcomes, empower employees to continually improve work processes, understand and monitor work processes to prevent error and rework, and improve systems functioning as a more efficient means to quality improvement (Osborne, 1992). According to Deming, the efficiency of a focus on systems functioning stems from the 85–15 rule, which holds that 85 percent of all problems stem from faulty systems and only 15 percent derive from an individual person or thing (Walton, 1990).

## BARRIERS TO TQM IMPLEMENTATION

For all the promise that a TQM philosophy holds for health care organizations, many obstacles must be overcome before TQM is truly effective. For example, some employees may believe that involvement in TQM simply creates more work with little payoff (Gaucher & Kratochwill, 1991), and others may regard TQM activities as "just another program." Indeed, the history of the JCAHO (Table 11-1) with its many quality programs reinforces this attitude. Therefore, an important early step in the implementation process is convincing management and staff that TQM is here to stay and that it will become permanently integrated into the organization's daily functioning.

Another barrier to TQM may arise from lack of genuine support by some members of mid- and upper-level management. Deming (1986) stated that the job of management goes beyond supervision to a focus on strong leadership and therefore management must have knowledge about, and be actively involved in, quality. Thus, managers must solidify their commitment to quality by "walking the talk" (personal communication with L. Solow, consultant, July 10, 1994). This phrase emphasizes the notion that managers must integrate TQM philosophies and techniques into their own daily routine before they can expect their staff to adopt such behavior. Organizations that expect good outcomes yet invest minimal efforts toward authentic implementation will see poor outcomes. Many companies do not see results because they do not integrate quality programs with their daily operations. Sometimes TQM is introduced as a special project with separate objectives and activities (Vanderpool, cited in Fuchsberg, 1992). For TQM to prosper, it must be fully integrated into operations and become not just another project, but a comprehensive process for meeting all of the organization's service objectives.

# Contributions of the Experts to Total Quality Management

| DEMING'S (1986) 14 POINTS | J. M. JURAN'S (1989) TRILOGY | CROSBY'S (1984) "FOUR ABSOLUTES" |
|---|---|---|
| 1. Create constancy of purpose. | *Quality planning* | *The first absolute: The definition of quality is conformance to requirements.* |
| 2. Adopt the new philosophy. | 1. Define your customers. | |
| 3. Cease dependence on mass inspection to achieve quality. | 2. Define customer needs. | |
| | 3. Design products and services to respond to customer needs. | The key to quality improvement is to "do it right the first time" (DIRFT). |
| 4. End the practice of awarding business on price tag alone. | | |
| 5. Improve constantly. | 4. Transfer the plans to the operating workforces. | *The second absolute: The system of quality is prevention.* |
| 6. Institute training on the job. | | |
| 7. Institute leadership. | *Quality control* | |
| 8. Drive out fear. | 1. Evaluate actual performance. | Prevention involves understanding and monitoring the process so the errors do not occur in the first place. |
| 9. Break down barriers between departments. | 2. Compare actual performance with quality goals. | |
| 10. Eliminate slogans, exhortations, and numerical targets. | 3. Act on the difference. | *The third absolute: The performance standard is zero defects.* |
| 11. Eliminate work standards (quotas) and management by objective. | *Quality improvement* | |
| | 1. Establish the necessary infrastructure to assure quality improvement. | The message of "that's close enough" will encourage people not to strive for quality. |
| 12. Remove barriers that rob workers, engineers, and managers of their right to pride of workmanship. | 2. Identify specific improvement projects. | |
| | 3. Establish project improvement teams. | *The fourth absolute: The measurement of quality is the price of nonconformance.* |
| 13. Institute a vigorous program of education and self-improvement. | 4. Provide resources, motivation, and training to teams. | |
| 14. Put everyone in the company to work to accomplish the transformation. | 5. Teams execute process improvement. | This price includes "all expenses involved in doing things wrong." Quality will cut these expenses. |

NOTE: Based on Deming, W. E. (1986). *Out of the crisis.* Cambridge, MA: MIT Press. Juran J. M. (1989). *Juran on leadership for quality.* New York: Free Press. Crosby P. B. (1984). *Quality without fears.* New York: McGraw-Hill.

Hospitals are often particularly resistant to the concept of empowerment, largely because of a traditionally hierarchical power structure and the individualistic nature of the physician's job. Management is often threatened by empowerment because of the perception that it forces transfer of some power and job functions to employees. Some managers may perceive this as working themselves out of a job. Organizational leaders ought to assure management that empowerment does not give employees an "open checkbook" or the ability to vote on every organizational decision (personal communication with T. Barb, hospital executive vice president, September 8, 1994). Rather, empowerment contributes to employee feelings of "ownership" in the organization's aim for quality and thus facilitates the continuous improvement of health care processes. Overcoming the psychological and "cultural" resistance to this perceived loss of control is perhaps the greatest challenge in the successful implementation of TQM in health care (personal communication with R. Lamkin, consultant, August 18, 1994).

Full adoption of the principles of TQM is a crucial link to its successful implementation. However, some fundamental contradictions in these principles challenge the efficacy of management in bringing about change (Kaluzny & McLaughlin, 1992). Kaluzny and McLaughlin outlined the following four contradictions:

- TQM is a participatory, decentralized approach to quality and productivity improvement—yet it must be managed from the top, intensely and in detail.
- TQM as a managerial innovation is seen as a paradigm shift that affects the whole organization, with the greatest payoffs derived in rationalizing multidisciplinary and interdisciplinary systems—yet it is most easily adopted one work unit at a time.
- TQM requires an environment of low threat and implied job security and takes time to implement and institutionalize—yet health care organizations are under siege of the realities of the marketplace, operating under severe time constraints to contain costs and improve quality.
- TQM depends on the strength of apparent outcomes—yet the strength of outcomes is likely to depend on the extent of adoption. (p. 380)

## PRELIMINARY FRAMEWORK FOR SUCCESSFUL IMPLEMENTATION

The implementation of TQM is a complex process with many important components, or dimensions. This chapter outlines an organizing framework for the most important of these dimensions that serves to diagram their relationships and interdependencies. Figure 11-1 presents the major elements of the framework. Its purpose is to organize the literature around

FIGURE 11-1

# A Preliminary Framework of TQM Implementation in Health Care Settings

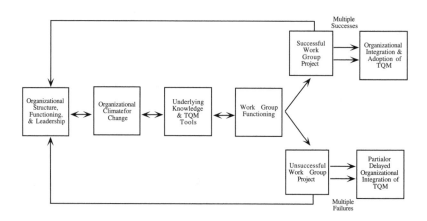

central components and to illuminate areas for future research. Current literature is rich with theoretical papers and "wisdom" (based on experience but not empirical research) discussing the important elements in TQM implementation. This literature stems largely from the experiences of health care and TQM professionals in the field. Although these "hands-on" experiences provide valuable guidance, the field still lacks empirical studies documenting the actual validity of many of the suggestions. Given the complexity of the hospital setting and of the TQM implementation process, it is difficult to study such a process empirically. However, the framework can be used to identify smaller components and related areas of influence that can be empirically tested. Each component of the framework is presented, followed by a discussion of the relationships among the components and the framework's utility in research and practice.

### Organizational structure, functioning, and leadership

Although many structural variables may influence the productivity and functioning of a hospital setting, four variables important to the successful implementation of TQM are discussed here: supportive leadership, employee empowerment, physician involvement, and interdepartmental collaboration.

**Supportive leadership style.** Continuous quality improvement depends on the strengths of the leaders implementing the TQM process. Because "health care tends to be more authoritarian than participative," behavioral changes must be demonstrated first at the top for TQM efforts to be truly successful (Brown, cited in Anderson & Daigh, 1991, p. 31). One of the most important components of TQM should be the "genuine, believable, and consistent" dedication of the administrators to the staff, because if employees know that they are valued and respected, they will apply this respect to the customers in turn (Rowe, cited in Anderson & Daigh, 1991, p. 31).

Coffey, Jones, Kowalkowski, and Browne (1993) have found that the success or failure of TQM is related to the attitudes and behaviors of the leaders. Managers need not pretend that they have the answers. The use of effective questions by administrators has been found to facilitate the improvement process by empowering staff to think critically and find solutions to problems. Coffey et al. suggested that effective questions should do the following:

1. Support the concept of empowerment (e.g., "Since you are closer to this process than we are, what are your findings and recommendations?")
2. Encourage individuals and groups to learn, share, and solve problems collaboratively (e.g., "What information and people would be helpful to make improvements?")
3. Encourage decisions based on data (e.g., "Can you explain the data to us?")
4. Seek ways to help remove barriers perceived by the team or individuals (e.g. "What barriers have you identified that we can help eliminate?")
5. Promote supportive behaviors (e.g., "How can we or your managers help?")
6. Stimulate creative thinking and paradigm changes (e.g., "What would you do if you had no constraints?" or "Can you think of other ways to improve this process?")
7. Support systems thinking (e.g., "What impacts, if any, will your recommended changes have on other processes?")
8. Value people (e.g., "What ideas do you have to provide greater opportunities for the people working in the process?")
9. Focus on customers (e.g., "What input have you gathered from the patients, physicians, or other customers about this issue?")
10. Make sure the improvements are maintained (e.g., "What measures are you putting in place to monitor this process?"). (p. 458)

Moreover, organization leaders must use policy to create a work environment that will foster the success of TQM implementation (Batalden & Stoltz, 1993). The policies should be built around a strong organizational mission and vision and a consistent definition of quality. It is imperative that employees have a clear sense of what is expected of them and how they can contribute to the quality improvement efforts. These principles must also be integrated with the values of the organization and work to instill a sense of shared ownership and commitment among all employees (Batalden & Stoltz, 1993).

**Empowerment.** TQM is built on the involvement and empowerment of employees at all levels of the organization. Empowerment is also said to be the bridge that carries organizations from the old system to a culture of continuous improvement (Dveirin & Adams, 1993). Empowerment is defined as a process by which individuals become a central part of the solution to their problems or those of their organization. Empowerment, in a psychological context, involves the process of gaining control over one's life. This serves to enhance wellness, increase self-efficacy, and foster a greater resiliency in the face of future difficulties. Rappaport (1987) highlighted the use of empowerment in community interventions, stating that empowerment is a process by which individuals gain "democratic participation in the life of [their] community" (p. 121). This concept also translates into the area of organizational behavior and functioning. Conger and Kannugo (1988) stated that employee empowerment is an essential area for improving managerial and organizational effectiveness; empowering employees increases their sense of self-efficacy and improves their motivation and productivity. This motivation also encourages employees to persist at work efforts that do not readily manifest tangible or positive results (for example, TQM activities such as work group meetings and ongoing data collection).

Dveirin and Adams (1993) outlined nine essential aspects of an empowering environment:

1. Employees participate in creating the organization's mission and vision.
2. Managers respect employees' judgment and capabilities and give them the authority to use such skills on the job without constant supervision.
3. Groups have a clearly established level of resource control.
4. Individuals and work groups have access to information that will facilitate their jobs.
5. Employees have access to education and training.
6. There is an environment of trust and respect.
7. Employees see that their efforts are making a difference.
8. There are meaningful incentives for being involved in TQM efforts (for example, education, training, recognition, reward).
9. Employees are involved in setting boundaries in which they are free to manage resources, manage their time, and make decisions.

Management should also survey employees about perceptions of empowerment and then focus on areas where it is weakest (Conger & Kannugo, 1988).

The successful implementation of TQM depends on the organization's abilities to empower employees to work actively to effect change in the organization. For employees to be authentically empowered, however, management must be decentralized and cooperative. Organizational change may make employees feel threatened and powerless. Unless employees are included in the process by being assigned to (or even better, volunteering for) work teams, they may generally resist TQM-related efforts and may show little enthusiasm for the mission and vision of the organization. However, when given the opportunity to work with others to implement changes to improve their environment and work processes, employees should show increased investment in the TQM process.

**Physician involvement.** Although physicians are just one group among many stakeholders involved in TQM implementation (for example, administrators, managers, nurses, technicians, secretaries), they play an especially important role in blocking or facilitating it. Often large hospital settings appear to "operate with two distinct lines of authority, the administrative staff and the medical staff" (Berwick et al., 1990, p. 160). Therefore, the involvement of physicians is a crucial step toward the organizational integration necessary for adoption of TQM. Strategies designed to increase the use and application of CQI through the health care setting may require tailoring for physicians (Kaluzny, McLaughlin, & Kibbe, 1992). Considerations of time, flexibility in scheduling, and a focus on increasing the perceived relevance of TQM activities to physicians must be addressed. Melum and Sinioris (1992) made the following suggestions for enhancing physician participation:

1. Select a few highly respected physicians to serve as TQM physician champions.
2. Have physician leaders serve on the TQM steering committee.
3. Take physicians to on-site visits of successful TQM health care organizations.
4. Have physicians participate in any early TQM organizational assessments.
5. Sponsor a physician TQM retreat for a cross-section of potential TQM champions.
6. Communicate TQM progress to the medical staff on a regular and timely basis.
7. Use existing physician communication vehicles and meetings.
8. Include physicians on quality improvement teams that are relevant to clinical practice.
9. Select improvement opportunities that are priorities to physicians and that have a high probability of early success.
10. Give physicians a major role in evaluating and improving the TQM process. (p. 132)

**Interdepartmental collaboration.** The continuous quality improvement of health care processes depends on the identification, cooperation, and collaboration of the hospital's internal customers (that is, departments within the hospital system whose products are necessary for another department to function). For example, the nursing department depends on the records department to provide timely delivery of records to provide the prescribed services. When initiating interdepartmental quality improvement efforts, many health care organizations experience common structural obstacles that challenge the team's success. One obstacle is that departments are generally organized by function (for example, nursing, radiology, admitting, records) rather than by process, which leads to minimal contact and limited knowledge of an employee's internal customers in other departments (D. Juran, 1994). A second important obstacle is lack of time to meet as a cross-departmental team. This is a particular problem in service settings because it is perceived as impossible to shut down or delay the process of care or to plan convenient times when the workload is light. A third obstacle stems from the value within the organization of devoting time to direct patient care. This may cause an employee to feel unsupported by colleagues and managers when pulled away from his or her direct patient care duties for a meeting (D. Juran, 1994). Juran, a quality improvement consultant at Beth Israel Hospital in Boston, who implemented an award-winning interdepartmental quality improvement project, has the following suggestions for interdepartmental collaboration:

- Choose projects that focus on frequently occurring problems that are quantifiable and of manageable size.
- Find a committed project leader who will drive the project on a daily basis and who will provide the follow through to make the project a success.
- Use data to determine whether the problem actually exists and to identify its cause and parameters (where, when, why).
- Use flowcharting and shadowing (experiencing the work of other team members) to understand a problem from all sides.
- Focus quality improvement meetings on the team's mission, being sure to provide a "defined purpose, ground rules, and a meaningful agenda" (p. 106).

## Climate for change

The organizational climate is an important component in the successful implementation of TQM. Florin, Giamartino, Kenny, and Wandersman (1990) defined *organizational climate* as a "perceptual measure of an individual's interaction with an organization's social environment" (p. 883). A climate that only superficially supports the implementation efforts will be insufficient for the true integration of TQM into the daily functioning of the organization. Of particular importance is an organizational climate that conveys commitment to TQM, patience, and persistence.

**Commitment to TQM.** Melum and Sinioris (1992) stated that "commitment starts with a dream of something better that motivates people to change" (p. 10). Therefore, the development of a vision statement, through the collaborative efforts of staff at all levels, is crucial. Five fundamental values must be incorporated into a quality vision statement: (1) commitment to excellence and continuous improvement, (2) commitment to employees and to their development and personal mastery, (3) commitment to a continuous learning environment, (4) commitment to customers and to meeting and anticipating their needs, and (5) commitment to the community and to a sense of public responsibility.

It is imperative that top-level management feel personally committed to TQM. However, their "support is not enough; action is required" (Deming, 1986, p. 21). Before employees are expected to learn and use TQM principles, management must show their commitment to TQM in their own functioning (Melum & Sinioris, 1992). Managers not only must serve as role models, they also must be able to provide a supportive climate by showing a willingness to remove the obstacles that would limit or prevent employee participation in TQM-related activities. In other words, management must be prepared to provide the time, education, and resources needed for TQM (for example, provide employees with time for training, meetings, and workshops, as well as the financial resources for projects and possibly even for overtime hours worked). Deming (1986) stated that "management should publish a resolution that no one will lose his [or her] job for contributions to quality and productivity" (p. 26). This would serve to "drive out fear" (one of Deming's 14 points) and promote a climate suitable for the desired changes.

**Patience and persistence.** Continuous quality improvements require a focus on long-term growth instead of short-term gain. Therefore, learning the main principles and tools of quality improvement is only the beginning. TQM requires a cultural transformation and new management behavior that encourages such a transformation. Behavioral change is often the most difficult hurdle to TQM implementation.

Organizations are very slow to change. Belasco (1990) argued that organizations are like elephants in that "they both learn through conditioning." When elephants are young, they learn that they are too weak to pull free from the stake to which they are shackled. After a while, they stop trying; yet as they grow older they passively stand shackled to a small stake from which they could easily break free. In Belasco's words, some companies are like powerful elephants who are "bound by earlier conditioned constraints" (p. 2) and who remain limited by the statement "but we've always done it this way" (p. 2). Although change is tough, it does happen, usually in many small steps. If attention is focused on these small wins, it becomes evident that slowly but surely, elephants can be taught to dance.

### Underlying knowledge, tools, and techniques

**Underlying knowledge.** Batalden and Stoltz (1993) presented a model describing the linkage of professional and improvement knowledge to the day-to-day organizational activities in a hospital setting. For example, improvements in medicine have resulted from the advancement of professional knowledge, which consists of the knowledge of the field's "subject and discipline in the context of a set of underlying values" (Batalden & Stoltz, 1993, p. 425). This expertise has been the impetus for outstanding advancements, such as the development of antibiotics, organ transplant techniques, and gene therapy. However, for the field to keep up with the challenges of cost containment and competition, there is continued pressure for further advancements. The effective application of a second body of knowledge, improvement knowledge, accelerates the rate with which professional knowledge affects continuous improvements in the quality of health care service (Batalden & Stoltz, 1993).

Improvement knowledge consists of four elements (Deming, 1986):

1. *Knowledge of a system:* For organizations to be successful, all employees must have systems knowledge and view the organization as a system of production—in Batalden and Stoltz's (1993) words, "a group of interdependent people, items, processes, products, and services that have a common purpose or aim" (p. 426). The hospital as a system for delivering patient care involves both the core processes of patient care (for example, admitting, assessing, planning, implementing care plans, evaluating progress, follow-up care, and discharging) as well as the supportive services (for example, transportation, nutrition, record keeping, and supplies).

2. *Knowledge of variation:* The ability to recognize variation in a process and to distinguish common cause from special cause variation allows for the maintenance of stable processes. "Common cause variation" refers to the expected variation that is inherent in the system or process and is therefore unavoidable. On the other hand, "special cause variation" originates outside the system and should be manipulated to restabilize system functioning (see Deming, 1986; Walton, 1990). However, the improvement of a process

requires not just maintenance, but a fundamental alteration of the process, which moves the acceptable limits of variation to a significantly lower level (Deming, 1986). Customers serve as a feedback mechanism for the success of changing systems, and their inputs are essential to determine whether the new system is effectively meeting customer needs.

3. *Knowledge of psychology:* This element of improvement knowledge includes the psychology of work, which involves the psychology of motivation and the design of the workplace. Most organizational motivation strategies involve plans that correct, improve, or reinforce the desired performance of employees (Batalden & Stoltz, 1993). However, because most variations in outputs are a function of a faulty process, not an individual worker (Deming, 1986; J. M. Juran, 1989), it follows that attempts to externally motivate employees through the use of rewards and recognition or warnings and probations would have limited effect. Motivating performance is thus best accomplished by focusing on ways to increase employees' intrinsic motivations, such as investment in a shared vision and curiosity in the process of testing and achieving higher levels of quality (Batalden & Stoltz, 1993).

The knowledge of psychology also involves an understanding of the various ways people respond to change. Feelings of confusion, insecurity, resentment, and being overwhelmed may influence people to resist changes in the workplace. Some employees, including managers, may feel that it is risky to participate in a process of improvement that may one day eliminate their jobs. Organizational leaders must have knowledge of the psychology of improvement to guide quality efforts to fruition.

4. *Theory of knowledge:* Improvement knowledge also involves the understanding of how to build a theory and how to link theory with action. Linking theory and action with prediction and measurement are fundamental elements in creating new knowledge that can be used to guide future improvements (Batalden & Stoltz 1993). One simple knowledge-building activity is the plan–do–check–act (PDCA) cycle, referred to as the "Shewart cycle" (or "Deming cycle" in Japan), which has been proven to be an effective strategy in process improvement (Batalden, 1992, cited in Batalden & Stoltz, 1993). This common model of the process of continuous improvement allows for effective organizationwide learning and communication. This circular approach to process improvement has four stages: planning to change a process, implementing process changes, checking and evaluating the results, and standardizing and maintaining the improvements in the process (Walton, 1990). Figure 11-2 presents the PDCA cycle and its important substeps.

FIGURE 11-2

# The Plan–Do–Check–Act Model and Its 12 Substeps

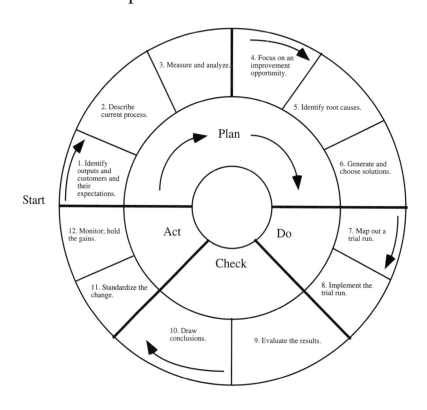

*Source: Albert Einstein Healthcare Network. (1990).* Health care managers guide to continuous quality improvement. *Reprinted with the explicit permission of the Albert Einstein Healthcare Network, Philadelphia.*

**Tools and techniques.** Seven basic tools can facilitate the improvement process by identifying and analyzing problems within a system (Deming, 1986; Walton, 1990). These tools are presented in Figure 11-3 and may be described as follows:

1.  Flow charts depict the steps in a process and can help to identify specific areas for improvement or links between steps that must be refined.

2.  Cause-and-effect diagrams (also called fishbone diagrams) are used to chart the causes of a desired or undesired effect (for example, high sales or low quality). The causes are also categorized to facilitate the

FIGURE 11-3
# The Seven Quality Control Tools

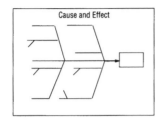

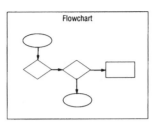

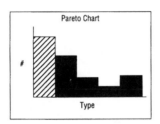

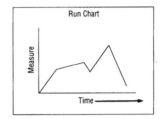

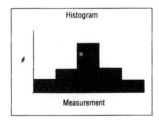

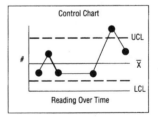

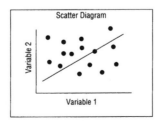

*Source: GOAL/QPC. (1989).* Hoshin planning: The developmental approach. *Reprinted with permission from GOAL/QPC, 13 Branch Street, Methuen, MA 01844-1953*

identification of categorical areas that require the most attention (often using method, labor, material, and machinery).

3. Pareto charts are bar graphs that reflect the magnitude or severity of several identified problem areas. According to the 80–20 rule (80 percent of the problem stems from 20 percent of the causes), the tallest bar represents the most important problem and should become a priority area for improvement.

4. Run charts plot the outcome of a process over time. Analysis of trends is useful in monitoring changes in process functioning.

5. Histograms, or frequency distributions, are created by measuring the frequency of certain process variables (for example, number of patients calls for nurse assistance per day). They serve as a pictorial representation of the amount of variability within a process.

6. Control charts are run charts with statistically controlled upper and lower limits. A process with variations within these limits is referred to as "in control." Variation within these limits is said to stem from "common causes" within the system and can only be affected by changing the system. Variation outside of the upper and lower control limits is referred to as "special cause" variation. This type of variation stems from sources outside the system (for example, broken machinery, unplanned events) and should be eliminated. The goal of quality improvement is to narrow the range of limits so that the process occurs with increasingly less variation while still remaining "in control."

7. Scatter diagrams are used to determine the relationship between two variables (for example, number of calls for assistance and patient satisfaction). The diagram can reflect a positive relationship (as $x$ increases, $y$ increases), a negative relationship (as $y$ increases, $x$ decreases), or no relationship.

### Work group functioning

Quality improvement teams (QITs) are the vehicles through which organizations continually improve. Although full adoption of TQM requires an organizationwide change, effective TQM implementation may also effectively occur "one work unit at a time" (Beer, Eisenstat, & Spector, 1990, cited in Kaluzny et al., 1992). The success of work groups depends on the type of project (for example, attainable versus overwhelming goals) and the character of the work group (for example, style of leadership, level of empowerment, and understanding and investment in TQM philosophies and methodologies). Kaluzny and McLaughlin (1993) suggested that strategies for TQM adoption should be tailored to the character of individual work groups and not uniformly to the entire organization. It also has been postulated that work teams with a formal structure and predictable task will have a more successful impact (Kaluzny & McLaughlin, 1993).

Given the importance of the functioning of individual work units, a focus on these groups appears to be an appropriate level of analysis for judging the initial success of TQM implementation. However, much of the work in this area is theoretical in nature and has not addressed the actual measurement of work group characteristics and functioning. The field of psychology is rich with research methodologies that measure the functioning of groups, organizations, and communities. Wandersman (1981, 1993a, 1993b) has studied individual participation and group functioning in a variety of settings (for example, communities, neighborhoods, and coalitions) and has summarized the essential components of effective associations (Wandersman, 1993a) (see Table 11-3). We posit that these same key elements are likely to relate to the structure and function of individual QITs within health care settings as well. For these teams to effectively bring about the desired change (output), they must be supported by the leadership, have the necessary resources (time, supplies, money) and guidelines, and have an appropriate cost–benefit ratio (Wandersman, 1993b).

In addition, the use of measures such as the Group Environment Scale (Moos, 1981), an analysis of the perceived costs and benefits of participating in TQM activities, and a measure of perceived empowerment will assist management in identifying both the ingredients for success and some areas for improvement. The process of TQM implementation will differ depending on the particular hospital setting. However, regardless of the setting, successful implementation will be facilitated by organizational leaders who understand the climate of their organization and work groups and who respond to areas that require attention.

### Cumulative project success as an agent for organizational adoption of TQM

Kaluzny and McLaughlin (1992) proposed a model that identifies the stages through which TQM becomes an integral part of a health care system. The stages include awareness, identification, implementation, and institutionalization. To ensure organizational adoption of TQM, an initial focus on the functioning of the individual work teams is required (Kaluzny & McLaughlin, 1992). Individual work groups are likely to be differently affected by initial TQM efforts, and therefore, certain work groups may have progressed further in the TQM adoption process than others. Kaluzny and McLaughlin (1993) predicted that the stage a work group is at when given a project is likely to affect the pace and effectiveness of the group's move as it adopts TQM.

TABLE 11-3

# Summary of Keys to an Effective Association

| ORGANIZATIONAL RESOURCES AND FUNCTIONING | GUIDELINES (BASED ON RESEARCH) |
|---|---|
| Resources | |
| Internal | Groups require enough members with the skills and contacts necessary to get the job done. |
| External | Groups require adequate assistance in terms of money, information, or supplies from other groups. |
| Structure and maintenance | |
| Leadership | Elected leaders should be responsive to members' ideas. |
| Committees | Interested persons should have a chance to participate, and the workload should be widely distributed. |
| Decision making | Everyone should have a say. |
| Incentives | Members must have good reasons for joining and staying involved. |
| Mobilization | |
| Time and energy | Many members commit themselves fully. |
| Assistance | Outside assistance from other community groups is obtained when needed. |
| Production | |
| Action strategies | The organization needs to produce the type of activities it was created to perform. |
| Maintenance strategies | Recruiting members, building team spirit, developing new leaders, and fundraising make an organization strong. |
| Output | |
| Goal attainment | The group must meet its initial goals and establish a track record. |

Therefore, initially targeting work groups that demonstrate the character and commitment to be successful will serve to move them closer to adoption. After the initial work groups have proven to be successful, then more-resistant work groups can be guided to success (Kaluzny & McLaughlin, 1993).

As our framework suggests, the success of an individual work group project relies on the degree to which all components of the framework (that is, organizational structure, functioning, and leadership; organizational climate; knowledge of TQM philosophies and tools; and work group functioning) are oriented to the successful implementation of TQM. Project success can be defined as meeting project goals and objectives in a timely and efficient manner with demonstrated sustained results in process improvement. The smoother the functioning of all areas of the framework, the greater is the likelihood of work group project success. Project success early in the implementation process can reinforce an enthusiasm and confidence in the TQM process that can influence improvements in the functioning of other components in the framework. In this way, multiple successful projects, stemming from and leading to improved functioning in other areas of the framework, influence the eventual integration and adoption of TQM into the organization's daily functioning. These successful visible results can serve to build momentum in the overall TQM implementation process. Conversely, multiple unsuccessful projects, perhaps stemming from weaker areas identified by the framework, can lead to a disenchantment or discouragement with TQM. This could cause a delayed integration of TQM into the organization's daily functioning.

### CONCLUSION

The TQM implementation process requires the coordinated functioning of the essential components presented in the framework. All components are interdependent. At the beginning of the implementation process, there is often a focus on the tools and knowledge necessary for TQM to take place. However, as the framework shows, the tools and knowledge are but one component. Organizational leaders also must invest time, resources, and expertise in the development of the organizational structure, climate, leadership, and work group functioning to maximize the success of TQM implementation efforts. The framework also highlights the importance of early work group projects in influencing more lasting structural and cultural changes throughout the organization. Therefore, organizational leaders should focus initial attention on providing work groups with the necessary resources, leadership, and knowledge to effectively and efficiently produce lasting improvements in the quality of designated processes.

The framework is useful on two important levels. First, such a framework can be helpful to a particular organization by providing a map of the crucial components necessary for TQM success. When the implementation process is slowed, leaders can look to the functioning of individual components and focus efforts toward those components that are barriers to, instead of facilitators of, TQM success. The development of valid indicators of adequate or supportive functioning of each of these major components is a useful area for future research.

The framework is also useful on the level of organizing TQM literature and identifying areas for future research. The framework identifies major components and relationships among components. In this way, the complex process of TQM implementation can be divided into smaller research questions to be tested empirically. Many experts state that because each hospital setting is different, leaders should be creative and flexible in their application of TQM strategies. Although such variation and complexity may make research and evaluation more difficult, it does not reduce the need for empirical research. Perhaps the TQM field can learn from the successful evaluation of complex community coalitions, which are evaluated with a system designed to measure the process, outcome, and impact of this complex process (see Goodman & Wandersman, 1994). Such empirical investigation of the key components of TQM probably will improve current implementation strategies and advance knowledge of the effect of TQM in hospitals.

TQM focuses on empowering employees to identify and implement improvement strategies that will continuously improve the quality of the product or services delivered by an organization. Although originally developed for use in manufacturing and industry, TQM is also a successful management strategy in health care settings. It is best thought of as a system of meeting quality work objectives, and not as a program or quick-fix. Given the complexity of some of the principles, the diversity of tools available, and the difficulty of bringing about organizational change, TQM cannot be implemented or understood overnight.

Some organizations move through the stages of the adoption process more rapidly than others. Factors such as organizational readiness, management commitment, employee empowerment, physician involvement, and work team character are essential variables in the adoption of TQM. The extent to which these and other key variables are managed successfully determines the extent to which TQM will succeed. Therefore, organizational leaders should examine and improve the functioning of each of these areas to increase the overall impact of TQM. Above all, organizational leaders must stay committed, empower staff at all levels of the organization to assist in the process, and continue to foster an environment that supports the successful implementation of TQM.

## REFERENCES

Albert Einstein Healthcare Network. (1990). *Health care managers guide to continuous quality improvement*. Philadelphia: Author.

Anderson, C. A., & Daigh, R. D. (1991, February). Quality mind-set overcomes barriers to success. *Healthcare Financial Management*, pp. 21–32.

Batalden, P. B., & Stoltz, P. A. (1993). A framework for the continual improvement of health care: Building and applying professional and improvement knowledge to test changes in daily work. *Journal on Quality Improvement, 19,* 424–447.

Belasco, J. A. (1990). *Teaching the elephant to dance: The manager's guide to empowering change*. New York: Penguin Books.

Berwick, D. M., Godfrey, A. B., & Roessner, J. (1990). *Curing health care: New strategies for quality improvement* (A report on the National Demonstration Project on Quality Improvement in Health Care). San Francisco: Jossey-Bass.

Coffey, R. J., Jones, L., Kowalkowski, A., & Browne, J. (1993). Asking effective questions: An important leadership role to support quality improvement. *Journal on Quality Improvement, 19,* 454–464.

Conger, J. A., & Kannugo, R. (1988). The empowerment process: Integrating theory and practice. *Academy of Management Review, 13,* 471–482.

Crosby, P. B. (1984). *Quality without tears*. New York: McGraw-Hill.

Deming, W. E. (1986). *Out of the crisis*. Cambridge, MA: MIT Press.

Dveirin, G. F., & Adams, K. (1993). Empowering health care improvement: An operational model. *Journal on Quality Improvement, 19,* 222–223.

Florin, P., Giamartino, G. A., Kenny, D. A., & Wandersman, A. (1990). Levels of analysis and effects: Clarifying group influence and climate by separating individual and group effects. *Journal of Applied Social Psychology, 20,* 881–900.

Fuchsberg, G. (1992, May 14). Quality programs show shoddy results. *Wall Street Journal*, p. 81.

Gaucher, E., & Kratochwill, E. (1991, May). Perceived barriers in implementing TQM. *The Quality Letter*, p. B1.

GOAL/QPC. (1989). *Hoshin planning: The developmental approach*. Methuen, MA: Author.

Goodman, R. M., & Wandersman, A. (1994). FORECAST: A formative approach to evaluating community coalitions and community-based initiatives. In S. Kaftarian & W. Hansen (Eds.), Improving methodologies for evaluating community-based partnerships for preventing alcohol, tobacco, and other drug use. *Journal of Community Psychology* (Special Issue), pp. 6–25.

Joint Commission on Accreditation of Healthcare Organizations. (1991). *Accreditation manual for hospitals*. Oakbrook Terrace, IL: Author.

Juran, D. (1994). Achieving sustained quantifiable results in an interdepartmental quality improvement project. *Journal on Quality Improvement, 20,* 105–119.

Juran, J. M. (1989). *Juran on leadership for quality.* New York: Free Press.

Kaluzny, A. D., & McLaughlin, C. P. (1992, November). Managing transitions: Assuring the adoption and impact of TQM. *Quality Review Bulletin,* pp. 380–384.

Kaluzny, A. D., & McLaughlin, C. P. (1993). TQM as a managerial innovation: Research issues and implications. *Health Services Management Research, 6,* 78–88.

Kaluzny, A. D., McLaughlin, C. P., & Kibbe, D. C. (1992). Continuous quality improvement in the clinical setting: Enhancing adoption. *Quality Management in Health Care, 1,* 37–44.

Melum, M. M., & Sinioris, M. K. (1992). *Total quality management: The health care pioneers.* Chicago: American Hospital Publishing.

Moos, R. H. (1981). *Group Environment Scale manual.* Palo Alto, CA: Consulting Psychologists Press.

Osborne, D. (1992, August). Why total quality management is only half a loaf. *Governing,* p. 65.

Rago, W. V., & Reid, W. H. (1991). Total quality management strategies in mental health systems. *Total Quality Management Strategies, 18,* 253–263.

Rappaport, J. (1987). Terms of empowerment/exemplars of prevention: Toward a theory for community psychology. *American Journal of Community Psychology, 15,* 121–146.

Shanahan, M. (1983). The quality assurance standard of the JCAH: A rationale to patient care evaluation. In R. D. Luke, J. C. Kreuger, & R. E. Modrow (Eds.), *Organization and change in health care quality assurance* (pp. 21–33). Rockville, MD: Aspen Systems.

Walton, M. (1990). *Deming management at work.* New York: G. P. Putnam's Sons.

Wandersman, A. (1981). A framework of participation in community organizations. *Journal of Applied Behavioral Science, 17,* 27–59.

Wandersman, A. (1993a). *Keys to an effective association* (Working paper for the Kellogg Foundation CBPH initiative).

Wandersman, A. (1993b). *Understanding coalitions and how they operate: An "open systems" organizational perspective* (Working paper for the Kellogg Foundation CBPH initiative).

# Chapter 12

# Managing in a Changing Health Care Environment

## *A Case Study*

**Michael A. Harris**

The health care delivery system in this country is going through some important changes. Managed care has arrived and people in the system are unsure of what changes will be made and how these changes will affect their work. Some people have a feeling of crisis, because hospital administrators are taking a close look at all departments with a view to downsizing. In such an environment, social work departments are as vulnerable as any other. At this time, it is appropriate that social work administrators take a good, hard look at themselves and their departments and determine how they can successfully compete with other professionals for a share of a much smaller pie.

In 1983 the Prospective Payment System (PPS) was enacted by Congress as one of the Social Security Amendments under Medicare. Until then hospitals received reimbursement retrospectively by Medicare for their costs. This was called "cost-plus reimbursement." The PPS established reimbursement on a fixed rate per case, set prospectively instead of retrospectively. This rate is based on a system of close to 500 *diagnosis-related groups* (DRGs), that is, "categories of illness calculated on the national average of cost per diagnosis" (Mizrahi, 1988, p. 2). Medicaid is also changing its policy to comply with the Medicaid Managed Care Act of 1991, which stipulates that half of the 2.9 million poor New Yorkers receiving Medicaid must enroll in managed care programs within five years (Kotelchuck, 1992). Medicaid will no longer pay on a fee-for-service basis but will pay a single price to health care plans for a package of services. Because of these changes, hospitals are under pressure to discharge patients "in a less-recovered state" (Mizrahi, 1988, p. 4). Hospitals lose a great deal of money if they permit patients to occupy hospital beds when they are either no longer in an acute condition or at the end of the length of stay based on the national average of cost, that is, DRG, for their particular illness. Fitzgerald, Moore, and Dittus (1988) observed that this change has shifted much of the rehabilitation from hospitals to nursing homes. Hospitals refer to patients who will be transferred to nursing homes as being on an alternative level of care (ALC) status.

Managed care companies are promising efficient delivery of service, and hospitals are doing everything in their power to reduce costs. Managed care, which was resisted by hospitals in the Northeast until recently, is making inroads, and hospitals are positioning themselves for a shift from inpatient to outpatient care; procedures that previously had involved a hospital stay are now done in an outpatient center, such as a clinic or physician's office. For inpatient procedures, medical teams are under pressure to stabilize patients and discharge them as quickly as possible. For many elderly people—and this population is ever increasing—this change means they are being discharged to home care or to a nursing home. Medicare does not cover long-term care, and middle-class people cannot afford it for any length of time; poor people cannot afford it at all. This leaves only one option, Medicaid, which is a means-tested program. This situation presents an opportunity for social work to take the lead in protecting patients' rights by making sure that discharge plans are made with the patients' well-being in mind and not just the hospitals' financial situation.

## OPPORTUNITIES FOR SOCIAL WORK MANAGERS

Opportunities for social work managers depend not only on their competence but also on their political skills. Social work managers often rise through the ranks; as they move up the organizational ladder, they need to "acquire and exercise political influence" within and outside their departments and organizations (Gummer, 1987, p. 23). Many managers tend to think of politics in its negative context, but as Gummer noted, "individuals must . . . view the use of power as an integral and legitimate part of their professional and organizational roles" (p. 25). This is especially true in a hospital setting where social work is only one of various disciplines involved, with physicians and nurses having a much larger share of power and control. How the director of the social work department exercises political power and decision making will determine to a large extent how social work will be perceived throughout the hospital and how successful social work will be in increasing its market share at a time of downsizing of hospital departments in general.

Organizational politics is only one responsibility a manager must master. Lewis, Lewis, and Souflee (1991) identified the effective manager as one who has skills in the following areas: the planning process (including needs assessment); goal determination; program formulation; implementation; evaluation; and assessment of social, political, legal, and economic consequences. All of these skills are needed if a manager is to "survive and achieve in today's human service organization" (p. 277).

## ADMINISTRATOR AS ADVOCATE

Perlmutter (1990) viewed the social work administrator as one who "must be proactive, with a vision of the future that serves to impel the organization forward to better meet clients' needs," and "an advocate for the constituency being served" (p. 145). She made three important points regarding the role of the administrator in the voluntary hospital sector, where the structure was developed in a different historical context: (1) The social work administrator must help voluntary agencies engage in strategic planning, as they examine their raison d'être, including the system variables of mission, services, and target populations. (2) Business as usual, or organizational maintenance, cannot be continued when the external environment is so dramatically shifting. (3) The planning must encompass not only the internal capacity but also the external capacity in the broader community as well.

In a medical hospital setting, discharge planning is critical to the success of the hospital; therefore, the social work administrator has the opportunity to move into the forefront by identifying and anticipating areas that will benefit from social work skills. Once identified, data must be gathered, analyzed, and presented to the hospital administration in a form that will be clearly understood.

### Case study

Research aimed at identifying elderly high-risk patients who are likely to present discharge problems was conducted by the Social Work Department of the Long Island Jewish Medical Center over a five-year period. "Since many hospitals have selected their Departments of Social Work to be responsible for discharge planning, both the issue and the field of social work have been placed in the forefront" (Auerbach, Cohen, Ambrose, Quitkin, & Rock, 1993, p. 34). A critical aspect of discharge planning is reducing the length of stay of ALC patients, who no longer have an acute medical condition but who cannot be discharged because they lack a safe alternative. These patients may have lived alone before hospitalization and may not be able to return to their home; rather, they may need home care or nursing home placement. These patients tend to be elderly and usually have limited financial resources. Because Medicare does not cover long-term care, these patients must usually apply for Medicaid. Medicaid approval or recertification takes time, usually more than a month, even when all the paperwork is correct and submitted to the proper place.

To determine how ALC influences length of stay, a multidisciplinary team was established at the medical center. The team quickly became aware of the complexity of the problems confronting adequate discharge planning; therefore, the "Department of Social Work Services began to design and implement [a computerized] . . . ALC data base/tracking system, supported by external development funds" (Auerbach et al., 1993, p. 34). These studies generated a rich database from which to produce the reports used to demonstrate the potential effectiveness for new programs.

The original studies, all published, were primarily descriptive and retrospective; the most recent study is prospective: "A cohort of elderly patients was followed from admission to determine which patients become ALC and with what associated attributes . . . . These findings have led the medical center to develop an acute care geriatric unit in cooperation with an affiliated nursing home" (Rock et al., in press).

The social work department at Long Island Jewish Medical Center, an urban teaching medical center, consists of approximately 200 social workers employed by the three divisions of the medical center and its satellites. Two recent changes resulted in the social work department increasing its prestige as well as its "market share." The first was the creation of the Medicaid Eligibility Program, which gave the department the responsibility of assessing applicants for Medicaid and filing applications where necessary for all inpatients over age 65, a task previously handled by the finance department. The second change was that the social work department was given the task of identifying and spearheading the creation of an inpatient geriatric unit as a proactive rather than reactive method of identifying ALC patients.

The social work department director Barry Rock and associate director Marian Goldstein have taken a proactive stance in identifying areas where social workers can make a positive impact. One area identified was length of stay. An interdisciplinary committee, known as the ALC Committee, was originally set up in 1987 to deal with DRGs, which had become the driving force in hospitals, and the discharge delays of ALC patients. The committee consisted of the hospital administrator, the director of social work services for the medical center's three divisions, the associate director of social work services for the medical hospital, social work managers, the social work Medicaid manager, the home care nursing manager, a nursing administrator, and representatives from utilization review.

Using the social work department's research combined with case review to identify areas where specific early interventions could be made, the committee was able to reduce the average length of stay from 15.6 days in 1989 to 10.4 days in 1994 ($p < .001$; Auerbach, 1995; Rock, Goldstein, Quitkin, & Auerbach, 1993), as is presented in Figure 12-1. The Medicaid Eligibility Program was an outgrowth of the ALC Committee.

Weissert and Cready (1988) identified having Medicaid as a predictor of patients who have a shorter length of stay. Speedy Medicaid approvals contribute to shorter lengths of stay. The Medicaid application process for elderly people and those with medical disabilities was originally handled through the financial aid office, and the staff tended to take what a family said at face value. It is not surprising that things moved very slowly; after all, patients and their families were under great stress because of the seriousness of the patient's condition, and Medicaid requires a great deal of documentation with financial information going back three years. The family of a patient who must enter a nursing home or who has a terminal illness may be facing guilt or denial in addition to the shock of the sudden deterioration of a loved one.

Social workers are well trained to handle these situations. To deal with the organizational issue of the financial aid office relinquishing part of its work, the social work director began building a data bank and was able to produce reports and graphs demonstrating the need to move the application process along by working with families in crisis. (At that time, social work was the only department collecting data.) It was agreed that one of the financial aid office workers would move over to the social work department to assist with training the two other Medicaid eligibility specialists (these three positions do not require a master's degree in social work [MSW]).

Because working with families in crisis was seen as key to moving the application along, a convincing case was made for having an MSW supervise the program, and in late 1990 the social work Medicaid Eligibility Office opened. The next year, the average length of stay dropped 2.5 days (Rock et al., 1993), and Medicaid approvals were obtained faster. Not only were applications

**FIGURE 12-1**

# Means and Standard Deviations of Length of Hospital Stay by ALC Patients, 1989–94

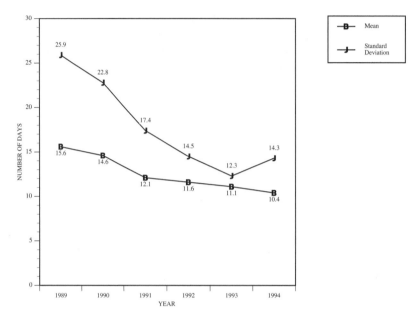

NOTES: $F = 5.3$, $p < .001$. ALC = alternative level of care status. Data points provided by Long Island Jewish Medical Center, from raw data collected by C. Auerbach, 1995, Wurzweiler School of Social Work, Yeshiva University, New York.

being completed (with required documentation) faster, but also the quality of the applications improved and thus, so did the Medicaid approval rate. The social work Medicaid Eligibility Program reduced the waiting period for Medicaid and thus the length of stay. Shorter lengths of stay benefit the patient as well as the hospital; they are both ethical and economical, a win–win situation for all. Furthermore, an Advocacy Program, staffed by volunteers under the direction of the Medicaid Eligibility Program social worker, was incorporated into the Medicaid Eligibility Program to assist patients with their Medicaid recertifications and problems with the system. This ensures that if patients return to the hospital, their coverage is still in place. The advocates also help outpatients apply for Medicaid as well as other entitlements.

Proactive leadership may also involve what appear to be relatively simple decisions. Ordinarily, a director would not be concerned with the assignments of a social work intern. However, the social work director had the foresight to realize that a social work intern on an administrative track would greatly benefit by attending the weekly ALC committee meetings on a regular basis. This enabled the intern to see an interdisciplinary committee in action. It turned out to be a wise decision, because just as the intern was about to graduate, the MSW in the Medicaid Eligibility Program decided to leave the medical center, and the intern was offered the job. The experience the intern had gained on the ALC Committee was a foundation that no amount of reading could have provided; it gave the intern a familiarity with the types and possible solutions of problem cases that would be dealt with in the program.

The department is about to increase its market share again with the advent of the Prenatal Care Assistance Program (PCAP), which will bring pregnant women and their families into the Medicaid Eligibility Program for prenatal as well as postpartum care. PCAP will enable poor families to receive the same quality of care that those with private insurance already receive without forcing them to negotiate the complicated Medicaid system alone. Medicaid has broadened the eligibility requirements for pregnant women and children by not demanding proof of the pregnant woman's citizenship, by increasing the amount of income a recipient is permitted to earn, by not investigating a recipient's resources (bank accounts and so forth), and by permitting the use of a simplified application and granting approval within about one month. The Department of Social Work Services handles the processing of the Medicaid applications for this category of patients.

### CONCLUSION

As lengths of hospital stay continue to decline, medical social work must evolve from tertiary care toward ambulatory primary care (outside the hospital setting) stressing psychological prevention, that is, health-inducing behaviors and stress management. We must look closely at multicultural issues and the effect they have on health care. We should investigate other countries with social work programs to see what can be learned from them. Finally, we must never stop advocating for better health (including mental health) care for our clients.

### REFERENCES

Auerbach, C. (1995). [Reductions in average length of stay.] Unpublished raw data.

Auerbach, C., Cohen, C., Ambrose, D., Quitkin, E., & Rock, B. (1993). The design of case management system for ALC patients: A preliminary report. *Computers in Human Services,* 9(1–2), 33–46.

Fitzgerald, J. F., Moore, P. S., & Dittus, R. S. (1988). The care of elderly patients with hip fracture: Changes since the implementation of the Prospective Payment System. *New England Journal of Medicine, 319*, 1392–1397.

Gummer, B. (1987). The social administrator as politician. In F. D. Perlmutter (Ed.), *Human services at risk* (pp. 23–36). Lexington, MA: D. C. Heath.

Kotelchuck, R. (1992). Medicaid managed care: A mixed review. *Health Pac Bulletin, 22*(3), 4–11.

Lewis, J. A., Lewis, M. D., & Souflee, F., Jr. (1991). Meeting the challenge of organizational achievement. In J. A. Lewis, M. D. Lewis, & F. Souflee, Jr. (Eds.), *Management of human service programs* (2nd ed., pp. 275–310). Monterey, CA: Brooks/Cole.

Medicaid Managed Care Act of 1991, 42 USCA §§1396a, 1396b.

Mizrahi, T. (1988). Prospective payments and social work: Obstacles and opportunities. In J. S. McNeil & S. E. Weinstein (Eds.), *Innovations in health care practice: Health/mental health conferences* (pp. 1–11). Silver Spring, MD: National Association of Social Workers.

Perlmutter, F. D. (1990). *Changing hats: From social work practice to administration.* Silver Spring, MD: NASW Press.

Rock, B. D., Goldstein, M., Harris, M., Kaminsky, P., Quitkin, E., Auerbach, C., & Beckerman, N. (in press). Research changes in a health care delivery system: A biopsychosocial approach to predicting resource utilization in hospital care of the frail elderly. *Social Work in Health Care.*

Rock, B. D., Goldstein, M., Quitkin, E., & Auerbach, C. (1993). *Comprehensive geriatric service proposal.* Unpublished manuscript, Long Island Jewish Medical Center, New Hyde Park, NY.

Weissert, W., & Cready, C. (1988). The determinants of hospital-to-nursing home placement delays: A pilot study. *Health Service Research, 23,* 619–647.

# Chapter 13

# Administering Alternative Social Programs

**Felice Davidson Perlmutter**

I n these times of increasing political conservatism and turbulence, social work executives are challenged continuously by the necessity of maintaining the integrity of their programs, while facing the realities of economic decline and fiscal cutbacks. The literature on social administration is replete with these concerns (Perlmutter, 1984; Slavin, 1980; Wilson, 1980).

During the 1980s, there was a proliferation of various types of new social agencies organized to serve new or existing needs in more flexible and appropriate ways. Although special attention must be paid to the role of all the people involved, including the organizers, board members, staff, and

*This chapter was originally published in Keys, P. R., & Ginsberg, L. H. (Eds.). (1988).* New management in human services *(pp. 167–183). Silver Spring, MD: National Association of Social Workers.*

consumers, the concern here is with the executives who are administering these programs. Generic technical skills that are necessary for administration are important in any organization, but this discussion will highlight the unique and overarching requisites that are inherent in alternative organizations that require special leadership skills.

A definition and description of alternative social programs are presented in this chapter and are clarified through case illustrations. Additionally, the implications of these programs for administration are discussed. Attention to this topic is of critical importance, because the mortality rate of alternative agencies is disproportionately high; not only is there a risk that an agency may not survive, but what is of equal importance is the risk of losing the unique attributes of the alternative organization and becoming a traditional bureaucracy just to survive.

## ATTRIBUTES OF ALTERNATIVE PROGRAMS

The social work profession should welcome alternative social programs, because, historically, most social agencies in the voluntary, nonpublic sector resembled these programs, particularly in their early stages of development. Various unsolved social problems served as the stimulus for the creation of voluntary social agencies when the treatment of, or response to, these problems appeared both pressing and possible. Furthermore, the founders, with the élan of a social movement, took the situation into their own hands to rectify the inequities in the larger society (Perlmutter, 1969).

Although the early social agencies in the voluntary sector and the new alternative agencies are similar, Grossman and Morgenbesser (1980) pointed out that the early voluntary agencies have themselves become sufficiently bureaucratized and static so that new agencies are now required to meet new needs. These new agencies differ from the traditional ones on many dimensions, the seven most important of which are as follows:

1.  The new programs are deeply committed to social change. They are concerned not only with changing the larger external systems, but with altering internal procedures and structures to ensure a democratic and egalitarian operation (Schwartz, Gottesman, & Perlmutter, 1988). The provision of service is necessary but not sufficient.
2.  Directly related to the first dimension is the focus on governance and policymaking. Alternative organizations often are reluctant to acknowledge the reality and legitimacy of authority and power as being instrumental for the achievement of the organization's goals because the values of equality and collegial participation are the overriding ones.

3.   The new programs are designed to meet the needs of special populations that are not being served by existing agencies in the voluntary or public sector. Usually, these groups have a characteristic that is not acceptable to, or accepted by, the larger society, thus making explicit a set of values that can be viewed as "precarious," in contrast to the "secure" values that underpin the traditional programs (Clark, 1956).

4.   The services themselves often are exploratory or innovative and are not available in the existing repertoire of the traditional agencies.

5.   The personnel in these organizations are either deeply committed from an ideological perspective or are closely identified with or even part of the group at risk. They include a broad range of people, from volunteers to paraprofessionals to professionals.

6.   The size of these organizations is a critical variable. Smallness is valued because it permits face-to-face interactions among the various participants and more individualized attention to the needs of consumers (Kantor & Zurcher, 1973).

7.   Alternative organizations usually are in a marginal position economically, because the resources available to the traditional health and welfare agencies, both from public and private funds, are not available to them. Thus, Parsons and Hodne (1982) pointed out that in the design and development of an alternative agency, the resource base must be as vital an aspect of the planning as is the mission.

These seven variables that characterize alternative programs will now be examined in greater detail within the context of two alternative organizations. (Note that the terms *programs, agencies,* and *organizations* are used interchangeably.)

Two alternative agencies serve as the basis for the case illustrations in this discussion. One is a direct service agency that provides services to a consumer group; the second is an indirect service agency that raises funds for alternative direct services agencies. Both are located in Philadelphia.

*The Elizabeth Blackwell Health Center for Women* is a nonprofit women-controlled facility originally organized in 1974 to provide abortion services to women in reaction to negative experiences in commercially run abortion programs. Over the years, Blackwell has broadened its repertoire of services. In addition to the original abortion program, it now includes pregnancy testing, routine gynecological services, a birthing center with full prenatal care, nutritional counseling, menopause workshops, an insemination program, and, most recently, testing for AIDS. The center is guided by the following three principles:

1. Health care is a right; the profit motive in health care can negatively affect equality of care;
2. The needs of the consumer should be the utmost consideration in organizing . . . health care . . . . Consumers should be active participants in their personal health care and participate in the decision-making activities of the health care system;
3. Health care should . . . emphasize maintenance of health and prevention of disease . . . and take into account physical, mental, social and environmental conditions. (Blackwell Health Center for Women, 1975, p. 1)

The facility is run according to two major assumptions that are explicated by feminist administrative theory (Ferguson, 1984): A nonhierarchical, participatory structure is essential, and the mission of the organization must focus on structural change, not merely on the provision of services.

The *Bread and Roses Community Fund* was founded in 1977 as a public foundation that provides financial support to organizations that are working for fundamental social change in the greater Philadelphia area. Special priority is given to small community-based groups that have limited access to traditional funding sources because they are considered too small, too new, or too controversial. The internal organization of the fund has been carefully designed to reflect its philosophy; it is thus unique as a fund that practices what it preaches vis-à-vis alternative agencies.

## UNDERSTANDING ALTERNATIVE ORGANIZATIONS

The seven attributes are discussed in the context of the following case illustrations.

### Social change

The commitment to external social change usually is the stimulus for the founding of an alternative organization, because there is a pressing problem that must be solved and little attention is being paid to it in the society at large. Although external problems have been the stimulus for the creation of all social agencies in the voluntary sector, a distinctive difference must be highlighted. That is, in contrast to most social agencies, alternative agencies are not content just to address a particular problem, they feel compelled to *push for change* in the larger society.

Blackwell was started with a mandate to offer abortion services to women that would respect the consumer as a person who not only needed to understand the process but who would be entitled to participate in the decision making that was needed in each case. Blackwell's philosophy is explicit regarding entitlement to care; health maintenance and the prevention of disease; and its nonprofit status, designed to provide care to women of all income levels, ages, racial and ethnic backgrounds, and lifestyles, including lesbians as well as heterosexuals.

Blackwell works to influence the extensive sophisticated and traditional medical system in Philadelphia. It has provided a broad array of nontraditional services that not only provide options for women but demonstrate the efficacy of alternative care. For example, not only was Blackwell a pioneer in the use of midwives, but it provides an out-of-hospital birth center. Although it is primarily a service delivery agency, it views its advocacy role as central to its existence; thus, its board of directors and staff members are actively involved in the political process at the state and local levels. The active anti-abortion positions at both the federal and state levels will undoubtedly require Blackwell's greater commitment to this external thrust, while it simultaneously struggles to meet the ongoing demands for service.

Bread and Roses is particularly interesting in regard to the external social change function. Not only does it fund organizations that are committed to social change, it is an activist group in that it plays a watchdog role and supports and encourages advocacy. The fund is particularly active in publicizing the problems in the community and the activities of the various organizations it supports. Several examples of the activities of its grantee organizations illustrate this thrust:

- The Kensington Joint Action Council organized a coalition of 33 North Philadelphia organizations in this low-income area to challenge the lending policy of a major Philadelphia bank that did not meet the requirements of federal law under the Community Reinvestment Act of 1977. The coalition won a $50 million, three-year settlement.
- The Disabled in Action, a group composed of people with various degrees of disability, has successfully brought to public attention the need for public transportation for people in wheelchairs and with other special needs.
- The Philadelphia Lesbian and Gay Task Force has released a study that documents the discrimination, harassment, and violence that gay men and lesbians have experienced in the community and has recommended various responses, including legislation and police training.
- The Action Alliance of Senior Citizens of Greater Philadelphia has played a major role in the struggle to maintain special programs and discounts for senior citizens, including discounts from the Philadelphia Gas Company and a special transit program provided by the state.

Thus, the role played by Bread and Roses in social change is perhaps best understood by examining the organizations it elects to support. All are dealing with complex problems and reflect precarious social values in this society.

## Internal governance

Internal change is addressed through a concern with governance and participatory democracy; alternative organizations are suspicious of hierarchy and authoritarian decision making. This is a critical dimension that requires the most sophisticated arrangement, because the method of dealing with decision making often determines an organization's capacity to survive. Two dangers exist. On the one hand, the system may be unable to delegate authority to any subgroup and may founder in the struggle to achieve a consensus; on the other hand, the participatory ideals may be sacrificed for the goal of survival. Both Blackwell and Bread and Roses have developed interesting, complex, and effective strategies for dealing with this central issue.

Blackwell has made a continuous and self-conscious effort to ensure a participatory, nonhierarchical structure that will effectively meet the organization's requirements while acknowledging the reality and legitimacy of authority and power as a functional imperative for accomplishing its goals. Its carefully planned system of checks and balances is designed to allow decisions to be made, when necessary, while ensuring participation, when possible.

First, the board of directors has special attributes. It is elected by consumers and is composed of individuals, primarily women, with special expertise or commitment to Blackwell's goals, who are representative, in terms of race, age, experience, and lifestyle, of the women to be served. Furthermore, one-third of the board is composed of elected staff members, and all board committees must include staff representatives (Blackwell Health Center for Women, 1976).

Second, every staff member is encouraged to participate in decision making, and mechanisms are continuously being created to help all levels of staff respond to issues that affect the organization. Thus, the administrative staff works to frame the questions, so all staff members can focus on an issue, consider options, voice opinions, and arrive at an agreement on the direction to be taken. New staff often have to "unlearn" attitudes of powerlessness that they bring with them from past experiences in traditional work environments and are reminded of the mechanisms provided for their direct involvement in decision making.

Third, in contrast to personnel procedures in traditional agencies, all staff members, except for the executive director, are hired and fired by a staff committee whose membership is rotated among all staff on a quarterly basis. This committee also sets the salary levels, within a range set by the board. Only the executive director is hired by the board, as is the usual procedure, but it should be noted that, even in this regard, the staff participates actively, because one-third of the board members are staff. Although Blackwell addresses the problem of participatory governance in numerous ways, at all levels, and on all issues, the ways cited here serve to illustrate the checks and balances in the organization.

Bread and Roses has equally sophisticated internal governance procedures that are designed to avoid elitism. It is an organization of approximately 500 members, consisting of three constituencies: donors, volunteers, and representatives of grantee organizations. At its annual membership meeting, two boards are elected, each with a clear mandate.

The board of directors is responsible for all policy and procedural decisions except for those dealing with funding. The board must be composed of a minimum of 18 members, with representation as follows: Four members must represent groups funded within the past year; nine are elected at large; two are donor members; two are from the Community Funding Board; and one is a staff representative, usually the executive director.

The Community Funding Board deals with all aspects of funding, including applications, allocations, grant-making policies, and procedural decisions. It must have a minimum of 12 members, all of whom are committed to and actively involved in social change activities.

Guidelines have been developed that ensure that diverse interests are represented on both boards. Thus, one-half of each board must be women; one-third must be people of color; and one representative must be a gay man and one must be a lesbian on each board.

Because Bread and Roses is a granting agency, similar to United Way, it has unique concerns. One priority is to ensure a broad donor pool so that a variety of interests can be served. Any person who contributes $50 or more can serve on the board—a critical stipulation, because more than 50 percent of the donors are wealthy. In this way, Bread and Roses has dealt with the problem of the control of policy by a small cadre of wealthy donors.

A sophisticated mechanism also has been developed that recognizes the special needs and conflicts of the wealthy donors who are struggling with their ideological commitments. Two types of services are available to donors. The first is a "Women and Money" group, which is self-led and self-directed; Bread and Roses serves an administrative function only in that it sends out the mailings. The group develops its own agenda, which serves both a self-help and an educational function. Bread and Roses is directly engaged in the second service—the sponsorship of two donor conferences each year. Workshops are presented, usually in the following three areas: (1) personal (for example, money and friends and money and family); (2) technical (for instance, how to manage wealth); and (3) political (such as which candidates are dealing with important social issues).

## Special populations

Blackwell and Bread and Roses serve special populations with unique needs. Blackwell was organized because the traditional obstetrical and gynecological services of the medical establishment were not meeting the special needs of women—not only the reproductive needs of the young, but the special needs of women of all ages who are at different stages in their lives. It seeks to serve women of all economic levels who might otherwise be deprived of services.

Bread and Roses defines its target populations as local advocacy organizations that, as described earlier, are too small, too new, or too controversial to receive traditional funding. Local advocacy organizations are active in human and civil rights, peace and disarmament, workers' rights, and environmental concerns, among several other issues.

## New services

Services to these special populations usually are not readily available in other settings. At Blackwell, the original concern with abortion services has been broadened to include a vast array of obstetrical and gynecological services. Two will be mentioned here because they are unique or controversial.

The first is an out-of-hospital birth center, staffed by certified nurse–midwives, that provides a unique alternative childbearing option. The second is a controversial artificial insemination program for fertile women, such as unmarried heterosexual women or lesbians, for whom pregnancy is socially unacceptable.

Bread and Roses does not itself provide services; however, it makes possible a broad array of services advocated for or provided by the numerous groups it funds. It must be noted that Bread and Roses is always seeking new groups to fund. It sees its function as providing seed money for organizations to help them get started, especially because groups usually need a history of accomplishment before they can seek funding from more conventional sources. Two different groups that were helped with seed money were an organization called "Peace Tools," which consisted of high school students seeking to use the arts as an alternative to drugs and gangs, and a new project introduced to a professional health society that focused on the consequences of nuclear activity as a health concern.

## Personnel

Personnel also are dealt with in a manner that differs from traditional settings. Blackwell's approach to personnel can be of heuristic value in other settings. The principles of staff participation in governance have been described, as has the intent that staff be representative of the women to be served by the agency.

This attention is illustrated by Blackwell's approach to salary. Because the organization is committed to a philosophy of equity, it limits the dramatic disparity usually encountered in professional settings. This was easier to achieve in the early years when the staff was relatively homogeneous. As the services became more diversified and more complex, so, too, did the staff.

Currently, the staff consists of physicians, social workers, health educators, nurse practitioners, options counselors, health care assistants, and clerical staff. Not only do the staff members have different levels of training, but many staff members have been with Blackwell for years, while others are new. This complexity generated tensions, and decisions had to be made about salary that would meet the needs of the staff while remaining committed to Blackwell's ideology.

The board and staff gave careful consideration to this issue and developed a mechanism for dealing with it in 1982. (Until that time, the only increases were across-the-board when there was money available or no increases when resources were lacking.) A formula was implemented, as follows: Each staff member receives a flat increase on the anniversary date of her employment, an amount ($300 to $500) based on the number of years she has been employed at Blackwell, and the board grants an annual cost-of-living increase, which, in odd years, is a percentage of the individual's salary and in even years is a percentage of the median salary. In this way the disparity issue has been addressed, at least in part. This solution has been accepted over the years, and the issue is no longer one of active concern.

At the outset, there was little differentiation among the staff, and jobs were evenly rotated. As the agency has grown and developed, however, it has been necessary to delineate staff roles more precisely. For example, some staff members began to play supervisory roles with students, volunteers, and other staff members. Although this change has introduced some hierarchical structure into the agency, the staff members relate to each other as peers because of the careful and deliberate protection of participatory and collegial mechanisms. Thus, regardless of level, all staff members have access to information and decision making and are eligible for board membership. Furthermore, the staff committee retains the responsibility for hiring and firing staff members.

Staff participation in decision making is not a process without cost, because it is difficult for staff members to move beyond their particular interests and knowledge of the organization, and they often do not have a broader, or long-range, organizational vision of Blackwell. Therefore, ongoing discussions and staff development are a necessity, more critically so than for most agencies. But the benefit of maintaining the commitment to participatory democracy and governance is the overriding concern. The issue of personnel is less instructive vis-à-vis Bread and Roses, because there are only three staff members, each with a separate portfolio (an executive director, a fund raiser, and a grants associate).

## Size of an agency

Smallness of size is an important characteristic of alternative organizations. It permits the implementation of the central principle of participatory democracy.

Despite its increasing size and complexity, Blackwell protects the capacity of its participants to have face-to-face interactions. The agency has grown dramatically in 11 years. Its annual budget has increased from $220,000 to $800,000; services have increased from 5,000 to more than 10,000 visits; and, what is most important, the personnel have increased from 8 to 35 full- and part-time staff members and from 12 to 40 volunteers and students. In addition, the board has increased from 15 to 21 members.

Blackwell may be at the point of making critical decisions regarding its future growth and development, for it is clear that continued expansion would have serious consequences for its ideological commitments. The carefully designed mechanisms for full staff participation, which depends on face-to-face contact, could be lost, to the detriment of the unusual design of this organization.

Although smallness of size is not a necessary attribute for the organizations that Bread and Roses funds, most of the groups are small because they have staked out a particular point of view and ideology. However, there is face-to-face contact between the organization and all the applicants for funding, and the grantees can remain directly involved through the governance mechanism. It should be noted that Bread and Roses operates with only three staff members and enhances its capacity through the effective involvement of a large cadre of volunteers.

## Resource base

Resources are limited in all human services systems, but the situation is more extreme for the alternative agencies. Although much attention has been paid to the fundraising strategies of these agencies, the problem is complex, because it entails not only sophistication in fundraising and development work but care to ensure that the mission of the organization is not distorted by the need to raise money (either in the amount of time consumed for this activity or its influence on policy).

Blackwell's funding sources have remained fairly consistent over the years. Approximately 80 percent of its money is generated from fees for the services it offers, thus providing the agency with a dependable base. The remaining 20 percent is obtained from foundations and private donations. Blackwell's basic strategy is to stay unrestricted by its funding sources so it will be free to set policy in any direction that meets women's special health needs. (Only on one occasion, one year after it opened, did the agency obtain governmental funds for a cancer screening program with a minimal grant of $2,500.)

Bread and Roses seeks donors from as broad an economic base as possible. Consistent with its philosophy, it values the smallest contributor and makes eligible for its board anyone who donates more than $50. Although it has attempted to diversify its base of support, at least 70 percent of its funds come from individual donors. Because more than half its income comes from a small number of wealthy donors, with gifts ranging from $500 to $10,000, it is critical that decision making and governance remain with a broad base of contributors—not just with people of means.

Bread and Roses recently joined with several other funds in Philadelphia that are seeking to be included in the payroll deduction programs of large corporations and businesses. In addition, it is part of the Donor Option Program, which allows contributors to United Way to designate agencies that are not members of United Way to which employee contributions may be allocated.

It is essential that Bread and Roses maximize the flexibility of its income strategy to protect the complex grant arrangement it maintains. In its early years all grantees received the same amount of funding; the current mechanism allows for three types of grants: donor advised, emergency and discretionary, and general fund distribution. Because donors can express their particular preferences and emergencies always arise in this vulnerable grantee population of agencies, the development of resources must be a creative and unorthodox process for this fund that serves unorthodox and nonmainstream agencies.

It is evident that both Blackwell and Bread and Roses have given much thought and planning to their financial strategies. Both recognize that fundraising is an essential element in the struggle of alternative agencies to stay alive.

## IMPLICATIONS FOR ADMINISTRATION

The egalitarian nature of alternative organizations, as well as their other characteristics, suggests that leadership and administration in these organizations is a unique phenomenon that must be carefully explored and developed. It can be conceptualized only partly in terms suggested for social administration, as succinctly formulated by Slavin (1980), or in broader generic administrative terms. The following comments explore this problem with the intent of stimulating further debate and discussion.

In an earlier article (Perlmutter, 1983), I discussed three types of constraints experienced by middle management and placed them in the following order: professional, organizational, and personal. Although these variables remain relevant for the discussion of the administration of alternative programs, a reverse, more appropriate, order is suggested: personal, organizational, and professional. Consequently, this section relates the needs of the agencies to these characteristics to sharpen their understanding as the basis for a better matching of executive leadership with program. I believe that special individuals are needed for these positions and that although the usual leadership traits discussed in the management literature may or may not be necessary, they are certainly not sufficient.

## Personal characteristics

Personal characteristics have been deliberately placed first in this ordering to acknowledge and emphasize that leadership in this system is unconventional and, to use a metaphor from the field of architecture, "form follows function." Characteristics that are discussed in this section include values and ideology, risk taking and flexibility, comfort with difference, and the capacity to tolerate an economically insecure situation. A charismatic leadership style also is considered.

Of greatest importance is the individual's personal ideology and value framework, because the change efforts of the agency are central to its existence. The emphasis of alternative organizations on social change in the larger system requires a person who shares this commitment on a personal level. However, it is not enough to be a social activist in the broader sense. It is essential that the administrator ideologically identify with the particular social problem that the alternative agency is addressing. The dual demands for leadership in a cause-oriented context are complicated enough when one works in a traditional setting, let alone a fringe one.

The second personal characteristic of importance is the interrelated capacity for risk taking and flexibility. The growth and development of alternative programs is unpredictable and dependent on a variety of factors. What is clear is that the environment of such programs is not stable. Not only must the leader be able to handle this instability, and perhaps even thrive on the challenge, but he or she must set the tone that helps all the personnel deal with this reality.

Third, the administrator of an alternative program must be comfortable with difference. This characteristic is particularly vital, because many different types of people are involved with the organization, as consumers, supporters, or board members. In fact, the capacity of the organization to attract different types of people is distinctly tied to its mission.

Finally, related to the risk-taking quality is the necessity, and the capacity, to tolerate periods of economic insecurity. Not only are these positions low paying, but the total economic base often is unstable and unpredictable.

These specific qualifications will undoubtedly limit the pool of potential candidates. Nevertheless, it is important that they be recognized at the outset to prevent the personal and organizational trauma that would result from naïveté.

The issue of charismatic leadership is not clear cut, as it may be in other settings. Although I suggested in an earlier article (Perlmutter, 1969) that charismatic leadership is appropriate at various stages in a traditional agency's development, the alternative agency is a different entity. Charismatic leadership may be dysfunctional in the alternative agency because it may dissuade or discourage other participants from remaining actively involved. It is not that leadership is not appropriate, but the nature of the leadership requires careful consideration and assessment.

### Organizational characteristics

It is necessary to understand the unique nature of the alternative agency to assess the implications for leadership. Not only is the organization dealing with complex social problems, something it shares with other human services agencies, but it is an agency whose mandate is not acceptable to the broader system. The implication of this fact of life is that the executive must, first and foremost, serve an ongoing watchdog/advocacy function because the broader system requires constant education and persuasion. In other settings, an organization's mission often is forgotten or ignored, but in the alternative agency, it glows like a beacon to light the way for all its participants.

Related to the advocacy role is the urgent need for constant fundraising and development work. Again, although this work is a requisite of leadership in all organizations, it is on the front burner at all times in alternative agencies. The readiness and capacity to seek new audiences cannot be overstated (Brawley, 1984), and the more creative and initiating the search, the better.

Finally, the continuous search for and development of new organizational responses to meet the mission of the alternative agency cannot be overemphasized. The agency can never rest on its laurels. Thus, for example, Blackwell's continuous evolution of new programs and new services demonstrates its capacity to seek new modalities to meet the evolving needs of its target population.

### Professional characteristics

It is not accidental that professional characteristics are discussed last in this listing of requisites for effective leadership in alternative organizations.

Although these characteristics may be desirable for the achievement of some organizational goals and standards, they are not required a priori.

However, it is important to examine the possible role and contribution of the social work administrator. It can be helpful to relate the trinity of social work values, skills, and knowledge to this analysis. Social work's values are clearly compatible with the social change and advocacy orientations of alternative agencies, as well as with the value of participatory democracy and self-management (Adizes & Borgese, 1975), a sine qua non of alternative agencies. The social work administrator must not only accept and be committed to this value, but he or she must be nonauthoritarian and ready to work in a non-hierarchical setting.

Focusing on the value of self-management leads directly to a consideration of the knowledge base of social administration. Attention to the formation of policies and the process of governance is essential and is linked to a focus on working with boards and lay committees. Furthermore, an understanding of social policy and the relevant legislation is necessary, especially because much activity may be taking place in the courts and be linked to entitlements. And last, but not least in the knowledge category, is an understanding of the planning process.

Administrative skills can be an important contribution to leadership in the alternative agency. Interpersonal skills must include the ability to work one to one with small groups and with broader community groups within and outside the power structure. In addition, mediating skills can serve a vital function, because, in many situations, sophisticated techniques are required to resolve conflicts. This is not to suggest that conflict cannot serve a positive function; in fact, this is an area in which social work administrators need to develop more expertise.

The final area of administrative skill is staff development; that is, the recruitment, deployment, and training of all kinds of personnel, including volunteers, paraprofessionals, and professionals. The staff development activity in an alternative agency will have some unique emphases, related to the particular characteristics of this type of organization. Of prime importance is the recognition that the personnel who are most likely to be recruited, at all levels and for all positions, will be ideologically committed to the program. Furthermore, a large proportion of the personnel cohort will be volunteers, who seek meaningful participation and responsible decision making in this social movement of their choice (Sills, 1957).

In addition to recognizing the importance of a sophisticated staff development program to help the volunteers and nonprofessional staff members in their demanding work (Schwartz, 1984), the executive must be sensitive to a variety of issues that directly affect the staff, including process versus product, the rotation of jobs, staff turnover, and staff burnout. There are no ready-made solutions, but a delicate balance exists in these small organizations in which the priority for providing direct service may come into conflict with administrative requirements for survival (Hooyman, Fredriksen, & Perlmutter, 1988).

Alternative programs serve a critical function in our rapidly changing and complex society. They must not only be encouraged to develop, but must be protected and nurtured. Leadership in this sector is a complex phenomenon that merits further research. It is hoped that this analysis of the administration of alternative agencies will be of heuristic value for that process.

## REFERENCES

Adizes, I., & Borgese, E. M. (1975). *Self-management: New dimensions in democracy.* Santa Barbara, CA: American Bibliographic Services-CLIO.

Blackwell Health Center for Women. (1975). *Statement of principles.* Philadelphia: Author.

Blackwell Health Center for Women. (1976). *Bylaws.* Unpublished manuscript, Philadelphia.

Brawley, E. A. (1984). *Mass media and human services: Getting the message across.* Beverly Hills, CA: Sage Publications.

Clark, B. R. (1956). Organizational adaptation and precarious values. *American Sociological Review, 21,* 327–336.

Ferguson, K. E. (1984). *The feminist case against bureaucracy.* Philadelphia: Temple University Press.

Grossman, B., & Morgenbesser, M. (1980). Alternative social service settings: Opportunities for social work education. *Journal of Humanics, 8,* 59–76.

Hooyman, N. R., Fredriksen, K. I., & Perlmutter, B. (1988). Shanti: An alternative response to the AIDS crisis. In F. D. Perlmutter (Ed.), *Alternative social agencies: Administrative strategies* (pp. 17–31). New York: Haworth Press.

Kantor, R., & Zurcher, L. (1973). Concluding statement: Evaluating alternatives and alternative valuing. *Journal of Applied Behavioral Science, 9,* 381–397.

Parsons, P., & Hodne, C. (1982). A collective experiment in women's health. *Science for the People, 14,* 9–13.

Perlmutter, F. D. (1969). A theoretical model of social agency development. *Social Casework, 50,* 467–473.

Perlmutter, F. D. (1983). Caught in-between: The middle management bind. *Administration in Social Work, 7,* 147–161.

Perlmutter, F. D. (1984). *Human services at risk: Administrative strategies for survival.* Lexington, MA: Lexington Books.

Schwartz, A., Gottesman, E. W., & Perlmutter, F. D. (1988). Blackwell: A case study in feminist administration. In F. D. Perlmutter (Ed.), *Alternative social agencies: Administrative strategies* (pp. 5–15). New York: Haworth Press.

Schwartz, F. S. (1984). *Voluntarism and social work.* Lanham, MD: University Press of America.

Sills, D. L. (1957). *The volunteers.* Glencoe, IL: Free Press.

Slavin, S. S. (1980). A theoretical framework of social administration. In F. D. Perlmutter & S. S. Slavin (Eds.), *Leadership in social administration* (pp. 3–21). Philadelphia: Temple University Press.

Wilson, S. (1980). Values and technology: Foundations for practice. In F. D. Perlmutter & S. S. Slavin (Eds.), *Leadership in social administration* (pp. 105–122). Philadelphia: Temple University Press.

# Chapter 14

# Higher Education Leadership and Management

**Frank B. Raymond III**

anagers

of human services agencies come from a variety of academic backgrounds. They may hold master's degrees in social work, business administration, public administration, health administration, and so on. Each of these disciplines has something unique to contribute in preparing human services managers. The administrators of the academic programs in all of these areas use many of the same managerial theories that are used in the administration of human services organizations. The structure of academia is significantly different from that of other institutions, however, and therefore academic administration is also different. The structure of the academy and the values that undergird it necessitate modification of the management principles that apply in other organizations. Academic administration is unique in this respect.

Administrators of academic programs that prepare students for roles in human services must manage their programs in ways similar to their counterparts in other academic disciplines. As an administrator, the dean of a college of social work has much more in common with the dean of a liberal arts college or a dean of an engineering college than with the administrator of a human services agency such as a mental health center or a family services agency. The unique features of management in higher education are the focus of this chapter.

Although there are a number of administrative roles within higher education, many of the management principles unique to higher education apply at all of these levels. The same values and organizational structures govern the administrative activities of the department chair, the dean, the provost, and the president. Each of these officials has to perform particular tasks that require specialized knowledge and skills, yet the organizational culture requires that they carry out similar managerial duties, but in ways that are different from those of administrators in other organizations. Academic organizations may range from small, simple programs to large, complex universities. Regardless of the complexity of the organization, however, similarities may be found in the relationships, duties, and functions assumed by academic administrators at all levels (Wolotkiewicz, 1980; see also Bennett & Figuli, 1990; Brown, 1984; Creswell, Wheeler, Seagren, Egly, & Beyer, 1990; Green, 1988; Miller, Hotes, & Terry, 1983; Seagren, Creswell, & Wheeler, 1993). This chapter examines the overarching principles of administration that apply to all of these positions.

Most academic administrators have little or no training in management to prepare them for their positions. Unlike business and industry, which identify and groom future leaders through career and succession planning, higher education follows a pattern of natural selection, with little planning or preparation by the individual or the organization (McDade, 1987). The careers of most academic administrators are rooted in the professoriate. However, according to a number of recent studies cited by McDade, the traditionally held view that administrators rise from faculty ranks and follow a path from professor to department chair, dean, provost, and eventually president, is incorrect. The actual experience of administrators does not follow a well-defined, hierarchical, linear model. Even though most administrators enter academia as faculty members, their moves into administrative roles generally do not follow a pattern of career development or involve progressive administrative training for higher positions. According to Gaff, Festa, and Gaff (1978): "Most academic administrators have not been trained in the skills demanded of them as educational executives; they have neither planned for careers in administration nor studied others functioning successfully in similar roles" (p. 88). Bennis (1973) cynically summed up the situation:

> I am more and more impressed with the almost total lack of rational
> career plan for academic administrators. Most of us got into this work

adventitiously, and most of us do what we have either observed others do when they were in these roles or emulate, incorrectly, some other shadowy figures of the past, fantasies of Harvard Business School products, General Patton, creatures of fiction or movies, or some atavisms of leadership and authority which never were. (p. 397)

Because most academic administrators have not benefited from systematic preparation or in-service training, as they enter their new roles they must draw on knowledge and skills they have acquired in other ways. This knowledge and skill level may vary among administrators, but as mostly former academicians they all share a certain base of values and operating principles inherent to the academy. For example, they adhere firmly to the principle of academic freedom. They believe in the faculty's authority and responsibility over matters of curriculum. They hold to the right of faculty to participate in decisions about tenure and promotion of colleagues. Beliefs in principles such as these provide the academic administrator with guidance in carrying out the responsibilities attendant to the position, but they can also make the role more difficult. Administrators in other organizations, where lines of authority are more clearly delineated, are able to apply traditional management theory to their work more easily than can be done in academic administration. The difficulties that this creates for the academic administrator are described next. The problems associated with moving from a faculty position to an administrative role are also discussed.

### MAKING THE TRANSITION TO AN ADMINISTRATIVE ROLE

Because most academic administrators have planned for and pursued careers as teachers, not administrators, it is often initially difficult for them to leave behind teaching and research activities. Many academic administrators often continue these activities, perhaps on a limited basis, after they have assumed management positions. Many administrators find it difficult to abandon the satisfactions that are derived from teaching and research activities, satisfactions that attracted them to the profession initially.

Whereas some academic administrators continue to teach by choice, others, particularly department chairpersons, teach out of necessity (Tucker, 1992). The department's student–faculty ratio may make it necessary for the chairperson to continue to teach. There are arguments for and against a continued teaching role for the academic administrator. On the one hand, teaching enables the administrator to stay in touch with the students and to know their needs, wishes, and attitudes. It forces the administrator to stay current in his or her discipline, which may not happen if full-time effort is devoted to administration. Finally, remaining in the classroom enables the administrator to maintain teaching skills. Because many administrators eventually leave these positions and return to full-time classroom teaching, it is reasonable for them to make efforts to keep their knowledge current and their teaching skills polished.

On the other hand, a strong argument can be made that academic administrators should not teach if they can avoid it. The mixing of roles violates a principle of management cited by some writers (for example, Gross, 1968) that although administrators should understand the types of activities to be performed by people under their direction, it is not necessary or even desirable for administrators to perform these activities personally. The administrator's role is to manage, not to engage in activities that are more appropriately carried out by others in the organization. When this principle is violated in academe, the result may be that the chairperson does neither job well. The teaching role suffers because the administrator is unable to devote sufficient time to class preparation, grading papers, meeting with individual students, and so on. Moreover, insofar as the administrator commits time to teaching functions, adequate time cannot be given to managerial tasks.

Newly appointed academic administrators who are grappling with this problem may solve their dilemma by assuming limited teaching roles. They may find that their personal needs are met through teaching one course a year or team teaching a course with another faculty member. Another alternative is for administrators to teach a course that is closely related to personal interests and day-to-day work and therefore would not require as much preparation time. In any event, administrators must not let classroom involvement impair their effectiveness in their primary role of administrators.

Academic administrators encounter similar problems when they attempt to maintain previous levels of research and scholarly activities. Most academicians expect that they will engage in research relevant to their discipline. Conducting research and publishing are essential for university tenure and promotion.

Often administrators are selected, in part, because of their demonstrated expertise as teachers and researchers. Consequently, when they enter administrative positions it may be as difficult for them to give up research as teaching.

Although academic administrators often endeavor to maintain their research activities, performance in this area generally plummets after they enter into administrative roles (Gandy, Randolph, & Raymond, 1979; Tucker, 1992). This decline is partly attributable to the diminished time available for research. A minority of administrators do continue to conduct research and publish at previous levels, but for most there simply is not enough time to perform administrative tasks effectively and to engage in research at previous levels.

Many academic administrators feel compelled to continue their research activities for practical reasons related to academic advancement. Most administrators eventually return to full-time teaching roles, and their experience in administration is not viewed as "time out" in the tenure and promotion process. Most educational institutions require that candidates for tenure or promotion demonstrate consistent acceptable research and scholarly performance. Performance gaps tend to be regarded negatively, even if spent in administration.

One way for administrators to maintain active involvement in research without jeopardizing administrative performance is through collaboration with colleagues in research efforts. Often junior faculty are pleased to be invited to join a seasoned veteran in research projects. In such a joint venture the administrator, as senior researcher, can assume major responsibilities for developing the conceptual framework and methodological design, whereas the junior colleague takes on some of the more time-consuming research roles, such as data collection and analysis.

Some administrators view research activities not as work but as a diversion from the humdrum tasks of administration. For them, research provides a creative outlet they may not experience in their administrative activities. Time spent in the laboratory, in the library, or behind the computer is relaxing, refreshing, and fulfilling. For these individuals, carrying out research activities during evening hours and on weekends is not tiring and onerous but invigorating and rewarding.

### RELATING TO OTHER SYSTEMS

Petit (1967), building on the earlier work of Parsons (1960), conceptualized the organization as a system with two levels of subsystems (graphically illustrated by three concentric rings). The work of the organization is done within the inner circle, the technical system, and managers at this level oversee the actual production and distribution of the product or services of the overall system. The technical-level managers in the university are the department chairpersons. The next outer circle illustrates the organizational system, and management at this level coordinates and integrates the task performance of the technical system. In the university the organizational-level managers are the president, the provost, and the deans. The outermost circle illustrates the institutional system, and managers at this level relate the organization to the environment. In the university, the board of trustees are the institutional managers.

The academic administrator who functions at any of these levels serves as a "boundary agent" responsible for establishing and maintaining relationships both upward and downward. When a faculty member moves from the ranks of teaching to an administrative role, the new job results in a different type of relationship with students, faculty, alumni, and the community. Furthermore, the new academic administrator must establish relationships with new systems, such as the university administration, accrediting bodies, advisory boards, and funding agencies. Both the restructuring of relationships and the establishment of relationships with new systems can be stressful. Moving from one administrative position to another also necessitates a realigning of relationships.

One of the most difficult transitions for a new academic administrator is that of relating differently to people who were formerly peers. This is particularly difficult when the administrative appointment is made from within the individual's own school. The assumption of the administrative role means that the relationships are no longer equal, and the administrator now has power and authority in the relationship. Even though former relationships can continue to exist, ways of relating inevitably change. The administrator cannot appear to "play favorites" or to be in alliance with certain individuals or factions. At the same time, the new administrator cannot begin relating to faculty in a cold, detached manner in order to affirm the separation of teaching and administrative roles.

Academic administrators usually have no previous experience to prepare them for establishing relationships with other systems. Even when the administrator has previously served in a lower administrative position, such jobs typically do not give one the opportunity to relate to higher university administration, advisory boards, or accrediting bodies. Under these circumstances the administrator must rely on whatever role models may exist, earlier experiences of a somewhat similar nature, knowledge that can be gleaned from the literature about academic governance, and, perhaps more than anything else, intuition and imagination.

The academic administrator, as a "boundary agent," often finds it stressful to develop and maintain these various sets of relationships with other systems. This stress can be ameliorated, however, by clearly delineating one's administrative role and setting priorities. As discussed earlier, the administrator in academe is often tempted to hold on to old roles, which may not be feasible. The adherence to these previous roles necessarily affects the nature of the relationships with the other parties involved. For example, the administrator who continues to teach relates with other faculty members at two levels, fellow teacher and administrator, and each relationship carries with it a different set of expectations. As a teacher, the administrator may play an equal role with faculty in determining curriculum content, developing course syllabi, and advising students. As an administrator, he or she may feel that curriculum decisions, course development, and academic advisement are functions that rightfully belong to the faculty. Such role confusion can be mitigated if the administrator is committed to full-time administrative work.

Clarification of management functions also helps the administrator identify priority tasks. Commitment to the performance of these tasks then thrusts the administrator into relationships with the appropriate parties and defines the nature of these relationships. For example, if one of the administrator's priorities is that of fundraising, this role will require the establishing of appropriate relationships with alumni groups, foundations, and public funding agencies.

The academic administrator can also lessen the burden of responsibility as "boundary agent" by creating organizational structures and making appointments to support the administrative objectives of the position. A dean, for example, may appoint an associate dean charged with specific administrative responsibilities. A department chair may create committees to develop policies, perform administrative activities, or provide technical advice (Tucker, 1992). In appointing individuals and groups to carry out such responsibilities, the academic administrator is, in effect, creating mechanisms for enhancing links with other systems such as faculty and students. Through appropriate delegation of authority the administrator becomes free to devote more time to fostering relationships with other entities, tasks that are essential to the administrative role.

### PROVIDING LEADERSHIP

With respect to leadership, the academic administrator also faces different challenges than managers in other organizations. Most of the literature on leadership in higher education draws on the general theories of leadership, usually focusing on the behavior or traits of the leader (Dill & Fullager, 1987). Studies have shown that effective academic leaders possess traits such as professional credibility, vigor, decisiveness, a willingness to take risks, and the ability to articulate a vision and persuade others to pursue it (Maxcy, 1991).

The literature consistently points out, however, that leadership in higher education differs from that in other organizations. Because academic administrators work within structures that are different from other organizations, their leadership roles are significantly different (Vroom, 1983). Both authority and leadership are shared more in academia than in other types of organizations. As Eble (1978) stated, "Administrative structures stand easily between a hierarchical model, in which one person serves another in a pyramid of authority, and the model of shared governance, in which chronic uneasiness exists about who serves whom" (p. 3).

The system of governance in higher education tends to negate the implementation of certain principles of management that would apply in other organizations. For example, whereas most managers exercise control over the organization's processes and products, it is generally understood in academe that the curriculum is controlled by the faculty. Also, administrators in most organizations have final authority in staffing decisions, but in higher education tenure and promotion committees exercise great control in this area. Finally, whereas administrators normally create supervisory systems to ensure quality control, there is little provision for supervision in higher education, where the right of "academic freedom" reigns paramount and can be used to justify a wide range of idiosyncratic job behaviors.

Clearly, administration in higher education requires a special type of leadership. Bensimon, Neumann, and Birnbaum (1989) recognized this and emphasized that academic administration calls for transactional rather than transformational leadership. Academic administrators may aspire to become transformational leaders, but this type of leadership is not compatible with the ethos, values, and organizational features of colleagues and universities. Three assumptions that underlie transformational leadership conflict with normative expectations in higher education: that leadership emanates from a single highly visible individual; that followers are motivated by needs for organizational affiliation; and that leadership depends on visible and enduring changes. In reality, the presence of two forms of authority in academe—administrative and professional—limits the administrator's authority and, therefore, the opportunity to be a transformational leader.

The effective academic administrator must be a transactional leader. Transactional theory views leadership as a mutual and reciprocal process of social exchange between leaders and their followers. The ability to exercise leadership is considered to be dependent on the group's willingness to accept the leader. The conceptual foundations of transactional theory are hence most appropriate to the unique features of academic organizations. The academic administrator who is a transactional leader is more appropriately seen as servant than as controller. Such an administrator focuses on two-way communication, social exchange processes of mutual influence, and facilitation rather than direction of the work of highly educated professionals (Bensimon et al., 1989).

One example of transactional leadership in higher education is the participation model (Moomaw, 1984) in which academic administration is characterized by open information, a clearly focused and shared mission, widespread delegation and acceptance of responsibility, broad involvement in policy formulation, clear evaluation procedures, and rewards for those who do well. Faculty tend to be most enthusiastic and most productive in their activities when they can participate in determining what is happening to them and their programs. This concept does not mean that faculty will want to take over the institution or that the administrator must surrender overall responsibility. Instead, it suggests that administrators should be aware that faculty are important to institutional creativity, problem solving, and new program implementation and that a system of decentralized leadership is most likely to bring about a high level of motivation. This model suggests that administrators should have confidence in their staff and listen to and respect their ideas.

Implementation of the participation model in higher education does not necessarily result in a completely open and democratic system of leadership. The administrator must know which activities to centralize and keep under control and which activities to decentralize and place beyond direct control. As a guiding principle, Moomaw (1984) suggested that broad statements of mission and goals, evaluation procedures, and leadership training should be centralized, whereas the administrator should decentralize problem-solving activities, the managing of daily activities, and planning to meet goals.

Through this type of leadership, the academic administrator can effectively address some of the authority problems inherent in academic administration. On the one hand, the administrator is able to make swift and tough decisions to respond to external demands placed on the organization. On the other hand, the administrator is able to respond positively to the demand of faculty for openness and participation in academic governance. Although the conflict resulting from these paradoxical needs will necessarily continue, the stress that the administrator feels around issues of authority will be mitigated.

### MANAGING PERSONNEL

One of the primary functions of managers in all organizations is that of personnel management, which includes hiring, developing, deploying, evaluating, and terminating staff (Weinbach, 1994). Academic administrators must perform this function, but it is different in higher education than in other organizations. Whereas the administrator is primarily responsible for the personnel management function in most organizations, all aspects of this responsibility are shared with the faculty in academic institutions. Faculty involvement in matters of personnel management goes far beyond the level of staff involvement inherent in most approaches to participative management sometimes used in other organizations. The value base of the academic world and the consequent structure and functioning of educational institutions result in a weakened role of academic administrators in performing personnel management functions. The respective roles of faculty and administration in matters of personnel management are usually more clearly articulated in schools that have unions than in those that do not. In all academic programs, however, it is essential that these roles be understood by the administrator and the faculty.

The first component of the academic administrator's personnel management functioning is that of hiring. This includes developing a system for recruiting faculty and staff, interviewing applicants, gathering and analyzing information on applicants, and making the final selection. Responsibility for hiring is usually shared in higher education. Normally a search committee, composed of faculty and perhaps students, is responsible for locating, recruiting, interviewing, and selecting applicants for the position to be filled. In reporting its selection of a candidate to the administrator, the search committee often presents more of a mandate than a recommendation. Although the administrator normally has final responsibility in hiring decisions, it would be foolish to ignore the recommendations of the faculty.

A second component of the personnel management function involves development and training of new employees. They must be oriented to the academy and be helped to understand how their roles relate to the overall operation. It is unfortunate that in higher education little attention is given to orienting new faculty. It is usually assumed that individuals who are very knowledgeable in a particular subject area automatically know how to teach this material, when in fact quite the opposite may be true. Few doctoral programs outside of the field of education prepare graduates to be teachers. Moreover, it is not unusual for newly hired faculty to be forced to discover for themselves their roles in the overall program structure, the expectations of them as teachers, the procedures for achieving tenure and promotion, and so forth. Often academic administrators, perhaps because of their appreciation of the value of faculty autonomy and independence, do not recognize that new faculty have special needs and that mechanisms must be developed to address them. In one study, the lack of this type of support was a major factor in attrition of new faculty (Rausch, Ortiz, Douthitt, & Reed, 1989).

One of the more encouraging recent developments in higher education to address the development needs of faculty is the use of mentors. Tierney and Rhoads (1994) described a number of innovative mentoring programs. These may range from programs that socialize new faculty to the academy to those that involve the mentor and protégé in ongoing research activities to enhance the protégé's research record. Faculty development needs may exceed the time and expertise of the academic administrator and may be met most effectively through mentoring by other colleagues.

Another personnel management function is that of developing and implementing a system to evaluate employees. In most organizations, administrators have a primary responsibility for evaluating those who work under their direction. In academe, however, the evaluation responsibility is shared with other people, including students, peer reviewers, tenure and promotion committees, and higher university administration officials. In some institutions evaluation may occur only when the faculty member is considered for tenure or promotion. In other schools faculty members may be evaluated excessively by different people or groups. Methods used to assess faculty may range from use of highly objective instruments to open-ended, subjective appraisals. This evaluation process can become frustrating not only for the faculty member but for the academic administrator whose involvement may be minimal. To lessen this frustration, the administrator should work with appropriate committees and institutional officials to develop a rational evaluation system that involves appropriate, clearly articulated roles for all the people involved in the evaluation process.

In carrying out the fourth aspect of personnel management, staff deployment, academic administrators generally have more circumscribed responsibility than is true for managers in other organizations. For example, the department chairperson's major role in this area is that of determining teaching assignments, and even this may be challenged by the faculty. Occasionally faculty members claim expertise in specific subject areas and resist teaching in other areas or having other colleagues invade their territory. Furthermore, because of the tenure and promotion system in most schools, the chairperson or dean may have little voice as to who advances to positions of greater responsibility in the school. Such decisions are usually shared with other faculty, broader university committees, and higher administration officials. Whatever the roles of the administrators and the faculty regarding assignment of tasks and appointment to positions, these roles should be explicated in the school's policy and procedures manuals and communicated to everyone.

Finally, personnel management includes the unpleasant task of dismissing employees when necessary. Normally this happens in an organization when an individual's performance is ineffective or when changes in the nature and scope of the organization render the individual's services unnecessary. In such cases managers must know how to protect the rights of employees and promote the good of the organization. In academia, however, termination of employees is not a simple matter. The tenure system requires that decisions relative to dismissal of faculty be shared with others. Whereas the president may have final authority in matters of tenure and promotion (subject to board approval), other administrators below the president have limited authority. Furthermore, once a faculty member is tenured, academic administrators, including the president, have little authority to terminate the individual. Normally, tenured faculty members can be terminated or dismissed only in cases of extreme failure to perform duties, misconduct, or bona fide reduction in staff. Hence, tenure achieves the original intent of protecting the academic freedom of faculty members and also enables tenured individuals to maintain faculty positions even when they are no longer effective educators. A common complaint of deans and department chairpersons is that they are "stuck" with certain tenured faculty who are unproductive and unmotivated.

Thus, in all aspects of personnel management, academic administrators have less autonomy in personnel matters than managers in other organizations because of the unique structure of higher education. It is essential that faculty be involved in all of the personnel management tasks. Administrators must work collaboratively with faculty in recruiting, developing, and evaluating academic personnel. This process, if carried out effectively, will result in high-quality, productive employees who will be retained or tenured.

## CONCLUSION

Academic administration differs from government and business administration in two important respects: the nature of those who are led and the nature of the enterprise itself. Faculty members are highly educated, independent professionals who are trained to challenge, question, criticize, and search for alternative solutions. They are attracted to higher education partly because of the autonomy that is available to them as members of the academy. The value system of higher education and the institutional configurations that reflect these values support faculty independence and lessen the authority of the administrator. Governance in higher education requires full participation of both the administrator and faculty, each carrying out particular management tasks that are complementary and that ensure the effective functioning of the academic institution as well as promoting the job satisfaction of each of its members.

Because of this system of governance, higher education administration is, in a sense, at the cutting edge of current management theory. During recent years a great deal of management literature has been devoted to the concept of participative management. Under this approach to management the administrator involves the people who are supervised in goal setting and decision making, in the belief that this process will make each individual and the entire organization more effective and efficient. Participative management techniques have been described in literature dealing with management by objectives (Koontz, O'Donnell, & Weirich, 1986), total quality management (Walton, 1990), and quality circles (Ingle, 1982). Each of these variations on the use of participative management has emphasized the application of the democratic process in the day-to-day running of the organization.

The assumptions, values, and principles that underlie all of these highly touted techniques of participative management are inherent in academic governance. Consequently, higher education has been characterized historically by its use of the participative management model of governance, and this type of administration has served the academy well. Although some of the techniques that are used in the management of other enterprises cannot be used in the administration of higher education, the system of governance that has proven effective in academia may provide a useful model for other organizations that strive to develop and implement democratic approaches to management.

## REFERENCES

Bennett, J. B., & Figuli, D. J. (Eds.). (1990). *Enhancing departmental leadership.* New York: ACE/Macmillan.

Bennis, W. G. (1973). An O.D. expert in the catbird's seat. *Journal of Higher Education, 44,* 389–398.

Bensimon, E. M., Neumann, A., & Birnbaum, R. (1989). *Making sense of administrative leadership: The "L" word in higher education* (ASHE-ERIC Higher Education Report No. 88-1). Washington, DC: George Washington University, School of Education and Human Development.

Brown, D. G. (Ed.). (1984). *Leadership roles of chief academic officers* (New Directions for Higher Education No. 47). San Francisco: Jossey-Bass.

Cresswell, J. W., Wheeler, D. W., Seagren, A. T., Egly, N. J., & Beyer, K. D. (1990). *The academic chairperson's handbook.* Lincoln: University of Nebraska Press.

Dill, D. D., & Fullagar, P. K. (1987). Leadership and administrative style. In M. W. Peterson & L. A. Mets (Eds.), *Key resources on higher education governance, management and leadership: A guide to the literature* (pp. 390–411). San Francisco: Jossey-Bass.

Eble, K. E. (1978). *The art of administration: A guide for academic administrators.* San Francisco: Jossey-Bass.

Gaff, S. S., Festa, C., & Gaff, J. G. (1978). *Professional development: A guide to resources.* New Rochelle, NY: Change Magazine Press.

Gandy, J. T., Randolph, J. L., & Raymond, F. B. (1979). *On minding the store: Research on the social work deanship.* Columbia: University of South Carolina, College of Social Work.

Green, M. F. (Ed.). (1988). *Leaders for a new era: Strategies for higher education.* New York: ACE/Macmillan.

Gross, B. M. (1968). *Organizations and their managing.* New York: Free Press.

Ingle, S. (1982). How to avoid quality circle failure in your company. *Training and Development Journal, 36*(6) 54–59.

Koontz, H., O'Donnell, C., & Weirich, H. (1986). *Essentials of management* (4th ed.). New York: McGraw-Hill.

Maxcy, S. J. (1991). *Educational leadership: A critical pragmatic perspective.* New York: Bergin & Garvey.

McDade, S. A. (1987). *Higher education leadership: Enhancing skills through professional development programs* (ASHE-ERIC Higher Education Report No. 5). Washington, DC: Association for the Study of Higher Education.

Miller, B. W., Hotes, R. W., & Terry, J. D. (1983). *Leadership in higher education: A handbook for practicing administrators.* Westport, CT: Greenwood Press.

Moomaw, W. E. (1984). Participatory leadership strategy. In D. G. Brown (Ed.), *Leadership roles of chief academic officers* (New Directions for Higher Education No. 47, pp. 19–30). San Francisco: Jossey-Bass.

Parsons, T. (1960). *Structure and process in modern societies.* New York: Free Press.

Petit, T. A. (1967). A behavioral theory of management. *Academy of Management Journal, 10,* 341–350.

Rausch, D. K., Ortiz, B. P., Douthitt, R. A., & Reed, L. L. (1989). The academic revolving door: Why do women get caught? *CUPA Journal, 40*(1), 1–15.

Seagren, A. T., Creswell, J. W., & Wheeler, D. W. (1993). *The department chair: New roles, responsibilities and challenges* (ASHE-ERIC Higher Education Report No. 92-1). Washington, DC: George Washington University, School of Education and Human Development.

Tierney, W. G., & Rhoads, R. A. (1994). *Faculty socialization as a cultural process: A mirror of institutional commitment* (ASHE-ERIC Higher Education Report No. 93-6). Washington, DC: George Washington University, School of Education and Human Development.

Tucker, A. (1992). *Chairing the academic department: Leadership among peers* (3rd ed.). New York: ACE/Macmillan.

Vroom, V. H. (1983). Leaders and leadership in academe. *Review of Higher Education, 6,* 367–386.

Walton, M. (1990). *Deming management at work.* New York: Perigree Books.

Weinbach, R. W. (1994). *The social worker as manager: Theory and practice* (2nd ed.). Needham Heights, MA: Allyn & Bacon.

Wolotkiewicz, R. J. (1980). *College administrator's handbook.* Boston: Allyn & Bacon.

# Chapter 15

# Social Work Education for Nonprofit Management
## *Do We Want It?*

**Eleanor L. Brilliant and Langdon L. Holloway**

Voluntarism and voluntary nonprofit organizations are a significant part of American life. In the early 1990s more than one million such entities were listed on the Master File of Tax-Exempt Organizations of the U.S. Internal Revenue Service (IRS). Relative to total economic activity, these organizations represented about 6 percent of the American gross national product. About two-thirds of the nonprofit organizations registered with the IRS are considered charitable organizations or social welfare–related organizations under the Internal Revenue Code (Hodgkinson,

Weitzman, Toppe, & Noga, 1992).[1] This large group includes nonprofit social services agencies as well as hospitals, nursing homes, advocacy organizations, and local community and civic organizations that frequently employ social workers. Indeed, more social workers report working in the nonprofit sector than in government or private business organizations (Gibelman & Schervish, 1993a, 1993b). This trend follows the explosive growth of the nonprofit sector that began in the late 1960s and continued through the 1980s (Salamon, 1992; Weisbrod, 1988).

Despite the importance of the nonprofit sector in service delivery and as an employer of social workers, the social work profession has given little systematic consideration to preparing social workers for managerial careers in this arena. Curriculum guidelines set by the Council on Social Work Education (CSWE) do not highlight the significance of nonprofit or voluntary agencies, either as workplaces for social work practice or in relation to the training of social work managers. Although the National Network of Social Work Managers has given some attention to nonprofit management issues, the profession as a whole has shown no commitment to the education of managers with specific nonprofit orientations. The purpose of this chapter is to shed light on some reasons for social work's ambivalence toward the voluntary sector and more specifically on the sector's potential as an employer of social work managers.

## NONPROFIT ORGANIZATIONS: THE THIRD SECTOR

Formal organizations in American life are generally classified into three major categories: public sector (government institutions), private or for-profit sector (business), and nonprofit sector (voluntary or nonprofit organizations). The first two sectors have been widely recognized for a long time. However, the conscious identity of the third sector has developed more recently and can be linked to the deliberations and studies of the Commission on Private Philanthropy and Public Needs initiated by John D. Rockefeller III in 1973. This commission, dubbed the Filer Commission because of its chairperson, John Filer (chief executive officer of the Aetna Life and Casualty Company), conceptualized the work of philanthropy and voluntary action as part of a sector equal in importance to the other two sectors (Brilliant, 1990, 1995a; Commission on Private Philanthropy and Public Needs, 1975).

American public policy recognizes the value of the nonprofit sector through the instrumentality of tax benefits (Hopkins, 1992; Weisbrod, 1988).

[1]These organizations are referred to respectively as 501 (c) (3) and 501 (c) (4) organizations in the U.S. Internal Revenue Code. It is the group of 501 (c) (3) organizations that are defined broadly as charitable, in line with the old tradition of the English Law of Charitable Uses (1601). For more discussion of this definition, see Brilliant (1995a), Hopkins (1992), or Simon (1987).

Nonprofit organizations generally do not pay taxes, and in return they are expected not to return any excess revenues (profits) to their employees, volunteers, or founders. In addition, the special subgroup of charitable [501 (c) (3)] organizations enjoys another tax benefit, namely, the tax deductibility of contributions made to them. This group of organizations serves a range of charitable, educational, and religious purposes that are deemed to be of particular public benefit (Hopkins, 1992; Simon, 1987). These organizations are also the locus of most human services activities.

## VOLUNTARY ACTIVITY AS A HISTORICAL ARTIFACT IN SOCIAL WORK

The social work profession is generally considered to have a dual heritage, emerging out of the charity organization society and the settlement movement. Public social welfare existed at the state and local levels in the late 19th century, but voluntary organizations and voluntary activity gave the initial shape to the new profession at the turn of the century (Bremner, 1988; Leiby, 1978; Lubove, 1969). This profession included both direct practice agencies like the Charity Organization Societies (which became Family Service Agencies) and settlements, as well as intermediary organizations like the early federated funds and planning councils, which raised money, coordinated social services, and provided concentrated advocacy efforts at the local level. It was assumed that these agencies had an important if sometimes controversial role to play in community life (Brilliant, 1990). Moreover, most social workers openly valued community work and voluntarism, even though some voices warned that public support was necessary to meet basic human needs.

It was not until the New Deal created America's version of a welfare state that the social work profession questioned the leadership role of voluntary agencies in meeting human needs. Social work leaders Frances Perkins and Harry Hopkins were instrumental in the development of New Deal policies, and the profession gradually accepted the primacy of the public agency. Since the 1930s, however, social work has equivocated about the role of the voluntary agency and voluntary action. Throughout the next four decades, community work (in various forms of community organization, development, and organizing) continued to be a recognized method of social work practice (Brilliant, 1990), although it sometimes appeared as though adherents of public social welfare programs denigrated the value of these methods. Since its origins at the end of the 19th century, the social work profession has been neither unified nor consistent in its attitude toward voluntary action and its closely affiliated manifestation in community work. Community organizations have been viewed both as partners with public programs and conservative forces within social work. They have also been seen as progressive forces. To a large degree in recent years, the issue has revolved around the extent to which community organizations and social services agencies are perceived primarily as potential activists organizing for social change (Biklen, 1983; Wineman, 1984) or as community organizations connected with the more traditional United Way system and business (Brilliant, 1990). In either case, however, focus on management issues of voluntary community organizations has not been given the same degree of attention within social work as it has been given by outsiders.

## GENERIC VERSUS SPECIFIC MANAGEMENT TECHNIQUES

Most of the influential writings on organizational management since the 1950s have come from social psychologists or experts in business management, including Peter Drucker (1954); Fremont Kast and James Rosenzweig (1979); Robert Katz (1955); David Nadler, Richard Hackman, and Edward Lawler (1979); Henry Mintzberg (1973); and George Strauss and Leonard Sayles (1980). In general, the implicit assumption made by these experts is that management theories are applicable across organizations of all three sectors. Recently, however, Peter Drucker wrote a book dealing specifically with nonprofit management (Drucker, 1990).

The question of whether the three sectors require different managerial skills and knowledge has not received wide attention in social work literature, although it probably has been discussed more extensively in the public administration literature. In a notable example, Allison (1983) wrote an article entitled, "Public and Private Management: Are They Fundamentally Alike in All Unimportant Respects?" He answered in the affirmative—that they are different in the more important ways. Allison used "private" to mean business organizations, and his argument implied that nonprofit organization management is similar to that of government in fundamental respects, particularly in the absence of a profit motive and embodiment of public purpose.

The question of the existence of a generic management technology is explicitly discussed in a recent book by Graham and Hays (1993). Graham and Hays reviewed the seminal framework of public administrative functions formulated by Gulick and Urwick (1973; they gave it the acronym POSD-CORB, which stands for planning, organizing, directing, coordinating, reporting and budgeting). The reviewers concluded that POSDCORB still has utility and can be related to new business management concepts of productivity and efficiency. Thus, they showed how POSDCORB can be adapted to include techniques of management by objectives (MBO) and motivational approaches that are in line with human resources management techniques of job design and performance appraisal, as well as the more amorphous issue of leadership identified in many business-oriented management schemata (Brilliant, 1986; Graham & Hays, 1993; Mintzberg, 1973). Many management texts in social work follow the model of one generic management approach, applicable to both the public and private sectors (Austin, 1981; Edwards & Yankey, 1991; Lewis, Lewis, & Soufleé, 1991). Keys and Ginsberg (1988) are among the few who make the distinction explicit.

Undeniably, the generic management elements outlined above can be used for organizational management in any of the sectors. What remain to be considered are the differences in skills and knowledge required in each of the sectors. (It should be noted that there may also be specific knowledge bases needed for management work in different types of organizations by product, that is, a hospital compared with an art museum, or a shoe store compared with a dress manufacturer—but this issue is beyond the scope of this chapter). In particular, what specific skills might be considered significant for managers in organizations of the third sector, especially those in social welfare or human services areas? To answer the question, one can begin by considering four salient characteristics of nonprofit organizations: (1) Their purpose is to serve the public good; (2) they are accountable to boards of directors and volunteers; (3) they generally acquire resources from multiple sources; and (4) they face legal constraints that prevent them from distributing surplus funds to staff, members, or volunteers.

These qualities in turn can be incorporated in a model for nonprofit management. In addition to the generic elements of POSDCORB, this model would include knowledge and abilities in the following five areas: (1) a values approach to motivation; (2) working with volunteers; (3) effective use of boards of directors; (4) nonprofit fiscal issues and procedures (specific accounting techniques and tax-related knowledge); and (5) fundraising, grantsmanship, and resource building.[2]

## NONPROFIT MANAGEMENT CONTENT IN THE SOCIAL WORK CURRICULUM

To obtain some current baseline data about social work education for nonprofit work, an exploratory survey was conducted by Langdon Holloway of the curriculum of master's degree programs related to management of nonprofit organization. A telephone survey of 55 social work programs selected randomly from 110 social work programs on the CSWE list

---

[2]Marketing probably also could be added here; it is a dominant characteristic of the business sector and is also used by the government.

(1994) of accredited master's degree programs was conducted. The goals of the survey were primarily to ascertain (1) whether the social work program offered a concentration (specialization) or subconcentration in nonprofit management; (2) whether the program had courses that were specifically designed for nonprofit management; and (3) the extent to which some content related to nonprofit organization management was included in the curriculum.

An effort was made to contact the dean or director of all 55 programs for a telephone interview. At least four attempts were made to reach the dean (or another knowledgeable person suggested by the dean); in the end, 39 interviews were conducted (70 percent of the original sample) in a four-week period in the spring term of 1995. Five small-sized programs, 17 medium-sized programs, and 15 large-sized programs were represented in the final sample.[3]

Twenty-three of the master's programs (or 59 percent of the sample) had a concentration (sequence) in administration or a macro concentration with a significant administration component. Almost all of the large schools had such a concentration; 50 percent of the medium-sized schools had one; and most of the small schools did not. However, the percentage of the student body taking a concentration in administration appeared low: It ranged from 5 percent to 15 percent in the large schools, was about 10 percent in the medium-sized schools, and was about 12 percent in small schools that offered the concentration. As anticipated, no program reported having a subspecialty in nonprofit management.

The survey asked about courses and course content on topics deemed relevant to nonprofit management, such as community organization and development, fundraising and grantsmanship,[4] fiscal management of nonprofit organizations, organizational management for nonprofits, executive director–board relations, and working with volunteers.

Of the topics related to nonprofit management, community organization and development was the most frequently offered as well as the most often taken. Twelve of the large programs offered specific courses on this topic; seven of the 17 medium-sized schools did; and three of the seven small schools did. Most of the medium-sized and large schools that did not offer separate courses had the topic included in other courses.

[3]*Size is defined in the following way: Small-sized programs have fewer than 110 full-time students; medium-sized programs have between 110 and 299 full-time students; and large-sized programs have more than 300 full-time students.*

[4]*Although we used the term "grantsmanship" in our survey, many respondents indicated that their courses used the title "grantwriting" or "resource development." There is no uniformity of title in many of the courses surveyed; however, similar content is apparently covered. The authors believe that further research on macro practice content would be useful.*

Fundraising or grantsmanship was offered in more than one-third of all the programs—in eight of the large schools and in six of the medium-sized schools. Three of the seven small schools offered courses in grantsmanship.

Fewer schools offered courses specifically on fiscal management for nonprofit organizations. Only five of the large programs, seven of the medium-sized programs, and none of the smaller programs did so. However, most respondents indicated that some of this content is offered in other courses.

On the whole, few of the programs offered specific courses on organizational management of nonprofit organizations. There were no specific courses offered by respondents of large programs; three of the medium-sized programs had such courses, and only one of the small programs did. This topic is known to be related to the voluntary sector. Many of the larger and medium-sized schools offered content on nonprofit management in other courses.

In general, fewer of the program directors interviewed indicated that their programs offered specific courses on working with boards of directors. Two of the larger programs, most of the other large schools, and most of the medium-sized and small schools reported that this topic is addressed in other courses—either foundation or advanced practice courses.

The least attention appears to be paid to the topic of working with volunteers. One large school had a specific course on this subject, and nine others taught the material in other administration classes. Several other programs provided some content on this topic in other courses.

Although increased attention has been given to the nonprofit sector in recent years by the government, the media, and interdisciplinary scholarship in America and elsewhere (Brilliant, 1995b), the education of social workers for managerial jobs in nonprofit organizations has apparently not yet benefited from the same interest. The exploratory survey confirmed anecdotal evidence (through classroom, conferences, and the literature) that social work programs place little emphasis on developing a cadre of social workers to manage voluntary human services agencies. Schools place students in voluntary as well as public agencies, but for the most part they do not have separate content focused on the differences between government and voluntary organizations. This finding therefore confirms our perception that many advanced social work students are relatively unfamiliar with the unique qualities of nonprofit human services agencies.

Nevertheless, the survey indicated that social work curricula frequently include some relevant material, particularly in the areas of community organization and development (which involves community-based organizations) and grantsmanship (which targets foundations for funding). The relative popularity of these two topics and of grantsmanship and grantwriting in particular probably reflects an increased emphasis on resource development in the human services. This emphasis is in line with the move to greater commercialization necessitated by fiscal uncertainty and cutbacks in government funding of human services (Salamon, 1992).

Community development and grantwriting skills also fit in well with the new emphasis on generalist practice, with its broader appeal to students. That there is somewhat less inclusion of fiscal management may be as a result of its greater specificity and technical nature; thus, it may not seem significant for the same range of students as the first two mentioned. The dearth of courses that specifically teach management of nonprofit organizations may be a result of the belief that there is a generic concept of management. However, the relative lack of emphasis on the study of boards of directors or volunteers is somewhat surprising, because these are skills that were once considered important community work (Brager, 1973; Kramer, 1969). Moreover, board–staff relationships have attracted significant attention in the 1990s; the executive of the United Way of America and officers of several other national nonprofit organizations have been accused of improper management practices, raising questions about board accountability (Brilliant, 1995b; Moss, 1995; Shepard, 1992).

### ARE VOLUNTARY AUSPICES THE EQUIVALENT OF CONSERVATIVISM?

In a sense, the dilemma over the value of nonprofit activity (versus public social welfare) is the obverse of another controversy that splits social workers along progressive–conservative lines, that is, whether formal organizations are capable of realizing progressive goals. One variant of this position is the well-developed thesis of Piven and Cloward (1991) that social movements can be effective only to the degree that they are not organized formally but continue to act from more loosely organized, mass protest strategies.

Beyond this issue, however, social work's attitude toward management of nonprofit agencies may be influenced by an underlying sense that reliance on the voluntary sector in the United States is tantamount to support of what was once called our reluctant welfare state (Wilensky & Lebeaux, 1958/1965). Voluntary agencies and voluntarism may be linked with the notion of philanthropy by the rich and old concepts of charity and thus may be contrasted with the value of public welfare institutions. This point of view is reflected in the attitude of a social work dean who stated that all social work students should be required to do field work in a public welfare setting. Whereas we would hardly disagree with this requirement, it does raise the question of what to do about training for work in the voluntary sector. More recently, support for the belief that emphasis on voluntary agencies is inherently conservative may be found in the pronouncement of the "points of light" philosophy by former President George Bush in 1990, as well as in the renewed interest in a nonpublic service provision that has been emphasized in connection with Newt Gingrich's Contract with America (1995). His approach appears to represent the extreme form of privatization that progressives fear generally (Starr, 1989), as distinct from an idea of partnership with government in the planning and delivery of social services (Brilliant, 1974; Salamon, 1987).

Calling voluntarism conservative may, however, be like blaming the baby for the spanking: It is in fact the government that is becoming more conservative and withdrawing financial support from the public and private sectors. It is certainly not the management of the voluntary sector that is causing the conservatism. In fact, organizations of the voluntary sector frequently serve as advocates for social change or against poor public services (Brilliant, 1990; Marris & Rein, 1967; Salamon, 1987). This has happened even while many voluntary agencies have been contracting with government in a "shadow state" that made this option financially attractive (Wolch, 1990). The potential for public–private partnerships has in fact been evident since the 1960s and throughout the 1990s, although some philanthropic leaders have clearly expressed concern about the dependence of the voluntary (third) sector on government funding (Commission on Private Philanthropy and Public Needs, 1975).

### COMPETITION

If social work has been reluctant to espouse the cause of management training and (possibly) to value scholarship explicitly focused on the nonprofit sector, other institutions have been eager to fill in the gap. In the mid-1970s, a major commission was initiated to consider issues of private philanthropy and public policy. Whereas the initial concern may have started with tax issues, eventually the Filer Commission (1975) broadened its scope of inquiry and produced an influential report, *Giving in America,* along with six volumes of in-depth research documents on the issues confronting the voluntary sector. In the years since this initial articulation of the notion of an identifiable nonprofit, or third, sector a host of institutions have sprung up as advocates for the sector. These include significant national membership organizations (for example, Independent Sector, 1993, and the National Committee on Responsive Philanthropy) as well as the academic centers for interdisciplinary research, education, and training related to the nonprofit sector and voluntary action (Brilliant, 1995b).

Altogether, there are approximately 35 of these academic centers, many of which provide specific training and degrees in nonprofit organization management (Independent Sector, 1993). Few of these centers appear to be connected to social work schools; one exception is the Mandel Center for Nonprofit Organizations, which is affiliated with social work through the combined structure of the School of Applied Social Sciences at Case Western Reserve University. Many academic centers include management training, which encompasses a wide sweep of nonprofit organizations ranging from the social services to the arts. It is less clear what role they actually play in educating health administrators, because there are many long-standing separate programs in health administration.

The academic centers mentioned above have a variety of structural arrangements with the universities to which they are attached. Many are in effect institutions of public policy, such as the Johns Hopkins Institute for Policy Studies. Some centers or programs are part of existing business schools that have added training for nonprofit management; others, such as the Indiana University Center on Philanthropy, have more of a focus on fundraising and philanthropic activities. Most of them have been effective in obtaining grants for their institutions, with support from corporations, private foundations, and wealthy individuals. Thus, they bring resources to their universities.

### CONCLUSION

Management training generally has had a marginal place in social work education, even though large numbers of social work practitioners rise quickly to supervisory or mid-management levels. Moreover, increasing numbers of social work students have been entering master's degree programs in social work with an interest in private practice rather than in any kind of agency-related work. In addition, although training managers with a social work value system seems critical for the delivery of effective human services, new emphasis on generalistic social work practice administration may diminish curriculum space available for specialized management training.

Those who believe that it is important to educate social workers for leadership roles as managers of the nonprofit agencies in which they work must confront two issues: the status of management education in social work schools and the need (if any) for separate training in nonprofit education. Although we believe that different abilities are needed in government and voluntary organizations (for example, working with volunteers or understanding government lines of authority), we also recognize considerable similarities in such basic management functions as outlined by the POSDCORB framework or the social psychologists' questions about motivating personnel.

Given the ambivalence of many social work educators about the role of nonprofit agencies, and the small student pool for the administrative concentration in the schools, it seems fiscally and ideologically risky to treat nonprofit management as a separate subconcentration. However, given the high percentage of social workers who work in nonprofit organizations and the possibilities they offer both for service delivery and social change activities, it is important to prepare managers of these organizations with social work values and a commitment to public benefit purposes. Social work education is after all concerned about social welfare programs provided under any auspices but driven by social work ethics and professional values. In contrast, academic centers that focus on management of nonprofit organizations have cut the pie by auspices rather than substantive focus or a clearly defined professional ethos.

Our research and the findings of our exploratory study suggest that most social work programs are likely to gain from strengthening particular course offerings in nonprofit management rather than attempting to compete programmatically with the more sector-oriented academic nonprofit centers. We should avoid subdivisions of our curriculum that could add to the difficulties of maintaining viable administration concentrations in current programs. However, schools should consider more-extensive development of courses such as fiscal management for nonprofit organizations or managing grassroots organizations. In addition, content on auspices that affect agency administration (for example, major characteristics of organizations in each sector such as government reporting or working with boards) should be strengthened throughout the curriculum. Also, where courses are available through nonprofit programs at the same university or college, cooperative arrangements with the school of social work should be encouraged. In that way, social workers interested in nonprofit management can enrich their knowledge with appropriate specialty courses, such as the law of tax-exempt organizations. Thus, students will be better prepared to work in either public or voluntary sector organizations. It must still be recognized, however, that inevitably more in-depth specialized knowledge must be acquired through actual field work or on-the-job training.

## REFERENCES

Allison, G. T., Jr. (1983). Public and private management: Are they fundamentally alike in all unimportant respects? In R. Stillman (Ed.), *Public administration: Concepts and cases* (pp. 453–467). Boston: Houghton Mifflin.

Austin, M. (1981). *Supervisory management for the human services.* Englewood Cliffs, NJ: Prentice Hall.

Biklen, D. P. (1983). *Community organizing: Theory and practice.* Englewood Cliffs, NJ: Prentice Hall.

Brager, G. (1973). *Community organizing.* New York: Columbia University Press.

Bremner, R. H. (1988). *American philanthropy* (2nd ed.). Chicago: University of Chicago Press.

Brilliant, E. (1974). Private or public: A model of ambiguities. *Social Service Review, 47*, 384–396.

Brilliant, E. (1986). Leadership in social work: A missing ingredient? *Social Work, 31*, 325–331.

Brilliant, E. (1990). *The United Way: Dilemmas of organized charity.* New York: Columbia University Press.

Brilliant, E. (1995a). The Peterson and Filer Commissions: Private charity and public inquiry. In *Non-profit organizations as public sectors: Rising to new public policy challenges* (Working papers, Spring Research Forum, Independent Sector, pp. 85–101).

Brilliant, E. (1995b). Voluntarism. In R. L. Edwards (Ed.-in-Chief), *The encyclopedia of social work* (19th ed., Vol. 3, pp. 2469–2482). Washington, DC: NASW Press.

Commission on Private Philanthropy and Public Needs (The Filer Commission). (1975). *Giving in America: Toward a stronger voluntary sector.* Washington, DC: U.S. Government Printing Office.

Council on Social Work Education. (1994). *Directory of colleges and universities with accredited social work programs.* Washington, DC: Author.

Drucker, P. (1954). *The practice of management.* New York: Harper & Row.

Drucker, P. (1990). *Managing the nonprofit organization: Principles and practices.* New York: HarperCollins.

Edwards, R. L., & Yankey, J. A. (Eds.). (1991). *Skills for effective human services management.* Silver Spring, MD: NASW Press.

Gibelman, M., & Schervish, P. H. (1993a). *What we earn: 1993 NASW salary survey.* Washington, DC: NASW Press.

Gibelman, M., & Schervish, P. H. (1993b). *Who we are: The social work labor force as reflected in the NASW membership.* Washington, DC: NASW Press.

Graham, C. B., Jr., & Hays, S. W. (1993). *Managing the public organization* (2nd ed.). Washington, DC: Congressional Quarterly Press.

Gulick, L., & Urwick, L. (1973). Notes on the theory of organization. In L. Gulick & L. Urwick (Eds.), *Papers on the science of administration* (pp. 3–13). New York: Institute of Public Administration.

Hodgkinson, V. A., Weitzman, M. S., Toppe, C., & Noga, S. M. (1992). *Nonprofit almanac 1992–1993: Dimensions of the voluntary sector.* San Francisco: Jossey-Bass.

Hopkins, B. R. (1992). *The law of tax-exempt organizations.* New York: John Wiley & Sons.

Independent Sector. (1993). *Academic centers and programs focusing on the study of philanthropy, voluntarism, and nonprofit activities.* Washington, DC: Author.

Kast, F. E., & Rosenzweig, J. E. (1979). *Organization and management: A systems and contingency approach* (3rd ed.). New York: McGraw-Hill.

Katz, R. L. (1955, January–February). Skills of an effective administrator. *Harvard Business Review,* pp. 33–42.

Keys, P. R., & Ginsberg, L. (Eds.). (1988). *New management in human services.* Silver Spring, MD: National Association of Social Workers.

Kramer, R. M. (1969). Ideology, status and power in board–staff relationships. In R. M. Kramer & H. Specht (Eds.), *Readings in community organization practice* (pp. 285–293). Englewood Cliffs, NJ: Prentice Hall.

Leiby, J. (1978). *A history of social welfare and social work in the United States.* New York: Columbia University Press.

Lewis, J. A., Lewis, M. D., & Soufleé, F. (1991). *Management of human service programs* (2nd ed.). Monterey, CA: Brooks/Cole.

Lubove, R. (1969). *The professional altruist: The emergence of social work as a career, 1880–1930.* New York: Athenum.

Marris, P., & Rein, M. (1967). *Dilemmas of social reform: Poverty and community action in the United States.* New York: Atherton.

Mintzberg, H. (1973). *The nature of managerial work.* New York: Harper & Row.

Moss, D. (1995, March 5). Vulnerable charities will track this trial. *USA Today,* p. 4A.

Nadler, D. A., Hackman, J. R., & Lawler, E. E. (Eds.). (1979). *Managing organizational behavior.* Boston: Little, Brown.

Piven, F. F., & Cloward, R. A. (1991). Collective protest: A critique of resource mobilization theory. *International Journal of Politics, Culture and Society, 4,* 435–458.

Salamon, L. M. (1987). Partners in public service: The scope and theory of government–nonprofit relations. In W. W. Powell (Ed.), *The nonprofit sector: A research handbook* (pp. 99–117). New Haven, CT: Yale University Press.

Salamon, L. M. (1992). *America's nonprofit sector: A primer.* New York: Foundation Center.

Shepard, C. E. (1992, March 23). United Way volunteers hear apologies from board. *Washington Post.*

Simon, J. L. (1987). The tax treatment of nonprofit organizations: A review of federal and state policies. In W. W. Powell (Ed.), *The nonprofit sector: A research handbook* (pp. 67–98). New Haven, CT: Yale University Press.

Starr, P. (1989). The meaning of privatization. In S. B. Kamerman & A. J. Kahn (Eds.), *Privatization and the welfare state* (pp. 15–48). Princeton, NJ: Princeton University Press.

Strauss, G., & Sayles, L. R. (1980). *Behavioral strategies for managers.* Englewood Cliffs, NJ: Prentice Hall.

Weisbrod, B. (1988). *The nonprofit economy.* Cambridge, MA: Harvard University Press.

Wilensky, H. L., & Lebeaux, C. N. (1965). *Industrial society and social welfare* (Rev. ed.). New York: Free Press. (Original work published in 1958)

Wineman, S. (1984). *The politics of human services: Radical alternatives to the welfare state.* Boston: South End Press.

Wolch, J. R. (1990). *The shadow state: Government and voluntary sector in transmission.* New York: Foundation Center.

# Reinventing a Government Human Services Unit

## *A Case Example*

George W. Appenzeller

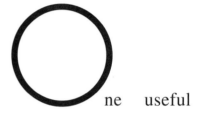ne useful

perspective for the human services manager attempting

to implement organizational change was provided by

Edward Fuchs. Fuchs (1993) summarized the principles

of the total quality management (TQM) approach to

excellence and the barriers to implementing TQM. The

principles he identified as critical to TQM were a strong

customer focus; definition and deployment to all employees of the goals and values that ensure success; enablement and empowerment of all employees; and definition, control, and improvement of all key business processes. The barriers he described as incrementation versus reengineering, lack of metrics (or means of measure) connecting quality approaches to business results, lack of focus on strategic planning and core competencies, and obsolete and outdated business cultures.

Appenzeller and Bond (1994) posited in "Total Quality Management and Honor" that the essential challenge to leaders of change in the workplace is an ethical one—to facilitate an examination of cultural values by managers and workers. This appendix describes a case example of a government unit that consciously addressed that ethical challenge and, aided by social work skills and values, succeeded in reinventing its own organization during this period of national concern and transition in management. The case analysis uses Fuchs's (1993) description of TQM and barriers to implementing TQM. The staff members involved found that social work values and skills appeared well suited to facilitating the change from a traditional management structure to a TQM structure.

### BACKGROUND

In 1984 South Carolina centralized the planning and financing of health and human services by creating the State Health and Human Service Finance Commission. The commission administers funds from Titles XIX and XX of the Social Security Act, the Child Care and Development Block Grant, and several Medicaid waiver programs for South Carolina. The commission also coordinates interagency efforts, develops annual plans for health and human services, and develops programs as required.

The Bureau of Community Services within the commission was created to administer Title XX and associated funds, which financed 23 services in a variety of public and private agencies, ranging from child welfare to home-delivered meals. This breadth of activity led to the establishment in 1985 of a Division of Quality Assurance in the bureau. The division's mission was to develop a comprehensive quality assurance system for the bureau's existing programs. During the last year of the development process, a new chief administrator came to the commission. In early 1989, as part of the new administrator's reorganization of the agency, the Bureau of Community Services gained responsibility for additional programs in long-term care, nursing homes, and home health services, as well as responsibility for developing a quality assurance system for these programs.

The division, with the bulk of the first quality assurance system just completed and turned over to other units to administer, prepared a plan for the development of a long-term-care quality assurance system, a lengthy and complex process. This plan was rejected in mid-1989. The new policy of the agency was that quality control was to be primarily a responsibility of service providers and state agencies with legal responsibility for licensure and certification.

Thus, at the start of the 1989–90 fiscal year, the division was left without a mission. By necessity, the division would have to reinvent itself or go out of business.

## THE REINVENTION DECISION

The division had several assets with which to work. The staff of 14, mostly licensed social workers, was organized into three departments, each supervised by a department head. The staff was experienced in working together and had developed a team approach to work. The division also had a substantial budget for training and travel. Finally, two permanent projects and one shorter term project had not been eliminated.

The division director, with the help and guidance of his three department heads, made the critical decision: Use the existing resources to try and reinvent the division so as to allow the operating unit to survive and become a useful part of the agency. The three projects in process would provide work during the period of change. The training and travel money would be used to purchase consultants, time, and space. The members of the division would do the reinventing work themselves; their knowledge, values, and expertise would provide the content, and the team approach would provide the method.

During the latter part of 1989, the division director prepared the staff, and in particular the three department heads, for the changes. He also discussed potential new missions for the division with his supervisor. By April 1990, the director felt that the groundwork for the transition had been accomplished and the reinvention could begin.

## THE REINVENTION PROCESS

The process started with a three-day retreat in May 1990. Two consultants, both with participatory management training expertise, facilitated the retreat. The retreat goal was for the staff to learn participatory management by planning their own future using androgological techniques. On the third day, the group formed two work teams. Each team would present a plan to the whole group regarding changing the division's purposes and implementing participatory management. Ideally, by the end of the third day the two work teams would merge the two plans in a consensus process. However, the consensus process never occurred, as some members of the teams defended their plans in an adversarial, competitive manner. At the end of the day, the division had, to some extent, broken into different camps, largely centered around the three departments. Evaluations and subsequent interviews with the participants clearly showed that, for many of the members of the division, the shift from an authoritarian management system to a participatory system was going to be difficult. Part of that difficulty was centered around the change in decision making. Whereas part of the difficulty came from a change in decision making, an equally important barrier was the change from a reward system based on adherence to abstract rules to a system based on determining and fulfilling concrete customer needs.

The director, although concerned with reaching the goal of a re-created division in a timely manner, strongly believed that the essential challenge to reinventing the division lay in dealing with the values of the division and its members. As a result, he made a decision to take the time to work through theses newly found problems and asked for the help of consultants in working with members of the division in the weeks after the retreat.

The director began coaching the department heads, sometimes on a daily basis, as a group and individually. The goal of the coaching was to help them evolve into resources for their departments and leaders of organizational change. Next the director asked the division to come up with a statement of identity. Developing the statement proved to be one of the most surprising events in the reinvention of the unit.

Four people volunteered to write a one-page statement of identity, without input or supervision. All had joined the division within the year, none had graduate degrees or training in TQM, all were women, and three were African American. Their statement, shown in the box on page 250, clearly expressed TQM values and practices and was adopted without significant change by the rest of the staff in June 1990.

While one team was developing the statement of identity, another team surveyed bureau staff to solicit ideas for helping staff or providers of bureau-funded services to do a better job. A management team, consisting of the division director and the three department heads, followed a similar pattern in surveying managers within the bureau. This team also looked for possible projects in the final report on the implementation of the quality assurance system that the division completed in 1989. All possible projects were placed in order by priority by the executive staff of the bureau, which selected 20 projects for the division to work on in fiscal year 1991–92.

Work teams were established for each project. An additional team was organized for technical and maintenance support for the division in areas such as database design and supply procurement. Each person was assigned to more than one team. To support the start of this new work process, the division as a whole met once a week. In these meetings, there was wide-ranging discussion of work progress, work methods, relationships of work teams to one another, and decision making around issues that affected the entire group. At first, the division director led the discussions. He gradually eased out of that role and, after eight months, members of the division took turns leading the meetings.

Training was judged to be a critical component of the reinventing process, and a great deal of training was made available from internal and

---

**Division of Quality Assurance**
**July 1, 1990**
**Division of Quality Assurance Critical Success Factors**

Outcome: Influence the ability of the services delivery system to provide positive outcomes for clients.

Critical Success Variables

I.     Identify trends and current needs of the target population.

    —Perform QA needs assessments within SHHSFC to determine information needs.

    —Identify and explore the quality gaps in the services delivery system.

    —Determine appropriate responses to quality needs.

    —Provide recommendations, based on current data analysis, for improving the ability of the services delivery system to provide better outcomes.

    —Identify methods and resources that would "fuel" quality recommendations, such as grants or reallocation of funds.

II.    Communicate and disseminate the services delivery quality information gathered.

    —Provide an annual QA report on a timely basis.

    —Provide annual reports.

All this should be done to enable providers to offer the best quality services to eligible citizens of South Carolina.

The components of the philosophy that drive the work of the QA Division are that
    The work should be of a practical nature.
    It should be valid and reliable.
    It should have a positive influence on the services the agency funds.
    It should promote creative solutions.
    It should be sensitive to the interest groups.
    It should be of relevance and significance to the mission of SHHSFC.

---

external sources. The training chosen by the staff was primarily devoted to increasing the skill levels and knowledge base of the employees in the types of services requested by customers. For example, a 30-hour course on statistics was made available because of the large amount of research, evaluation, and database services being requested. (The training program proved popular with other parts of the agency and other agencies and eventually became a product provided by the division on an ongoing basis.)

Initially, the new operational method for the division was met with enthusiasm by most employees. However, under the surface there was a great deal of tension. The department heads seemed to feel stripped of authority but not responsibility. Some of the nonmanagement staff seemed to feel that making management decisions was not work that they were paid to perform. Both groups were correct in their assessment as long as their frame of reference remained the traditional management structure. In addition, many of the employees had spent much of their working lives in agencies that provided human services and in which meeting process rules and regulations were of primary value. For these personnel, the change was especially wrenching. For many, these feelings were not always clearly articulated, thus leading to a great deal of confusion, and even anger, for some members of the division.

By the end of the fiscal year 1991–92, all of the department heads had moved to positions in traditionally structured organizations, In two cases the positions carried substantially more responsibility and income. Over the next two years, two other people left the division to return to units managed in a manner with which they were more familiar. Thus personnel, properly and rightly so, chose to leave the division when they felt uncomfortable with the management methods being implemented.

To replace the supervisors, two people from the division were promoted and a person was brought in from another division. All three supervisors demonstrated enthusiasm about the new values. Another significant personnel change occurred when, with support from the administration of the agency and as part of an overall study of appropriate pay levels throughout the agency, all but one of the positions in the division were upgraded to higher pay levels.

### REINVENTION RESULTS

By the end of 1994, the division had achieved a reasonable degree of adherence to Fuchs's (1993) principles. All the work in the division is driven by customer needs. Every year the staff re-evaluate the goals and values of the division. This process culminates in an annual three-day retreat in the spring. At the retreat the year just ending is reviewed, new goals and values are put in writing, the process of developing a work plan for the next fiscal year begins, and training chosen by the staff is delivered. During the year, all work requiring more than one person is done in work teams, and team leaders are chosen by the division as a whole. Within the context of state and commission rules and regulations, the division regularly reviews and improves the key processes through which it operates. The 1994–95 work plan's mission, goal, beliefs, and products statements are provided as an illustration (see box on page 252).

---

### The Division of Quality Assurance
### 1994/95 Plan

#### *Mission*

Assist the Bureau of Community Services, and other organizations as authorized, to improve the quality of health and human services by foreseeing the need for changes, by providing accurate information quickly, and by evaluating proposed and actual changes in the health and human services system.

#### *Goal*

Provide the service delivery system, at all levels, with quality support services.

#### *Beliefs*

1. Quick access to current, useful information is vital in the rapidly changing health and human services field.

2. Being proactive and foreseeing change in health and human services will guide the direction and quality of the delivery of services more effectively.

3. Comprehensive planning activities based on sound information will improve the quality of services.

4. Good teamwork is critical to quality products. Placing the highest value on our employees, our people resources, is our most effective vehicle to improving quality.

5. Our responsibility is to support the agency in any way requested, but further, to search for ways in which support is or will be needed and to provide it.

#### *Products*

Provide the following support services in a practice-oriented manner, sensitive to the diversity of the state, and adhering to proven standards of validity and reliability. These support services should be positive influences, offering creative win/win solutions.

1. Exploratory and descriptive studies
2. Information dissemination
3. Database development
4. Evaluation
5. Technological support
6. Regular reports

---

## BARRIERS TO REINVENTION

The description of the process that occurred appears to bear out Fuchs's (1993) delineation of barriers to implementing TQM. Initially, an attempt was made to have personnel slowly adapt to TQM-based management philosophy through a training and joint planning process. What actually occurred was that many staff members were unprepared to shift from lifelong habits of competitiveness to total cooperation virtually overnight. Yet until individual competition was left behind, reinvention could not occur for the division as a whole. The incremental approach had to be abandoned, and the volunteer group sat down and reinvented the division of behalf of everyone.

The scarcity of metrics connecting quality approaches to business results is a problem endemic to government and another barrier to reinvention. After all, there are no financial metrics available for determining success in government, at least in the way that businesses can use financial methods. There are, however, other means. In the case of the division, two metrics were chosen. First, was the division allowed to continue to exist as an operating unit by senior management of the commission? Second, did existing customers return and were new customers for division services attracted?

A major issue for the group at the beginning of the process was the lack of focus on strategic planning and core competencies, resulting from very human concerns regarding the lack of work assigned to the division other than the three projects in process at the start of the reinvention process. However, once the members of the division accepted responsibility for the operation of the division, the focus on strategic planning and core competencies increased, The division now places a significant amount of structured attention on these two subjects in the annual review process and as a result of the insistence on training and education by the individual staff members.

The most difficult barrier to overcome was that of obsolete and outdated business cultures, at least outdated and obsolete in terms of the new direction being taken by the division. The major upheaval caused by individuals having to face a change from the prevailing bureaucratic culture cam close to destroying the entire process. Some individuals liked the new values immediately, some adapted to them over time, and some chose to find places where the values they were comfortable with prevail. It is hoped that everyone ended up where he or she could be the most happy and productive.

### REFERENCES

Appenzeller, G., & Bond, J. (1994). Total quality management and honor: A collection of short essays. *South Carolina Business Journal, 13*(3), 12.

Fuchs, E. (1993). Total quality management from the future: Practices and paradigms. *Quality Management Journal, 1*(1), 26–34.

# Index

# About the Editors

**Leon Ginsberg, PhD, MSW,** has served as Carolina Research and Carolina Distinguished Professor since 1986. From 1977 to 1986 he was commissioner of the West Virginia Department of Human Services and chancellor of the West Virginia Board of Regents for Higher Education. From 1968 through 1977, he was dean of the School of Social Work at West Virginia University and, before that appointment, he was associate professor of social work at the University of Oklahoma. He is the author of 10 books on social work statistics, management, rural social work, public welfare, and aging, as well as the author of many articles in professional journals on social work subjects. He authored *Social Work Almanac,* the second edition of which was published in 1995, and edited *Social Work in Rural Communities*, the second edition of which was published in 1993. His book on social welfare policy, *Understanding Social Problems, Policies, and Programs,* was published in 1994.

Dr. Ginsberg has been a member of NASW for more than 30 years and served recently as secretary of the national Board of Directors. He has been a board member and treasurer of the Council on Social Work Education and has served as a member of and a consultant to the Commission on Accreditation. Dr. Ginsberg has served as a Fulbright Professor in Colombia, as an educator in Romania, and as a visiting professor in Mexico.

**Paul R. Keys, PhD, MSW,** is dean of the College of Health and Human Services and professor, Southeast Missouri State University, Cape Giradeau. From 1992 to 1994 he was vice president of the GARIOA/Fulbright Alumni Association. For the academic year 1990–91, he was a GARIOA/Fulbright Senior Research Scholar of the Faculty of Integrated Arts and Sciences, Department of Social Welfare, Japan Women's University, Tokyo, where he wrote the report "A Study of Japanese Management Applications to American Public and Nonprofit Health and Human Services Organizations." Dr. Keys is a member of the National Advisory Council of the National Network for Social Work Managers (NNSWM), NNSWM book series editor, and cofounder of the NNSWM/NASW National Management Conference. He has written numerous articles and is the founding editor of the *Journal of Multicultural Social Work.* He is the editor of the book *School Social Workers in the Multicultural Environment: New Roles, Responsibilities, and Education Enrichment* (1994).

# About the Contributors

**George W. Appenzeller, MSW, ACSW, LSW,** is director of the Division of Quality Assurance, South Carolina Department of Health and Human Services, Columbia. He has been an active member of NASW for many years. Currently, he is vice president of the National Network of Social Work Managers.

**Yvonne Asamoah, PhD, MSW,** is a member of the faculty of the Hunter College School of Social Work. She teaches in psychology of human behavior and social environment. She has published articles, presented papers, and consulted on issues of multiculturalism in the human services.

**Joseph J. Bevilacqua, PhD,** is a nationally published protagonist for reform and innovation in such areas as community mental health and services for homeless people, children, and chronically mentally ill people. He has served as South Carolina Commissioner of Mental Health and director, Rhode Island Department of Mental Health, Retardation, and Hospitals.

**Eleanor L. Brilliant, DSW,** is professor and chair of the Administration, Policy, and Planning Sequence in the master of social work program of the Rutgers University School of Social Work, New Brunswick, New Jersey. An active member of NASW, she has served as treasurer of NASW's national Board of Directors and president of the New York State chapter. Her recent work includes an article on voluntarism (and voluntary agencies) for the 19th edition of the *Encyclopedia of Social Work* and a book, *The United Way: Dilemmas of Organized Charity*. She is currently writing a historical analysis of the public policy impact of two significant commissions concerned with the role of the American nonprofit sector, the Peterson Commission (1969) and the Filer Commission (1973–77).

**Edgar Colon, DSW, ACSW,** is associate professor, Social Work and Urban Studies, Southern Connecticut State University, New Haven. He teaches administration, research, human behavior, and public policy analysis. Dr. Colon is a nationally recognized figure in the areas of organization development and workplace diversity. In addition to his long-standing academic career, Dr. Colon has served as associate director of Social Work and Discharge Planning at Lincoln Medical and Mental Health Center, a 700-bed Level 1 trauma center in New York City. During his tenure at Lincoln, Dr. Colon also served as director of the Children's Outpatient Psychiatric Service and chief psychiatric social worker on the faculty of New York Medical College, Valhalla. Dr. Colon is consulting editor for the *Journal of Multicultural Social Work*. His current professional memberships include NASW, American Society of Public Administration, and the National Network for Social Work Managers.

**Anthony A. Cupaiuolo, DSW,** is professor and director of the Edwin G. Michaelian Institute for Public Policy and Management, Pace University, White Plains, New York. Formerly special assistant to the commissioner of the New York State Department of Social Services, he has lectured and written extensively on public sector management and on the legal and community relations issues related to group homes. He has also established and serves as the director of a special program at Pace University to teach Japanese local government officials about U.S. public administration.

**Richard L. Edwards, PhD, ACSW,** is dean and professor, School of Social Work, University of North Carolina at Chapel Hill. A frequent contributor to the management literature, he is coeditor of *Skills for Effective Human Services Management* and the editor-in-chief of the 19th edition of the *Encyclopedia of Social Work*. He is also past president of the NASW.

**Burton Gummer, PhD,** is professor in the School of Social Welfare, Nelson A. Rockefeller College of Public Affairs and Policy, the State University of New York at Albany. He is the author of *The Politics of Social Administration* and numerous articles on social welfare administration and planning. His "Notes from the Management Literature" is a regular feature of *Administration in Social Work*, of which he is an associate editor.

**Michael A. Harris, MSW,** a graduate of Hunter College School of Social Work, is a social worker in the Medicaid Eligibility Program of the Department of Social Work Services at Long Island Jewish Medical Center, New Hyde Park, New York. He is also chair of the Queens Medicaid Advisory Council and a member of the New York Citywide Medicaid Advisory Council.

**Catherine M. Havens, JD, MSW,** is assistant professor, School of Social Work, University of Connecticut, where she formerly was associate dean. She has been chair, Community Organization Sequence and the Substantive Area in Women's Studies. She developed the course, "Women and Social Work Administration," which has been offered at the School of Social Work for 17 years. Dr. Havens teaches community organization, women's policy and leadership issues, social welfare policy, and law and social work. Her publications include "The Impact of Women in Appointed Executive Office" (with L. Healy) in *Impact of Women in Politics*, edited by S. C. Dobson.

**Lynne M. Healy, PhD, MSW,** is professor, School of Social Work, University of Connecticut, West Hartford, where she chairs the Administration Concentration and is founding director of the School of Social Work's Center for International Social Work Studies. Her research and publications focus on human services management, women and leadership, and international aspects of social work education. She is a member of the editorial board of *Administration in Social Work* and with Barbara Pine coedited the first publication of the National Network for Social Work Managers, *Managers' Choices.*

**Langdon L. Holloway, MSSW, ACSW, BCD,** has practiced social work for 20 years, with a concentration in mental health and chemical dependency. She is a doctoral candidate at Rutgers University School of Social Work.

**Michael J. Kelly, PhD, MSSW,** is professor of social work, College of Environmental Sciences, Missouri University, Columbia, and lead faculty member for planning and administration. He has conducted formal mentoring research and demonstration projects for private for-profit and not-for-profit organizational and public–private coalitions for more than 15 years. Dr. Kelly's other current research interests include organizational excellence, knowledge-intensive organizations, service quality, and electronic online services.

**Kim Kiely** received a BA degree in interdisciplinary studies in communications, law, economics, and government from The American University in Washington, DC, and an MPA in government from Pace University, White Plains, New York. She is currently a program associate at a private foundation that supports innovative educational projects.

**David S. Liederman, MSW, MEd,** is executive director of the Child Welfare League of America (CWLA), the oldest and largest voluntary organization in North America devoted to developing and improving services to abused, neglected, and deprived children. Mr. Liederman serves as CWLA's national spokesperson and travels thousands of miles annually around the United States speaking out for children. In addition to his duties as CWLA executive director, he is national cochair of Generations United, a coalition of more than 100 national organizations established to promote cooperation between generations. Mr. Liederman served two terms in the Massachusetts House of Representatives; in 1975 he was named chief of staff to Governor Michael Dukakis of Massachusetts. He has also served on the faculties of Yeshiva University in New York City, City University of New York, and Boston University.

**Grant Loavenbruck, DSW,** who has a 30-year career as a social work practitioner and administrator at the national, state, and local levels, is currently director of special projects at the Edwin G. Michaelian Institute for Public Policy and Management, Pace University, White Plains, New York. He is a member of NASW and the Council on Social Work Education and most recently was the deputy director of United Neighborhood Centers of America.

**Erin E. Morrissey, MA,** is a doctoral candidate in clinical–community psychology, University of South Carolina, Columbia. At Duke University she was project coordinator of a study investigating the mental health services needs of rural youths. She also has evaluated substance abuse coalitions, family-based abuse intervention, and a family support program for families with mentally ill members.

**Felice Davidson Perlmutter, PhD,** professor of social administration at Temple University, Philadelphia, is active in teaching and lecturing on administration of the social services. She is the author of seven books and 70 articles on social administration, social policy, and nonprofit organizations. She is a Fulbright scholar who has extensive international experience as a teacher and researcher.

**Barbara A. Pine, PhD, MSW,** is professor, School of Social Work, University of Connecticut, West Hartford, where she was formerly chair of the Administration Concentration. A social worker for 26 years, her teaching, research, and practice interests include social work management, primarily program planning, strategic planning, and organizational improvement; foster care, special needs adoption, family reunification, and social work values and ethics. Dr. Pine's most recent publications include *Returning to Stay: A Guide to Strengthening Family Reunification Services* (with R. Warsh and A. Maluccio) and *Teaching Family Reunification: A Curriculum Sourcebook* (with R. Warsh and A. Maluccio).

**Kaitlin A. Post, MBA,** is assistant professor and director of special projects for the College of Health and Human Services, Southeast Missouri State University, Cape Giradeau. She is a specialist in grant writing and program development. Ms. Post has more than 20 years' experience in not-for-profit administration, including directing several formal mentoring projects for publicly funded agencies. Current research interests include service animals, case management for multiple diagnoses cases, and public–private sector cooperative programs.

**Frank B. Raymond III, DSW,** is dean of the College of Social Work, University of South Carolina, Columbia. He is currently vice chair of the South Carolina State Health and Human Services Finance Commission Advisory Board, vice chair of the South Carolina Institute on Poverty and Deprivation, and chair of the education committee of the Public/Academic Consortium of the South Carolina Department of Mental Health. Dr. Raymond has written many articles and book chapters as well as three books. He is a member of NASW, the Council of Social Work Education, the National Association of Christians in Social Work, and the National Association of Deans and Directors of Schools of Social Work.

**David I. Siegel, DSW,** is associate professor, Department of Social Work, West Chester University of Pennsylvania, where he teaches courses in social welfare policies and services. He has completed a proposal for a new Master of Social Work Program. His research interests include poverty, organizational dynamics, and addictions.

**Abraham Wandersman, PhD,** is professor of psychology, University of South Carolina, Columbia. He received his PhD from Cornell University in the following areas of specialization: social psychology, environmental psychology, and social organization and change. He has been interim codirector of the Institute for Families in Society at the University of South Carolina. Dr. Wandersman has conducted research on environmental issues and community responses. He also conducts research and program evaluation on citizen participation in community organizations and coalitions and interagency collaboration. He is coauthor of *Prevention Plus III* and many other books and articles.

*New Management in Human Services, Second Edition*

Designed by The Magazine Group.

Composed by Patricia D. Wolf, Wolf Publications, Inc., in Times and Futura Condensed.

Printed by BookCrafters on 60# Lakewood.